CHINA'S ARCTIC
AMBITIONS

BEYOND BOUNDARIES: CANADIAN DEFENCE
AND STRATEGIC STUDIES SERIES

Rob Huebert, Series Editor

ISSN 1716-2645 (Print) ISSN 1925-2919 (Online)

Canada's role in international military and strategic studies ranges from peacebuilding and Arctic sovereignty to unconventional warfare and domestic security. This series provides narratives and analyses of the Canadian military from both an historical and a contemporary perspective.

UNIVERSITY OF CALGARY
Press

CHINA'S ARCTIC AMBITIONS

and What They Mean for Canada

P. Whitney Lackenbauer, Adam Lajeunesse,
James Manicom, and Frédéric Lasserre

Beyond Boundaries:
Canadian Defence and Strategic Studies Series
ISSN 1716-2645 (Print) ISSN 1925-2919 (Online)

University of Calgary Press
2500 University Drive NW
Calgary, Alberta
Canada T2N 1N4
press.ucalgary.ca

LIBRARY AND ARCHIVES CANADA CATALOGUING IN PUBLICATION

Lackenbauer, P. Whitney, author
    China's Arctic ambitions and what they mean for Canada / P. Whitney Lackenbauer,
Adam Lajeunesse, James Manicom, and Frédéric Lasserre.

(Beyond boundaries : Canadian defence and strategic studies, ISSN 1716-2645 ; no. 8)
Includes bibliographical references and index.
Issued in print and electronic formats.
ISBN 978-1-55238-901-0 (softcover).—ISBN 978-1-55238-902-7 (Open Access PDF).—
ISBN 978-1-55238-903-4 (PDF).—ISBN 978-1-55238-904-1 (EPUB).—
ISBN 978-1-55238-905-8 (Kindle)

    1. Arctic regions—Foreign relations—China. 2. China—Foreign relations—Arctic
regions. 3. Arctic regions—Politics and government. I. Lajeunesse, Adam, 1982-, author
II. Manicom, James, 1979-, author III. Lasserre, Frédéric, 1967-, author IV. Title.
V. Series: Beyond boundaries series ; no. 8

G606.L33 2018   919.8   C2017-907112-2
                                                                    C2017-907113-0

The University of Calgary Press acknowledges the support of the Government of Alberta through the Alberta Media Fund for our publications. We acknowledge the financial support of the Government of Canada. We acknowledge the financial support of the Canada Council for the Arts for our publishing program.

This book has been published with the help of a grant from the Canadian Federation for the Humanities and Social Sciences, through the Awards to Scholarly Publications Program, using funds provided by the Social Sciences and Humanities Research Council of Canada.

This book has been published with the support of St. Jerome's University Aid to Scholarly Publishing Grant.

 Canadä Canada Council Conseil des Arts
for the Arts du Canada

Printed and bound in Canada by Marquis
♻ This book is printed on Enviro Schoolbook paper

Copyediting by Kathryn Simpson
Cover image: Timo Palo, "Drift ice camp in the middle of the Arctic Ocean as seen from the deck of icebreaker *Xue Long* [*Snow Dragon*]," 2010, Photograph. Wikimedia Commons.
Cover design, page design, and typesetting by Melina Cusano

Table of Contents

Illustrations

Abbreviations

ADIZ — Air Defence Identification Zone

ARCTML — Arctic Change and its Tele-impacts on Mid-Latitudes

ACIA — Arctic Climate Impact Assessment

CHARS — Canadian High Arctic Research Station

CAST — China Association for Science and Technology

CIMA — China Institute for Marine Affairs

CNPC — China National Petroleum Corporation

COSCO — China Ocean Shipping Company

CSCL — China Shipping Container Lines

CHINARE — China's National Arctic/Antarctic Research Expeditions

CACPR — Chinese Advisory Committee for Polar Research

CAA — Chinese Arctic and Antarctic Administration

CCP — Chinese Communist Party

CTBT — Comprehensive Test Ban Treaty

DoC — Declaration on the Conduct of the Parties

EU — European Union

HPH — Hutchison Port Holdings

IPCC — Intergovernmental Panel on Climate Change

IAEA — International Atomic Energy Agency

IMO — International Maritime Organization

IMF	International Monetary Fund
ITK	Inuit Tapiriit Kanatami
MFA	Ministry of Foreign Affairs (China)
MTCR	Missile Technology Control Regime
NPT	Nuclear Non-Proliferation Treaty
NLCA	Nunavut Land Claims Agreement
OECD	Organisation for Economic Co-operation and Development
OOCL	Orient Overseas Container Line
PLA	People's Liberation Army
PLAN	People's Liberation Army Navy
PRC	People's Republic of China
PRIC	Polar Research Institute of China
PSC	Politburo Standing Committee
RFMO	Regional Fisheries Management Organization
SAO	Senior Arctic Official
SIIS	Shanghai Institutes of International Studies
SDI	Spatial Data Infrastructure
SOA	State Oceanic Administration
SOE	State-Owned Enterprise
SLBM	Submarine Launched Ballistic Missiles
LOSC	UN Law of the Sea Convention
UNEP	United Nations Environment Programme
WWF	World Wildlife Fund

Acknowledgements

The genesis for this book project was a report, prepared under contract W6431-13-0111 for the Canadian Forces Aerospace Warfare Centre, which Whitney Lackenbauer completed in January–March 2013 based upon an extensive review of existing scholarship, media commentaries, public speeches, and conversations with Chinese officials and scholars at workshops and conferences. The opinions expressed therein were entirely those of the author and, as is the case with this book, should not be misconstrued as the official position of the Government of Canada. Lackenbauer wishes to thank Adam Lajeunesse and James Manicom for helping to draft portions of various chapters in that report. Kristopher Kinsinger, Tom Themeles, Kylie Bergfalk, and Timothy Wright provided research assistance in compiling and indexing media and academic literature on the topic.

This book is a significant expansion of that original report and draws extensively on the work of other scholars and commentators to whom we are deeply indebted. In particular, it builds upon David Wright's invaluable translations of Chinese commentaries for the US Naval War College, and Linda Jakobson's pioneering work for SIPRI (which served as the initial catalyst for intensified Western interest in China's Arctic aspirations). It also draws upon research collected by Manicom and Lackenbauer pursuant to their Centre for International Governance Innovation grant on "The Internationalization of the Arctic Council: Regional Governance under a Global Microscope," including the exceptional research assistance of Alladin Diakun.

In the final stages of revising the manuscript, Frédéric Lasserre used funds from his Social Sciences and Humanities Research Council of Canada grant to pay for research on recent Chinese academic literature by Ph.D. candidate Linyan Huang, and in Chinese language newspapers.

We are grateful for a St. Jerome's University Aid to Scholarly Publishing Grant that helped to subvent publication costs, as well as to Laval University.

Introduction

Canada's North covers 40 per cent of our territory and is home to more than 100,000 people, more than half of whom are Indigenous. For Canadians, the North captures our imagination like no other part of our country.

As the Arctic attracts increased economic activity, as its resources are increasingly sought after and as its navigation routes open and its ecosystems become increasingly fragile, what is Canada's responsibility?

We see the North as an essential part of our future and a place of extraordinary potential.

PAMELA GOLDSMITH-JONES,
Parliamentary Secretary to the
Canadian Minister of Global Affairs,
October 8, 2016[1]

For China, Arctic affairs can be divided into those of a regional nature and those of global implications. It has been China's position that the former should be properly resolved through negotiation between countries of the region. China respects the sovereignty and sovereign rights of Arctic countries, and hopes that they can collaborate with each other and peacefully resolve their disputes over territory and sovereignty.

YANG JIAN,
Vice President of the Shanghai Institutes
for International Studies,
"China and Arctic Affairs," *Arctic Yearbook* (2012)[2]

Over the past decade, politicians around the world have been paying increasingly close attention to the Arctic. Global climate change has attracted researchers anxious to better understand the essential role the region plays in global ecosystems. Meanwhile, newly accessible resources and transportation routes have drawn the attention of state and private enterprise looking to profit from these same changes. In Canada, questions of northern sovereignty, security, and development are now central policy considerations. For politicians looking to prove their nationalist *bona fides* a strong statement on the centrality of the Arctic to the nation is a common refrain. In academia and the media, an ever-expanding number of commentators point to the complex array of regional opportunities and challenges emerging in the face of rapid environmental change but fail to reach consensus on what it means for Canada or for the world.

Whether viewed as a barometer for the global climate, a scientific or resource frontier, a transit route to elsewhere, a tourist destination, or a homeland, the Arctic has captured the attention of the world – from Baffin Island to Beijing. With the attention of the world now on the region, Canada's historic and ongoing dilemma is how to balance sovereignty, security, and stewardship in a manner that protects and projects national interests and values, promotes sustainable development and healthy communities, and facilitates circumpolar stability and cooperation.

The salience of the Arctic in Canadian political discourse has certainly grown since Stephen Harper became prime minister in 2006 and trumpeted "use it or lose it" as the "first principle of sovereignty." Coupled with resource development and the idea of Canada as an "Arctic superpower," Canadians have been inundated with strong, muscular messages aimed at a domestic audience suffering from deep-seated anxiety about sovereignty loss at a time of economic uncertainty.[3] The ground had been already laid by commentators conjuring various would-be challengers to that "sovereignty" in the early twenty-first century.

Along these lines, the United States was recast in its traditional role of seeking to undermine Canada's position that the Northwest Passage constitutes internal waters, while also challenging Canadian ownership of a section of the Beaufort Sea (with all its potential resource riches). In practical terms, however, the United States – Canada's primary trading partner, with which we share the world's longest undefended border – remains an unlikely candidate to threaten Canada's territorial integrity or sovereignty.[4]

In the early twenty-first century when Denmark sent naval vessels to Hans Island, a tiny rock subject to competing claims with Canada, some Canadian commentators quickly cast this quiet neighbour and NATO ally as a potential threat. Rob Huebert, a political scientist at the University of Calgary and frequent commentator on circumpolar affairs in the national news media, published a memorable description likening the Danes to Vikings who had returned to steal our Arctic.[5] Huebert went on to say that this admittedly small issue might have significant knock-on effects, capable of creating larger doubts about Canada's claim to the entire Arctic Archipelago. These fears grabbed headlines for a short time before reassuring diplomatic statements, and the sober realities about the extent of the Hans Island dispute (which was confined to ownership of the insignificant rock itself), silenced the alarm.[6]

In 2007, Russian explorer Artur Chilingarov's flag-planting exploit at the North Pole brought into sharp relief his country's military revitalization plans, its resumption of strategic bomber flights in the Arctic, and its belligerent political rhetoric. The latter was (and is) designed to reassure Russian citizens that the Putin government is strong and will defend its Arctic resources against potential foreign encroachment. While there were striking similarities between Russian and Canadian political rhetoric on Arctic sovereignty and security,[7] Russian activism created obvious conditions for Canada to resurrect the Russian bear as a potential adversary. Following the Ilulissat Declaration in May 2008, which committed the Arctic states to peacefully resolving their disputes, anxieties about regional conflict were dampened and have remained subdued. Voices indicating that Canada and Russia actually had common, vested interests in circumpolar stability made the Russian threat seem less acute,[8] although the ongoing geopolitical tension sparked by Russia's 2014 invasion of Ukraine has resurrected debate about whether it portends the emergence of a "new cold war" in the Arctic.[9]

The official national policy document *Canada's Northern Strategy: Our North, Our Heritage, Our Future*, released in 2009, as well as Arctic foreign policy statements made by various officials at that time, all sent positive signals about Canada's sovereignty position and opportunities for international cooperation. Canada's dual messaging under Prime Minister Harper – emphasizing sovereignty, national security, and national interests on the one hand, and international cooperation and stewardship on the other – revealed Canada's complex perspective and position on Arctic issues.[10] Nevertheless, it seems that Canadian interest in the Arctic cannot be sustained, at least in academic and media circles, without a threat narrative.

The rising interest of "new actors" in circumpolar affairs – particularly China and other East Asian states – offers new uncertainty and thus the possibility of a new threat narrative. Accordingly, Canadian commentators have been particularly suspicious of China's intentions and agenda (or hidden agenda) with respect to Canada's Arctic waters, resources, fisheries, and continental shelf claim. Indeed, as China expands its influence and investments across the circumpolar Arctic, the question of Chinese intent has become more pressing.

This book represents our attempt, from a Canadian perspective, to answer some of the most critical questions surrounding Beijing's new Arctic interests, namely: is China a revisionist actor in the Arctic? What are its intentions for the region? And what does it all mean for Canada? To do so we explore China's motives and how its interests and activities in the North relate to its broader geopolitical objectives, revealing how these *actually* intersect with, and may affect, the interests of Canada and the other circumpolar states. Throughout this book we carefully analyze contemporary Chinese and Western social science literature and commentary; articles in the Chinese and Western media on Arctic issues; discussions with Chinese and North American Arctic specialists; and secondary sources on Chinese foreign and security policy. These sources are then filtered using *Canada's Northern Strategy* and *Canada's Arctic Foreign Policy Statement* – the two principle documents framing Canada's approach to the Arctic over the last decade.[11]

Canada's Northern Strategy and Arctic Foreign Policy

The essentials of Canada's Arctic policy are encapsulated in the Department of Indian [now Indigenous] Affairs and Northern Development's *Canada's Northern Strategy*.[12] This strategy emphasizes four main priorities: exercising Canada's Arctic sovereignty, promoting social and economic development, protecting Canada's environmental heritage, and improving and devolving Northern governance. Through these mutually reinforcing pillars, the government emphasizes the importance of exerting "effective leadership both at home and abroad in order to promote a prosperous and stable region responsive to Canadian interests and values."[13] The document reinforces a message of partnership: between the federal government and Northern Canadians, and between Canada and its circumpolar neighbours. Although the strategy trumpets the government's commitment to "putting more boots on the Arctic tundra, more ships in the icy water and a better eye-in-the-sky," it also emphasizes that Canada's disagreements with its neighbours are "well-managed and pose no sovereignty or defence challenges for Canada."[14]

The "use it or lose it" messaging that the Harper Government had frequently mobilized in earlier years to justify the government's agenda[15] was absent from the 2009 *Northern Strategy*. Instead, the document stressed opportunities for cooperation in the circumpolar world. The strategy casts the United States as an "exceptionally valuable partner in the Arctic" with which Canada has managed its differences responsibly since the Second World War. It also emphasizes opportunities for cooperation with Russia and "common interests" with European Arctic states, as well as a shared commitment to international law. Implicitly, this document confirms that bilateral and multilateral engagement is key to stability and security in the region. "We're not going down a road toward confrontation," Foreign Affairs Minister Lawrence Cannon emphasized. "Indeed, we're going down a road toward co-operation and collaboration. That is the Canadian way. And that's the way my other colleagues around the table have chosen to go as well."[11] If China, or any other state, was perceived as a threat, that fear is not apparent.

In August 2010, the Department of Foreign Affairs and International Trade (now Global Affairs Canada) released its own *Statement on Canada's Arctic Foreign Policy*, articulating Canada's international efforts pursuant to the Northern Strategy.[16] This document emphasizes the importance of the Arctic in Canada's national identity and its role as an "Arctic power," and again, the overall message is one of cooperation, with the Arctic presented as "a stable, rules-based region with clearly defined boundaries, dynamic economic growth and trade, vibrant Northern communities, and healthy and productive ecosystems."

Other dimensions of the *Statement on Canada's Arctic Foreign Policy* reflect the interaction between domestic and international agendas in Canada's Arctic strategy. Trade and investment in resource development – one of the primary catalysts for the surge in Arctic interest over the previous decade – are upheld as main priorities. Perhaps more than any other element, this creates the need for broader international cooperation in the region since it is unlikely that Canada can "create appropriate international conditions for sustainable development" in a region beset with intense competition and conflict. Furthermore, international events (particularly the catastrophic oil spill in the Gulf of Mexico in April 2010 and debates over oil drilling off the west coast of Greenland) have generated public concerns over the potential environmental consequences of oil and gas development in the Arctic. "On the controversial issue of hydrocarbon development, we are realistic," Inuit spokesperson Mary Simon explains. "We need non-renewable resource development if we are to achieve economic self-sufficiency. But the terms of such development must ensure the protection of our environment and the continuation of our way of life. On that, there can be no compromise."[17] Cooperation with foreign companies, Chinese or otherwise, will therefore have to be coordinated at a federal, territorial, and even community level. This logic continues to hold, even with the shift to a Liberal government under Justin Trudeau.[18]

Although none of Canada's Arctic foreign policy statements to date make specific mention of China, these documents clearly stake out a cooperative framework open to foreign investment – from both other circumpolar states as well as emerging powers in "central Asia and Eastern Europe."[19] Canada has declared its Arctic open for business and, as has been the case in decades past, is looking to foreign investors and shippers to assist in developing the region. Historically, this meant a reliance on American and (to a lesser extent) European resource companies. As we discuss in more detail in chapter four, however, Chinese state-owned enterprises (SOEs) have emerged as some of the world's best capitalized and most risk-tolerant operators. Cooperation in the Arctic will therefore mean more than working with our traditional partners; Canada will have to manage relationships with new actors in the Arctic, and China represents one of the most important of these.

0.1 Canada's International Focus in the Arctic, *Statement on Canada's Arctic Foreign Policy*, 2010.

The Statement on Canada's Arctic Foreign Policy (2010) notes that as Canada "advance[s] the four pillars of our Northern Strategy, our international efforts will focus on the following areas:"

- engaging with neighbours to seek to resolve boundary issues;
- securing international recognition for the full extent of our extended continental shelf;
- addressing Arctic governance and related emerging issues, such as public safety;
- creating the appropriate international conditions for sustainable development;
- seeking trade and investment opportunities that benefit northerners and all Canadians;
- encouraging a greater understanding of the human dimension of the Arctic;
- promoting an ecosystem-based management approach with Arctic neighbours and others;
- contributing to and supporting international efforts to address climate change in the Arctic;
- enhancing our efforts on other pressing environmental issues;
- strengthening Arctic science and the legacy of International Polar Year;
- engaging Northerners on Canada's Arctic foreign policy;
- supporting indigenous permanent participant organizations; and
- providing Canadian youth with opportunities to participate in the circumpolar dialogue.

Competing Frames: The View from the Ivory Tower

Framing issues – setting the story lines or "schemata of interpretation" used to explain and provide a perspective on how to organize or sort a series of events or information – inherently involves the selection, emphasis, exclusion, interpretation, and presentation of "some aspects of reality while excluding other elements."[20] Alarming news media headlines framing the Arctic as a theatre of conflict, with global players "scrambling" to secure access to the rich resources of the region, imply that competition, rivalry, and potential conflict represent the most relevant frameworks through which to view regional geopolitics.[21] After the May 2008 Ilulissat Declaration, when the Arctic coastal states committed to the peaceful, "orderly settlement of any possible overlapping claims" in the Arctic Ocean, as well as the dismissal of any need for a "new comprehensive international legal regime to govern the Arctic Ocean,"[22] the dominant narrative of conflict among Arctic states seemed less sustainable. Adapting the Arctic-in-peril frame to accommodate new non-Arctic state actors in Arctic political transportation, and economic development discussions as potential destabilizing forces, with (allegedly) little vested interest in the regional status quo, provided a revised pretext for anticipatory action by Arctic states such as a Canada to defend their rights. "Future hazardous events/conditions must somehow be made known and identifiable in the present before it makes sense to talk about various forms of mitigating strategies," Chih Yuan Woon observes in his study of media framings of the Arctic. In the case of Canada's leading newspaper, "the logics of preemption and preparedness saturate" framings of the "so-called 'China threat,'" invoking Canada's need to defend national sovereignty by "seeking recourse to law and order in order to rein in China's growing ambitions in the Arctic."[23]

The emergence of China as a major Arctic player and partner in Arctic development has actually led to mixed reactions in the Canadian media and among the general public. In large measure these impressions have been shaped and guided by an ongoing debate among Arctic experts analyzing China's global and regional aspirations and agenda. Gang Chen, a researcher at the East Asian Institute, National University of Singapore, observes:

> As an East Asian power that has neither Arctic coast nor the
> Arctic Council membership, China's open statement of not

having a strategic agenda regarding the melting Arctic has been interpreted in dichotomous ways: some take it as a genuine expression from the Chinese government while others regard it as a tactic taken by the rising power to hide its real intention there due to its limited influence in the remote Arctic region. Such a divergence over whether China is following an Arctic strategy to secure its long-term economic interest or even geopolitical influence is analogical with, and to some extent, can be perceived as part of the early debates over whether China has a calculative grand strategy.[24]

This split in interpretation is clearly evident in Canadian commentary. On the one hand, alarmists – centred around what we will label the "Conflict School" of David Wright and Rob Huebert – suggest that Canadians should be wary of East Asian states (particularly China) as revisionist actors with interests counter to those of Canada. On the other hand, commentators like ourselves argue that Canada's national interests in the Arctic are generally compatible with those of East Asian countries and see opportunities for collaboration and mutual benefit.

David Wright, a military historian specializing in diplomacy and warfare in imperial China and the conquest dynasties, is not an Arctic expert but his linguistic skills have made him a leading commentator on what Chinese academics are writing about Arctic issues. His overarching message is that Canadians must recognize the attention that "astute and acutely observant geostrategic thinkers" in China are paying to the region. "The Canadian Arctic has what China wants: natural resources and the possibility of a major new shipping route," Wright argues. "China knows that Canadian control over these resources makes Canada a major international player, a country with natural resource wealth and geostrategic advantage befitting its sheer geographical size, but out of proportion with its relatively small population."[25] He noted in March 2011 that "there is at present quite a bit of room for discussion and debate in China over this issue, both in the halls of power in Beijing and, to a surprisingly open and public extent, in academic journals and popular news media." While pointing out that Beijing has yet to formulate an official Arctic policy, Wright asserts that "what non-official observers are writing should worry Canadians." Amplifying the voices of the most aggressive Chinese analysts, Wright pointed to China's perceived entitlement to the resource riches of the Arctic as the world's most populous country, as well as its desire to see most of the Arctic Basin remain "international territory" and to dilute Canada's sovereignty over the Northwest Passage to the point of "meaninglessness."[26]

Wright highlighted these concerns in a study for the US Naval War College, recommending that:

> American policy makers should be aware that China's recent interest in Arctic affairs is not an evanescent fancy or a passing political fad but a serious, new, incipient policy direction. China is taking concrete diplomatic steps to ensure that it becomes a player in the Arctic game and eventually will have what it regards as its fair share of access to Arctic resources and sea routes. China has already committed substantial human, institutional, and naval resources to its Arctic interests and will continue to do so, likely at an accelerated rate, in the future.[27]

Wright's warnings echo the work of political scientist Rob Huebert, who has sounded the alarm about East Asia's Arctic intentions for more than a decade. As part of the "sovereignty on thinning ice" narrative that he developed in the early 2000s,[28] Huebert frequently cited the purportedly unannounced arrival of the Chinese research vessel *Xue Long* at Tuktoyaktuk in 1999 as an example of Canada's negligible control over activities in the region, and the host of sovereignty related challenges *potentially* posed by Asian states with cutting-edge icebreaking capacity, an insatiable appetite for resources, and little vested interest in the status quo.[29]

As a regular fixture in the Canadian media on Arctic issues, Huebert has consistently framed twenty-first century Arctic dynamics through a threat narrative. For example, in portending a "new Arctic age" in August 2008, Huebert stressed that the region was "on the verge of becoming a more complicated and crowded area" and Canadians had to know how "to meet many challenges." To control its Arctic, he asserted, Canada needs to act decisively to deal with "some of the challenges we know about: climate change, resource development, globalization (the South Koreans are entering the market to build ice-capable vessels, the Japanese are investing heavily in the study of Arctic gas hydrates off the coast of Canada, and China is going to become an Arctic player as well), Russia is on the rise again, and laws governing the maritime Arctic are in flux."[30]

Huebert has continuously reiterated his concerns about East Asian interests in the region in his regular public and policy-related presentations and media statements since that time. Commenting on the "real possibility" of future tension in the Arctic in early 2012, he emphasized China's looming impact on Arctic security. "What we're seeing with the Chinese is that they've made it very clear that they want to be major players in the Arctic for reasons of transportation, natural resources, scientific research, and strategic concerns," Huebert noted. "They will be there. They're spending the money. Their navy is being modernized as we speak at a time when the American navy is facing huge budget cuts."[31]

Other commentators have carried this line of argument to its logical conclusion. In 2006, Canadian writer and historian Victor Suthren (the director general of the Canadian War Museum from 1986–97) justified the need for naval investments by linking China, terrorism, and the Arctic in a curious fashion:

> Canada's Arctic is melting into an ice-free major-ocean coastline that will provide the government of the day with the challenge of policing three busy ocean coasts; the extraordinary economic expansion of China is now being followed by heavy defence expenditures on developing a large and capable Chinese blue-water navy; and the vital seaborne trade that lies at the heart of Canadian economic well-being will see the flow of thousands of containers into our ports increase fivefold within our lifetimes. A seaborne terrorist attack on North America is increasingly a possibility.[32]

The following year, Rear Admiral Tyrone Pile, the commander of Canada's Maritime Forces Pacific, told the *Calgary Herald* editorial board that the Chinese Navy would soon have twice as many submarines as the US Navy, leading the newspaper to speculate that China might project its power "as Great Britain and the US once did." Indicating that China was aware that the Northwest Passage could soon be navigable and would "trim thousands of kilometres from Asia to Europe by bypassing the Panama Canal," the paper raised troubling questions: "how prepared is Canada to enforce its sovereignty claims in the region, if foreign ships, Chinese or otherwise, try to take advantage of this Arctic melting – without the formality of Ottawa's approval? What if those vessels are supported by their country's warships?" The editorial concluded that Canada had to achieve regional dominance in its northern waters to "deter a future Arctic sovereignty challenge."[33]

These threat narratives continue to emerge and, in many cases, dominate the Canadian popular media. A *Winnipeg Free Press* editorial on "China's Arctic Ambition" from 2014 is a case in point, beginning with the straight-forward assertion that "China has become increasingly vocal in asserting its right to a leadership role in how the Arctic is developed, challenging the very idea [that] the resources of the high north belong exclusively to those with sovereign claims on the territory." This apparent challenge to the sovereign rights of Arctic states such as Canada is predicated on China's alleged desire to have "the polar region internationalized, similar to the Antarctic, with its resources shared by anyone with the means and ability to develop and extract them for a profit." Although the editorial is silent on *who* in China has made these claims, the message is clearly designed to provoke public anxiety. After all, it asserts, "China also claims non-Arctic nations have a legitimate stake in northern development for reasons other than resource extraction or free navigation of the seas. These include concerns about climate change and environmental monitoring, protection of marine and land-based wildlife, and the welfare of indigenous peoples." While legitimate issues, the paper concedes, they are "merely an attempt [by China] to disguise its goal of easy access to the enormous potential wealth in the Arctic." After listing a series of benign Chinese activities in the Arctic, including bilateral research and trade initiatives with European Arctic states and Russia and the construction of a new Chinese icebreaker, the editor jumps to the conclusion that "by words and deeds, then, China has made it clear it will not be an idle observer. It wants a direct role in Arctic development and it is challenging the very idea of sovereignty, a proposition that is supported by countries around the world." For the *Free Press* editorial board, this requires a call to action. "For some countries, the future of the Arctic is up for debate and interpretation," it suggests. For Canada, however, the alleged threat posed by China to Canada's Arctic sovereignty requires "a speedier resolution" of the longstanding issues about Northern development "rather than allowing the outliers an opportunity to control and manipulate the dialogue."[34]

This belief in a Chinese drive to secure Canadian resources for itself, or to challenge Canadian control over the Northwest Passage, is a common theme in Canadian media. Diane Francis, a regular commentator for the *National Post*, asserted (falsely) that China has called the Northwest Passage an international strait and is building an icebreaker fleet to use it.[35] Robert Sibley, writing in the *Ottawa Citizen*, suggested in 2015 that Beijing is "eyeing the region with military strategies in mind," while Michael Byers and Scott Borgerson suggest that Russian naval vessels, or those of "other unfriendly nations," may barge through the passage.[36] Reports of Chinese interest in building a research station in the Canadian High Arctic are also met with skepticism in some circles, with Huebert acknowledging benefits of international scientific cooperation but asking: "Do you necessarily want to give a state that is that authoritarian a set of abilities to observe within the North?"[37] In 2016, the Chinese publication of an *Arctic Navigation Guide (Northwest Passage)*, indicating Chinese interest in planning voyages through Canadian waters, also generated suspicion in some media outlines, with Huebert warning that China's encouragement of commercial shipping through the North American polar route could pose "the biggest direct challenge to Canadian sovereignty in the Northwest Passage" if Chinese-flagged vessels sailed without Canadian consent, threatening to undermine Canada's legal position on "internal waters."[38] Commentators also suggest that Chinese behaviour elsewhere in the world might impinge upon Canada's Arctic sovereignty. "China has – so far – respected the fishing and continental shelf rights of the five coastal states" in the Arctic Ocean, Michael Byers noted in July 2016. "But if China rejects the application of the UN Convention on the Law of the Sea in Asia," as it seemed to do by rejecting the judgment of the Permanent Court of Arbitration when it ruled against China's claim in the South China Sea, "can any country rely on it respecting those same promises in the Arctic?"[39]

In contrast to these China-as-threat narratives, other experts offer a more optimistic appraisal of China's Arctic interests. Responding to scenarios positing China as a challenger to Canada's Arctic sovereignty, Frédéric Lasserre rebutted "prevailing assumptions in the general literature [in 2010] … that the Chinese government and Chinese shipping companies are merely waiting for the Northwest Passage to open up a bit more before launching full-scale service across Arctic Canadian waters between Asia and Europe." He found no evidence that shipping companies' strategies seriously contemplated the passage as an attractive deep-water transit route, or that China sought to claim territorial rights in the region. Consequently, Lasserre saw China's growing interest in Arctic affairs as "a good opportunity for Canada to voice its desire to foster cooperation in the region" and to advance its interests through enhanced polar shipping regulations, scientific collaboration, and adherence to international law.[40] His subsequent publications, often co-authored with colleagues and graduate students, have reaffirmed these themes.[41] Similarly, Whitney Lackenbauer has been sceptical of the China-as-threat narrative, noting emerging opportunities in Canada and the other Arctic states to realize their national goals, maintain their leadership role in regional governance, and accommodate growing international interests in the circumpolar North by constructively engaging with China and other Asian states.[42] His work with James Manicom suggests that non-Arctic states have legitimate interests in (and can make substantive contributions to) the region, as long as they respect the Arctic states' sovereignty and sovereign rights to exclusive economic zones (EEZs) and extended continental shelves as scripted in international law.[43] Several other Canadian authors also suggest that China's Arctic interests do not inherently pose a threat to Canada or to circumpolar stability – and might even serve as a basis for improved Sino-Canadian relations.[44]

This more optimistic messaging fits with the European scholarly literature, which tends to avoid alarmist rhetoric. Linda Jakobson and Jingchao Peng of the Stockholm International Peace Research Institute observed in 2012 that, while non-Chinese observers refer to Beijing's "more assertive" Arctic actions, "China's Arctic policies are still in a nascent stage of formulation." They emphasize that "China has not published an Arctic strategy and is not expected to do so in the near to medium-term." Nevertheless, in a low-key, measured, and pragmatic way Chinese officials have taken steps to investigate and "protect" China's regional interests, emphasizing the global impacts of the melting sea ice. Jakobson and Jingchao place the Chinese Government's key interests in three broad categories:

1. to strengthen its capacity to respond appropriately to the effects that climate change in the Arctic will have on food production and extreme weather in China;

2. to secure access, at reasonable cost, to Arctic shipping routes; and

3. to strengthen China's ability as a non-Arctic state to
    access Arctic resources and fishing waters.[45]

The growing literature on China's Arctic interests tends to focus on these themes through prisms of geopolitics, international relations (particularly in seeking to discern China's orientation as a status quo or revisionist actor), and political economy. Given the absence of an official Chinese Arctic strategy, scholars tend to describe, and in many cases rank, what they see as the relative priorities that China does or should place on science, climate change, resource development, polar shipping lanes, regional governance, socio-cultural issues, and other geostrategic considerations.[46] In general, most Asian and Nordic scholars place less emphasis on traditional security and more on economic considerations, particularly related to energy and mineral resources, as well as prospective contributions that Chinese inclusion in regional affairs can offer to multilateral regimes and bodies such as the Arctic Council.[47] Other scholars focus on China's interpretations of the law of sea and international law more generally, discerning potential implications for Arctic governance or, conversely, how Arctic cooperation may offer models for ocean governance and peaceful conflict resolution in the South China Sea.[48]

The deluge of recent scholarship suggests that China's growing Arctic interests over the last decade, even if they represent a tiny part of the global power's foreign policy more generally, are a source of tremendous interest for Arctic states and other stakeholders. During his July 2010 High North study tour in Norway, Chinese Assistant Foreign Minister Liu Zhenmin explained his country's focus on Arctic cooperation:

> The first reason is China's geographical location. China is separated from Arctic by only one country, Russia. The most northern part of China is around 50 degree of north latitude. As a country located in north hemisphere, China is seriously affected by climate and weather in Arctic.
>
> The second reason is scientific research requirement. Arctic is a unique place for global climate research and environment assessment. Airspace and outer space observation in Arctic is important for over Arctic flight and satellite.

Third, potential impacts on China. In case the Arctic shipping routes open someday, global shipping, energy activities and trade will be affected. We feel we are part of the world, changes in the Arctic will affect China.[49]

The reaction of the Arctic states to this growing Chinese interest have ranged from caution to full-blown hostility. This book argues, however, that the basis for this China-in-the-Arctic alarmism is speculative and imprecise, originating from (and largely reflective of) generalized discourses associated with the "rise of Asia" and Arctic change and sovereignty. Despite substantial allusions in academic and popular commentaries to China's potential as a revisionist actor in the region, there is a striking lack of substantive discussion about how or why China constitutes an alleged threat to Canada's Arctic interests.

Canadian Public Opinion of China

At the grassroots level, polling data shows that Canadian public opinion tends to sync more with the alarmist school of thought regarding China's presence in the Arctic. Essentially, most Canadians seem to be conditioned to conflate external interests in the Arctic with threats – a conflation that is continually reinforced, albeit with scant evidence, by certain elements of the media, themselves fed fresh analysis by the "Conflict School" and other academic circles.

A 2011 survey, conducted by Ekos Research for the Munk-Gordon Arctic Security Programme, clearly indicated popular antipathy towards Chinese involvement in the circumpolar world. The pollster provided respondents in each of the eight member states of the Arctic Council with a list of countries and asked which one they would be most and least comfortable dealing with on Arctic issues. Respondents in every nation except Russia identified China as the least desired partner (see figure 0.2). Furthermore, Canadians expressed the lowest levels of support for including non-Arctic states in the Arctic Council and granting them "a say in Arctic affairs" (see figure 0.3).[50]

The foundation undertook a second survey in 2015, though this version did not specifically reference China. It showed that support within Canada has grown for "countries that do not have an Arctic territory" to gain a say in "Arctic affairs" (26 per cent in southern Canada and 32 per cent in Northern Canada). Although this may indicate a modest swing from the data collected

0.2 Least Preferred Partner in Dealing with Arctic Issues, *Rethinking the Top of the World*, WDGF survey, 2011.

"Which of the following countries would you be least comfortable with (your country) dealing with on Arctic Issues?"

	FIRST CHOICE	SECOND CHOICE	THIRD CHOICE
Northern Canada	China	United States	Russia
Southern Canada	China	Russia	United States
Denmark	China	United States	Other
Finland	China	Other Europe	United States
Iceland	China	United States	Russia
Norway	China	United States	Other Europe
Russia	United States	Scandinavia	China
Sweden	China	United States	Other Europe
United States	China	Russia	Other Europe

0.3 Support for Inclusion of Non-Arctic States, *Rethinking the Top of the World*, WGDF Survey, 2010.

"Do you think non-Arctic states, like China or organizations like the European Union, should be invited to join the Arctic Council and have a say in Arctic affairs?"

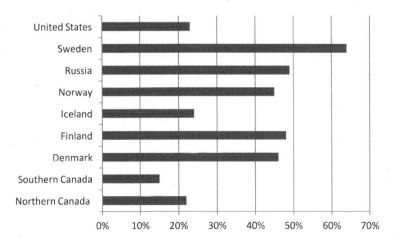

four years earlier, the more general question posed in this survey makes it impossible to gauge Canadian feelings about China in particular.[51]

Around the time of the Munk-Gordon Foundation's initial 2011 survey, Canadian popular opinion regarding China more generally seems to have deteriorated. The *2012 National Opinion Poll: Canadian Views on Asia*, commissioned by the Asia Pacific Foundation of Canada and conducted by Angus Reid, confirmed that "Canadians across the country are increasingly attuned to Asia and to Canada's place in the Asia Pacific region." This was particularly true of Northern Canada, where 57 per cent of respondents reported that they paid more attention to Canada's relations with Asia over the previous year than they had in the past.[52] In addition, 12 per cent of Canadians polled expressing "warm" (favourable) feelings towards China, while 29 per cent of Canadians indicated "cold" (unfavourable) ratings of China. This fit with a general trend of favourable or "warm" feelings to Western countries and unfavourable "cool" feelings to Asian countries, except Japan. Since 2012, Canadian attitudes towards China, and Asia more generally, have warmed.

In part, these feelings were due to Canadian perceptions of a shift in the international order that placed China in an increasingly powerful position. Two-thirds of Canadians polled believed that China's global influence would surpass that of the United States over the next decade. While more than a third of Canadians described the US as "in decline," 42 per cent perceived China as "growing" (tied with India atop the list) and 30 per cent described it as "strong." Nonetheless, Canadians ranked China the "least favourable" overall. The leading factor contributing to this outlook was the perception of Chinese governance. Here, 45 per cent of respondents described China as authoritarian, 37 per cent as "corrupt," and 34 per cent as "threatening." Only 4 per cent described China as "friendly." While 5 per cent expressed a general feeling of admiration towards China, 22 per cent said that they "disliked" the country.[53]

The *2012 National Opinion Poll* also found that Canadians tended to focus on economic relationships. In particular, Canadians consider China to be important to Canada's prosperity (second only to the United States in perceived importance). Accordingly, more than half of Canadians polled saw China's increasing economic power as more of an opportunity than a threat, perceiving opportunities for trade and investment, and for diversification of global economic and political relationships. A majority of Canadians (and 63 per cent of northerners) believed that "Canada must act now to take advantage

0.4 Canadian Opinion on China, Asia Pacific Foundation of Canada, 2012.

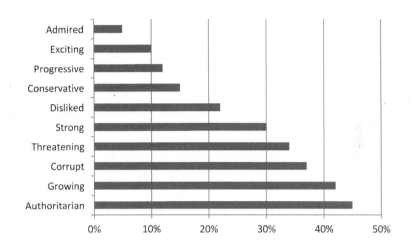

of Asia's need for energy resources," but this did not extend to receptiveness for foreign ownership of Canadian resources by state-controlled companies. Most Canadians remained "unconvinced that the economic benefits of Asia's investment in Canada's energy sector outweigh concerns about foreign ownership of our natural resources."[54]

Accordingly, the Asia Pacific Foundation concluded that Canadians retain "a lingering hesitation and concern about Asia, particularly China." Although aware of the benefits of Asian foreign investment in Canada, the poll found that "fewer than one-in-five Canadians would be in favour of state-controlled companies from China ... buying a controlling stake in a major Canadian company." It also noted a six point increase in the proportion of Canadians worried about China's military power in the Asia Pacific region.[55] As with leading pundits and scholars, China's behaviour in its region colours perceptions of China intentions elsewhere.

By 2016, however, the Asia Pacific Foundation surveys indicated that Canadians tended to "feel more connected and positive toward Asia than they did two years ago, and are more optimistic about future relations with the region," with increasing numbers supporting trans-Pacific cooperation. Indeed, 48 per cent of those polled believed that "economic and political relations with Asia should be Canada's top foreign policy priority." Looking specifically to China, "Canadians have warmed to the country since 2014" with nearly half of Canadians polled (49 per cent) perceiving the "growing importance of China as more of an opportunity than a threat," and with one-quarter of respondents suggesting that the Canada-China relationship is improving and another 46 per cent suggesting that it is stable. Furthermore, 20 per cent of Canadians polled supported a closer economic relationship with China, with another 50 per cent indicating that they "could probably be persuaded to support a closer economic relationship with China if more information was available." While almost half (46 per cent) of Canadians support a free trade agreement (FTA) with China (up from 36 per cent in 2014), an equal number opposed this potential relationship. Among northern Canadians, 51 per cent considered that Asia was important for their territory's economic prosperity (down from 61 per cent in 2014), while 46 per cent believed that it was not.[56]

According to the 2016 poll, Canadians continued to find various aspects of engagement with China to be disconcerting. Nearly half of those polled anticipated "a significant military conflict in the Asia Pacific" in the next decade, suggesting a persistent wariness about China's growing military power (which 65 per cent of Canadians polled cited as a threat to regional stability with direct implications for Canada). Although Canadians remained "relatively positive on private investment from Asia," the APFC found that the vast majority of Canadians remained "distrustful of foreign state-owned enterprises (SOEs) investing in Canada," with only 11 per cent of those polled supporting investment by Chinese SOEs in Canada. Furthermore, fewer Canadians believed that China's human rights record was improving, and about half indicated that they would be willing to sacrifice economic opportunities to promote political rights such as freedom of speech, expression, and political association. In summary, the APFC concluded that its "2016 poll results reflect a public that wants a government that can multi-task across a range of core policy issues, and is open to the development of a mature relationship with Asia: one that is nuanced and takes into account Canadian values and national interests."[57]

The Chinese Threat

How Canada should conceive of and approach China – whether as a friend, strategic partner, revisionist actor, competitor, potential adversary, or a mix of these frames – is a topic of ongoing academic discussion and debate. "China's resumption of power and influence is one of the transformative developments of this century," Asia-Pacific expert Paul Evans noted in his study on Canada's engagement strategies with China since the 1970s. "Its political power is that it is becoming a rule maker, and occasional rule breaker, with a major hand in defining the rules, norms, and institutions of global order in ways that only decades ago seemed unimaginable."[58] The rise – or global spread – of Chinese power and influence has catapulted the country from a secondary or tertiary place in Canadian diplomacy to a "top-tier policy priority for Ottawa," with questions abounding about whether China's participation in international institutions will conform with "a Western-led liberal order" or whether it will instead "try to create an alternative set of institutions, norms, and rules." In any case, Evans observes, "it is certain that Chinese views, interests, and priorities will be increasingly visible and influential. Canada and the West are no longer dealing with just an important country and trading partner; they are dealing with a great power with global weight."[59]

In his important book *Middle Power, Middle Kingdom: What Canadians Need to Know about China in the 21st Century*, former Canadian diplomat David Mulroney notes that by the time Prime Minister Harper finally visited Beijing in December 2009 Canadians were already "well into a Chinese discovery of Canada as a destination for investment in resources." Mulroney notes that "this was the latest step in an ambitious effort that saw China's major state-owned enterprises expanding their global reach, deploying vast and growing reserves of cash to secure footholds in key markets." Whether in the mining, petroleum, shipping, banking, or manufacturing sectors, this "rush to go global" and concomitant activities in Canada said "much about what China was, what it is now and what it is becoming." Chinese investment also generates significant debate, Mulroney observes, with SOEs either representing "admirable free-market offspring born of Deng Xiaoping's reforms, or Trojan horses, vehicles for bringing the very worst of the Chinese Communist system into the Canadian economy." Both views have merit, the former ambassador in Beijing suggests: the tethers connecting SOEs to "the center of power in Beijing" may be longer now, but they still bind these companies to state priorities.[60] As Evans observed in 2014, a significant number of Conservative politicians in Canada "continue to see China as godless, totalitarian, a security threat, and ruled by an illegitimate and morally unacceptable government."[61] Ongoing concerns about China's human rights record, commitment to global environmental health and the mitigation of climate change, and challenges to the liberal international order will continue to complicate our bilateral relationship – but, as Mulroney acknowledges, "not engaging China just isn't an option."[62]

Although polls suggest that most Canadians seem to view China's engagement in Arctic affairs with skepticism and even distaste, there is a striking lack of substantive discussion in academic and popular commentaries about how or why China constitutes a perceived threat to Canada's Arctic interests. While China's dictatorial form of government and poor human rights record suggest that its actions should be monitored with greater scrutiny than those of other Asian states, its growing interest in the Arctic does not necessarily imply malevolent intent, nor do its economic investments mean that Beijing is surreptitiously gaining control over sparsely populated regions of Canada and/or other circumpolar nations.[63] Rather, China's interests should be viewed through a more global lens that takes into consideration the country's continuously evolving economic, political, and security requirements and aspirations. These are often not Arctic-centric but rather hinge on trans-regional issues such as climate change, maritime shipping, environmental protection, regional inter-governmental cooperation, and scientific research exchange and cooperation.[64]

Since the 2008 Ilullissat Declaration, wherein the Arctic coastal states pledged to respect international law and downplayed the idea of conflict among themselves, China has emerged as a kind of threat du jour. Its sheer size and wealth, coupled with the fact that it is not actually an Arctic state, make its Arctic ambitions suspect. Yet, our closer examination of its investment patterns, political statements, and activities in the North paint a different picture. Rather than a threat to Canadian sovereignty or security, Chinese involvement in the Arctic should be seen as an opportunity that, if managed well, can facilitate northern development and strengthen Canada's legal position vis-à-vis the Northwest Passage, all the while improving international cooperation in the fields of science, fisheries preservation, and environmental protection.

This Book

Chapter one sets China's Arctic ambitions in the context of debates over Chinese foreign policy, and suggests a disconnect between the reaction to China's purported interests in the Arctic and its foreign policy tradition. It also questions the assumption that China is a revisionist territorial actor, motivated by resource concerns that could potentially dominate the Arctic Council and circumpolar affairs more generally. These notions contrast starkly with China's behaviour towards territorial and maritime disputes around the world, its resource procurement strategy, its track record in international institutions, and its emerging perspective on Arctic governance. Although many commentators have raised alarms over China's Arctic interests in recent years, we observe that the Arctic does not factor highly on China's national agenda relative to domestic, regional, and global priorities – including bilateral relations with some Arctic states.

Chapter two critically examines Chinese scientific interests in the Arctic and shows that China perceives its northern interests in global terms. China established a research station at Svalbard in 2004 and has been conducting research trips to the Arctic (using the *Xue Long* icebreaker) since 1999.[65] From a research standpoint, however, China is best considered as a polar state rather than an Arctic one. Analysis reveals that China's Antarctic interests predate its Arctic interests, and that the Chinese polar research budget still reflects a 4:1 ratio in favour of Antarctic research.[66] Furthermore, its interests intersect with extensive multilateral scientific cooperation that already exists in the Arctic, reflecting the coordination work of the Arctic Council as well as the recent International Polar Year.

Chapter three explores questions of shipping and sovereignty. With the world's largest export economy, China is aware of the global shifts that could be brought by year-round trans-Arctic shipping (particularly through the Northern Sea Route) and the effects this would have on global trading patterns. China has a direct interest in the prospect of a new international maritime trade route in the region and has already benefited from pioneering commercial transits through the NSR that have carried iron ore and condensates from Norwegian and Russian ports to Shanghai.[67] Accordingly, this chapter examines the international legal regime that applies to the Arctic waters, with particular emphasis on substantive issues related to maritime zones and jurisdictions, principles for the delimitation of maritime boundaries, the regime for the high seas, and the need to balance coastal state rights with the traditional freedom of the seas.

Chapter four looks specifically at the question of Arctic resources and Chinese interest therein. As a major mineral and hydrocarbon importer, China perceives resource supply through a security lens as well as an economic one. In the wake of the Ukrainian crisis, China has acted to secure long-term energy contracts in exchange for financing development in the Russian Arctic and sub-Arctic. Furthermore, China's demand for both strategic and base minerals from around the world will mean that, as Arctic deposits become increasingly feasible for extraction, its interests will increase accordingly. China recognizes that the vast majority of Arctic resources fall under Arctic states' control but, given the capital-intensive nature of Arctic development, it is likely that China's financial resources will play a significant role in the form and pace of Arctic resource development over the next decade.

Chapter five looks specifically at China's interests in the Arctic Council and the range of Chinese perspectives on Arctic governance more generally. Rather than perceiving Chinese state and scholarly ideas as a threat to Canada's interests, the decision to accept China as an observer to the Council does not risk opening the door to Chinese dominance in Arctic affairs. Arctic states would have run a greater risk trying to exclude China from the Council, thus forcing Beijing to pursue its interests through other multilateral or bilateral fora. Instead, Canada should embrace China's participation as an Arctic Council observer as an opportunity to involve it in matters of genuinely global importance, from shipping to trans-boundary pollutants.

Readers may be surprised that we have not included a chapter on defence or "hard" security issues. After all, the extent to which the Arctic is becoming "militarized" and whether we should expect international conflict or co-operation in the region has been hotly debated in the twenty-first century. Although most experts now downplay the probability of Arctic armed conflict,[68] a few prominent commentators continue to pose questions and frame popular debates that get picked up in non-Arctic states.[69] Thus, when Chinese commentators suggest the Arctic's potential military value,[70] they tend to simply echo Russian and Western statements.[71] Indeed, it is remarkable how few Chinese officials have made public statements on Arctic defence issues. In a presentation to the Second Sino-Canadian Exchange on Arctic Issues, a Chinese delegate explained that China is committed to pursuing a policy which is defensive in nature. Accordingly, the presenter laid out China's policy concerns over the Arctic:

- Concerns over the Arms Race and territorial wrangling in the Arctic, which may undermine the peaceful and stable environment of the Arctic.

- Concerns [that] Non Arctic countries are unjustifiably impeded from playing a certain role in the Arctic, especially in affairs of a trans-regional nature such as climate change and maritime shipping.

- Concerns over discriminatory laws, regulations or high standards [that] may be adopted by Arctic Coastal States, which may impair the rights of other states under the Convention, or restrict the developing states to conduct relevant activities in the arctic, especially marine scientific research.

- Concerns that excess claims for extension of the outer continental shelf may encroach the area in the Arctic Ocean, which is the common heritage of mankind.[72]

We do not anticipate that these concerns are likely to provoke Chinese military action in the Arctic in the foreseeable future.[73] In any case, China has no naval or air force capability to project power in or over the Arctic Ocean, and – simply put – its defence priorities lie elsewhere.

In the end, this study generally concurs with the main findings of Jakobson and Jingchao, who anticipate that "pragmatic considerations will be the main drivers of China's Arctic policies" and that the Arctic is not likely to become a main priority in Chinese foreign policy over the next decade." While access to Arctic resources is leading to more Chinese investments in co-development projects with Arctic states, we agree that – all things considered – it is "hard to envision China being genuinely assertive in the Arctic."[74] While drawing heavily upon the invaluable translations of Chinese studies and documents by David Wright up to 2011, this study differs substantively in its overall analysis of what the myriad of Chinese statements about the North actually mean when placed into a broader context. Our own assessment of Chinese academic and media articles on the Arctic suggests a growing awareness of potential opportunities associated with emerging shipping routes, resources, and polar science, as well as perceived roles for China in regional affairs as a "responsible actor" that respects the sovereignty of Arctic states and will abide by applicable international rules.[75] Accordingly, we arrive at a different assessment than that of the "Conflict School," which anticipates Chinese activism and even aggression to pursue its Arctic interests. Rather, we feel that, if managed properly, the relationship between China and the circumpolar states can be a productive and cordial one, with benefits for every partner over the longer term.

Situating the Arctic in China's Strategy

The global expansion of China's political and economic influences has moved China's strategic concerns from regional to global. Since the start of reform and the open-door policy, China's foreign policy has been aimed at creating peaceful international environment [sic] and favourable regional surroundings for domestic economic and social development. Over the past three decades, China has orientated itself as a regional power instead of a global power and showed more interest in East Asian affairs rather than issues in other parts of the world. In the new century, China's fast-growing economic and diplomatic strength and influence gradually can be detected in almost every corner of the world. Its global interest is growing rapidly due to the heavy dependence upon overseas supply of energy and raw materials as well as reliable maritime transportation. Although China now still orients itself as a regional power rather than a global power, more and more of its strategic concerns are moving beyond the periphery of East Asia to faraway places like Africa, Latin America, and ultimately, the Polar regions.

GANG CHEN,
"China's Emerging Arctic Strategy" (2012)[1]

China's activities and interests in the Arctic are often set against the backdrop of broader trends in the global political economy, and often implicitly framed through particular assumptions about what China's growing economic might and international assertiveness mean generally. This chapter attempts to lay these assumptions bare and give scrutiny to their foundations by holding China's purported interests in the Arctic against its observed foreign policy tradition. Although much has been made of China's Arctic interests in recent years, it is worth considering that the Arctic does not factor very highly on China's national agenda. Indeed, this chapter illustrates the disconnect between the common assumption that China's behaviour towards its own neighbours is, in any way, a bellwether for its behaviour towards Arctic countries.

In 2013, an economic survey by the Organisation for Economic Co-operation and Development (OECD) indicated that China's staggering growth will almost certainly continue.[2] China's GDP is $13.39 trillion (USD) – although that represents a modest $9,800 per capita (its population in 2013 was 1.355 billion).[3] The country weathered the post-2008 global economic crisis well compared to other OECD countries. The National Intelligence Council (senior experts in the US intelligence community who provide advice to the Director of National Intelligence) noted in *Global Trends 2030* that "China's contribution to global investment growth is now one and a half times the size of the US contribution."[4] In the World Bank's baseline modeling of future economic multipolarity, China – despite a likely slowing of its economic growth – will contribute about one-third of global growth by 2025, far more than any other economy.[5]

On March 5, 2013, at the opening of the National People's Congress, China announced an official defence budget of $114.3 billion – an increase of 10.7 per cent over 2012 and nearly four times its budget in 2003 (though still only 2 per cent of its GDP). This defence budget is the second-largest in the world, and China's military-spending growth is roughly consistent with its rising GDP. "Since the early 1990s, China has been surprisingly forthright about the reasons it is strengthening its military: to catch up with other powers, to construct a more capable and modern military force in order to assert its outstanding territorial and maritime claims, and to secure its development on its own terms," American defence analysts Andrew Erickson and Adam Liff observe. "It also wants to acquire prestige as a full-fledged 'military great power' – a status its leaders appear to increasingly see as necessary to enhance China's international standing." However much of a force China has become in its "Near Seas" (the Yellow, East China, and South China Seas), these analysts believe that its capabilities to engage in combat operations overseas will remain limited.[6]

Chinese grand strategy is guided by the underlying principle of maintaining external stability to promote domestic development. Recent statements indicate that China's foreign policy is designed to "safeguard the interests of sovereignty, security, and development" – core ideas that the state councillor for external relations Dai Bingguo defined in December 2010 as China's political stability ("the stability of the CCP leadership and of the socialist system"); sovereign security, territorial integrity, and national unification; and "China's sustainable economic and social development."[7]

Events in recent years reflect an emerging duality. On the one hand, Beijing maintains a rhetorical commitment to the notion that China is still a developing country, and uses this as a pretext to avoid incurring the costs of leadership on the international stage. On the other, the government is fostering a domestic nationalist narrative that celebrates the considerable achievement of lifting 300 million people out of poverty. This narrative includes the deliberate separation of Chinese civilization from that of the West and the use of Western powers (particularly Japan) as focal points for popular hostility centered around a jingoistic nationalism. Problematically, the principal targets of this narrative – Japan and, occasionally, the US – are also two of China's most important trading partners.

Beyond these relationships Chinese strategists view the world as a series of concentric circles of decreasing priority, much as their forefathers did.[8] Therefore East and Central Asia are of primary importance, followed by Africa, Europe, and the Americas. China's emergence as the centre of the global supply chain, however, has forced Chinese leaders to adopt a more global perspective. In this context China's global strategy is still under development. Although its most important relationships are still close to home, it is increasingly called upon to involve itself in global affairs. At minimum, scholars expect China to be more assertive in its "near-abroad."[9]

China's growing importance in the global economy, and its increasing activity in the international sphere, provokes a variety of reactions among observers.[10] Its rise has occurred within the context of the post-war, liberal democratic international order led by the United States, which established the rules, norms, and institutions defining the parameters of acceptable behaviour within the international system.[11] Some commentators worry that China may challenge this prevailing order simply by virtue of its rise; therefore some accommodation of this power's preferences is a prerequisite to avoiding the dissatisfaction that precedes great power conflict.[12] Other, more hawkish voices see confrontation as inevitable and even necessary. A common denominator, however, is anxiety in the face of China's rise. As Ikenberry notes, the Western realist fear is that "the drama of China's rise will feature an increasingly powerful China and a declining United States locked in an epic battle over the rules and leadership of the international system ... that will end with the grand ascendance of China and the onset of an Asian-centered world order."[13] For other commentators, a state can be described as being status quo oriented when it follows the rules of the game and it accepts the logic of those rules.[14] It is thus debatable whether China can appropriately be described as a status quo rising power.[15] On the one hand, evidence from its behaviour in international institutions suggests that it accepts the basic organizing principles and institutions of liberal world order.[16] Indeed, China has arguably been "the biggest beneficiary of the existing system over the past three decades," and thus should have little incentive for "grand revisionist ambition," desiring simply to have a seat at the table.[17] On the other hand, China does appear to seek to modify certain aspects of the international economic order, evidenced by its calls to end the reign of the US dollar as the reserve currency and by its efforts to reform the International Monetary Fund (IMF) governance structures.[18] Indeed, some point to very clear limits to the degree to which China has been 'socialized' into the international system.[19] For instance, although China has signed treaties underwriting the international human rights regime, its compliance has not extended to practical implementation.[20] What then should we make of China's behaviour and interests in the twenty-first century?

Getting to Today: Chinese Strategy in the Reform Era

Chinese strategy is rooted in the pragmatic foreign policy that marked the post-1979 reform era. This policy is characterized by the pursuit of "comprehensive national strength" through economic reform and military modernization. Peace was a prerequisite for this pursuit, which would produce an increase in wealth permitting China to modernize its military forces and rise to great power status. This "calculative strategy" was marked by market-oriented growth based on the maintenance of good relations with the major powers; military force and PLA doctrinal modernization, combined with restraints on the use of force regionally and globally; and an increased involvement in the international community, defined by a strategy of maximum gain for minimum commitment.[21]

To this end, China has sought pragmatic participation in international regimes, often aimed to maximize benefit at minimum constraint.[22] Of particular relevance in the security realm are Chinese calculations and behaviour in arms control institutions, given the American concerns over Chinese proliferation. Under Mao, China denounced the Nuclear Non-Proliferation Treaty (NPT) as discriminatory and part of a great power plot to monopolize nuclear weapons.[23] With the onset of reform however, and the corresponding drive to better its international status, China became more willing to embrace those treaties that brought better international standing and enabled it to expand its capabilities. China adopts an instrumental approach to international institutions. For instance, China joined the International Atomic Energy Agency (IAEA) in 1984 in order to acquire the advanced nuclear plants needed to power its modernization drive, rather than for reasons of international prestige. Instead of joining the highly constraining NPT, Chinese leaders made public statements against nuclear proliferation, which permitted Chinese assistance to Argentina and Brazil's "peaceful" nuclear development programs, from which it gained foreign capital.

Only after the Tiananmen Square incident, when its international prestige was at its lowest since the Cultural Revolution, did China sign the NPT (1992), declare its intention to abide by the Missile Technology Control Regime (MTCR, 1991), and announce that it would work on the Comprehensive Test Ban Treaty (CTBT, 1993). This allowed China to shed some of its pariah status at low financial cost because the opening of the Chinese economy had brought other sources of foreign exchange, decreasing the need for weapons sales. Beijing's preoccupation with international status is particularly important as it indicates that Chinese behaviour is increasingly influenced by international perceptions.[24] This observation is consistent with scholarship that treats international institutions as social environments – in which allegedly fixed interests and identities evolve through institutional learning and norm diffusion – rather than purely instrumental ones.[25] In the post-Cold War period China's arms control policies have been a function of pragmatic policy objectives as well as prevailing international opinion. For example, when faced with mounting US pressure to sign the CTBT, China agreed in 1996, but only after conducting six nuclear tests in two years over the course of negotiations that were frequently stalled.

Although military modernization was the last of the four reforms embarked upon, it remains an important priority. Initiated in 1985, China's modernization program was guided by a strategic shift from Maoist notions of "people's war" to the more pragmatic pursuit of "people's war under modern conditions." This highlighted a shift from defending against a large-scale Soviet invasion to planning for small-scale regional or local wars.[26] Rather than pursue the total annihilation of an enemy, the aim in local or limited wars would be to assert Chinese resolve and to deliver a political or psychological shock. The goal was to defend Chinese influence and interests, not expand its territory; thus Beijing must possess the capabilities to manage conflict escalation. "People's war under modern conditions" had elements of population-based guerrilla-style "people's war," as well as an emphasis on superior firepower and positional warfare.[27] The 1991 Gulf War provided a snapshot of what future wars would be like, and had serious ramifications for the strategic thought of the People's Liberation Army (PLA). The response was the doctrinal modification of "people's war under modern conditions" to "local war under high-tech conditions." This marked the end of the primacy of manpower over technology, and the PLA subsequently began investing in advanced military hardware and technology systems. For Chinese military planners, the primary lessons of the Gulf War were fourfold: electronic warfare and high-tech weaponry were decisive to a conflict's outcome; air and naval power were critical to combat and power projection capabilities; overall capability was a function of rapid response and deployment; and logistical support continued to be vital.[28] These have had several strategic and operational implications for the PLA, particularly the Navy (PLAN).

The PLAN's modernization is characterized by its quest for a "blue water navy." The navy anticipates its most likely combat scenarios to be against Taiwan and the US Navy or in the South China Sea against the coastal states of the area that dispute its maritime claims. Thus it has focused on expanding its operational capabilities from coastal to offshore defence. To meet this goal, the PLAN purchased four diesel *Kilo* class submarines and two *Sovremenny* destroyers from Russia to bolster its indigenously developed *Jiangwei* guided missile frigate and *Luhu* guided missile destroyer. Both indigenous ships possess improved cruise missiles, radar systems, and anti-submarine warfare capabilities.[29] China has also pursued a submarine-launched ballistic missiles (SLBM) capability, is deploying a new generation of nuclear-powered attack submarines, advanced diesel submarines, and is now a world leader in cruise missile technology. The anticipation that it might possess an anti-ship ballistic missile capable of striking American aircraft carriers is also of concern to American defence planners. In 2012 China began sea trials of an aircraft carrier purchased from Ukraine, and recent reports indicate that the country has now begun construction of the first of four planned domestically built carriers.[30] Until recently, it was widely believed that China's defence planning was oriented towards coercing the surrender of Taiwan with massive ballistic missile strikes while raising the costs of American intervention with its considerable submarine and cruise missile threat. However, recent platform deployments such as at-sea replenishment and the aforementioned aircraft carrier suggest that Beijing is also preparing to coerce regional states and to deploy farther afield to protect China's growing interests overseas.

To lessen concerns about its growing military, China embarked on a diplomatic offensive to engage East Asian states.[31] This policy built on credit earned during the 1997 Asian Financial Crisis and exploited American distraction from East Asia during the wars in Iraq and Afghanistan. China became more willing to pursue confidence-building measures with ASEAN states, as its foreign policy behaviour became more internationalist. The primary outcome of the ASEAN-China dialogue has been the Declaration on the Conduct of the Parties (DoC) in the South China Sea, signed by all claimants except Taiwan in November 2002. According to one scholar, China's agreement was in part a function of the regional balance of power, inasmuch as the US had by then ruled out a withdrawal from the Asia-Pacific region, as well as a more general acceptance of international norms of behaviour.[32] Parties pledged to resolve their border and jurisdictional disputes by peaceful means and by consultations. They are also agreed to begin developing confidence-building measures in the areas of resource exploitation and management, fisheries, and environmental management, as well as to work on a consensus basis towards the adaptation of a code of conduct.[33]

Despite this diplomatic offensive and ostensibly internationalist orientation, China has asserted its maritime claims in the East, and the South China Sea in particular, with unprecedented vigour.[34] According to analysts who anticipate regional conflict, China has fulfilled the long-held prophecy that it would become more belligerent in the East and South China Seas once it accumulated sufficient military power.[35] In this view, China has employed its more capable marine survey vessels to assert its maritime jurisdiction and sovereignty claims in the South China Sea against Vietnam and the Philippines and in the East China Sea against Japan. Particularly provocative actions included cutting the cables of Vietnamese survey vessels, detaining fishermen, operating a drilling rig in waters claimed by Vietnam, and forcing the release of Chinese fishermen detained by these countries.[36] A recent edict from Hainan province requires "all foreign vessels that seek to fish or conduct surveys in waters claimed by China to obtain advance approval.[37] There has also been speculation about an Air Defence Identification Zone (ADIZ) in the South China Sea following China's unilateral declaration of an ADIZ in the East China Sea.[38] This has resulted in a number of dangerous armed confrontations at sea and renewed support from East Asian states for the American military presence.

The Obama administration responded by "rebalancing" its military forces from counter-insurgency operations in the Middle East to the deployment of sea power to the Asia-Pacific region. In his address to the Australian Parliament in November 2011, President Obama stated unequivocally that "reductions in US defense spending will not – I repeat, will not – come at the expense of the Asia Pacific."[39] The Obama administration subsequently outlined a "rebalance" of its military forces towards the Asia-Pacific region, including the deployment of 60 per cent of the Navy and Air Force to the region.[40] These dynamics set the stage for the most important bilateral relationship in world and, in the view of many analysts, serve as a barometer for China's intentions and conduct in other parts of the world.

Newly appointed Chinese President Xi Jinping outlined his key foreign policy strategy one year after he rose to power at the 18th Party Congress. At a conference attended by high-level party elites and influential state-owned companies in October 2013, Xi called for an effort to improve ties with China's neighbours, in an apparent return to the "Smile Offensive" that China followed between 2002 and 2009.[41] Despite bilateral antagonism with the United States over Washington's rebalance, Xi has strengthened the relationship by adopting a harder line on North Korea following Pyongyang's third nuclear test in early 2013. Finally, like all Chinese leaders before him, Xi will remain preoccupied with domestic concerns, particularly strengthening the Communist Party. To do so, Xi needs to be seen acting on the endemic corruption that runs through China's system and implementing the considerable economic reforms the country needs to rebalance its economy to a more sustainable growth pattern. Unlike previous leaders however, there is a new confidence about China embodied in Xi's vision of the "Chinese Dream." China believes it is entitled to greater prestige and early indications, embodied by the bilateral Sunnylands Summit with President Obama, suggest that world leaders are prepared to accommodate this Chinese request.

China's Regional Diplomacy as Bellwether for Arctic Policy

Arctic scholars often look to China's posture on maritime boundary disputes in its own backyard as an indication of its expectations for the circumpolar world. China's decision to use its influence in regional institutions like the East Asian Summit and the ASEAN Regional Forum to bully rival claimants does not sit well with commentators concerned about the current state of Arctic governance. This connects with deeply engrained suspicions of Chinese intentions by virtue of its size, political orientation, and the pace of its emergence – and consequently the power and influence China can bring to bear on regional politics. This perspective seems informed by a view of China that accepts the more hawkish assumptions on one side of the "China debate" in Western academic literature. In this view China is a strategic animal, playing the long game of international politics with aplomb, seeking to capitalize on windows of opportunity to pursue its interests, which are informed by its great power ambitions. When it comes to the Arctic, two commentators conclude, "it appears that China has identified the Arctic as a strategically and geopolitically valuable region and aims at projecting its influence through regional political and economic partnerships," using "China aid ... to gain a foothold."[42] This perspective is based on an inherent mistrust of Chinese intentions that is distinct from what the behaviour of the nation might dictate. As historian David Wright predicts, "reticence and restraint on China's part will not likely last indefinitely." "Beijing will likely become much more assertive."[43] This position also has traction in policy and business communities. Roger W. Robinson of the MacDonald-Laurier Institute recently suggested that China is playing a "long con" in the Arctic, "lulling target states into a sense of security, commercial benefit, and complacency."[44] And, in a much-debated new book entitled *Merger of the Century*, *National Post* business reporter Diane Francis raises the spectre of China as a "wolf at the door," in the Arctic, with Canada as its prey.[45]

The key driver for those who anticipate heightened Chinese assertiveness is resources. In a recent article, Singapore-based political scientist Gang Chen summarizes:

As the world's second largest economy, China today has insatiable appetite [sic] for energy, minerals and other resources, which helps explain the significant increase in its diplomatic, commercial and civic activities in Africa, Latin America and the Middle East. Having emerged from an inward-looking weak economy to the largest exporter in the world, China's global interest is growing rapidly due to its heavy dependence upon overseas supply [sic] of energy and raw materials. For the last two decades, relations between China and other resourceful continents have reached unprecedented levels of economic and political significance, propelled by China's increasing involvement in these regions and the economic complementarity based on China's engorgement of raw materials and a flood of cheap Chinese products. Despite its constant effort to expand and diversify commodity supply [sic] from various parts of the world, in the long run, energy and natural resource scarcity could become a formidable bottleneck for China's sustainable development due to its astronomical economic scale, lower than world average per capita resource reserves and inefficiency in using these raw materials. Meanwhile as a mercantile state that is increasingly dependent upon foreign trade, China needs reliable and convenient sea lanes to secure its maritime transportation based on affordable cost.[46]

One of China's most important global priorities is the procurement of affordable commodities to support its growing consumption (although this does not necessarily need to lead to assertive foreign policy behaviour, as evidenced by the case of Japan).[47] Likewise, Chinese energy security has been characterized by the attempts to respond to the challenge brought on by its 1993 shift to net oil importer status. As such, its strategy has several elements. Chiefly, Beijing has endeavoured to develop its indigenous energy sources efficiently and has aimed to diversify both primary and imported supplies. This has required investment in overseas oil and gas resources through its major petroleum corporations, the construction of infrastructure to bring domestic resources to market, and the opening of the Chinese energy industry to foreign corporations. The goal is to minimize the vulnerability of the Chinese economy to fluctuations in the global energy market, helped in part by the establishment of a strategic oil reserve (which is being quickly topped up in the wake of oil's 2014 collapse). According to the IEA, China's response to its energy concerns has been consistent with other nations in similar situations, such as Japan.[48]

China has access to domestic energy resources but its oil fields are mature and its gas reserves are far from the markets on the eastern seaboard. China's energy links with Central Asia also have a strategic element. The region has traditionally been free of US interest and control, aside from the period during combat operations in Afghanistan. By importing oil overland via pipeline, China can avoid the major seaways, which are policed by the US Navy. Oil transported by seas would be vulnerable to embargo if relations with the US soured over other issues (such as Taiwan) or in the unlikely event that the Indian Navy tried to close the Strait of Malacca over a border dispute. Given its preference for self-sufficiency, this vulnerability is a concern. While it is not a serious problem in peace time, access to secure, land-based reserves reassures Beijing that it would not be cut off in times of conflict.

Nevertheless, a growing percentage of Chinese natural gas and oil comes via sea lanes, a situation that has created a pretext for greater Chinese interest in global maritime security. China thus contributes to the security of the Malacca Strait, through which 80 per cent of its imported oil and much of its trade passes, as well as to counter-piracy operations in the Gulf of Aden. Access to affordable energy resources is required for economic growth, which in turn is intimately tied to the legitimacy of the Chinese Communist Party. Chapters three and four take up the issue of China's resource and shipping interests in the Arctic more generally. Suffice to say however, there is little evidence that resources are a primary driver of Chinese assertiveness towards its neighbours. Moreover, there is little prospect that the resource value of the South China Sea is sufficient to dramatically affect China's growing consumption or force a confrontation.[49]

The Arctic in China's Grand Strategy

While China has clearly demonstrated belligerent behaviour in its own coastal seas, and the pursuit of natural resource is undoubtedly a critical dimension of China's overall orientation, these facts alone imply neither a revisionist nor even an aggressive stance in Arctic affairs. Indeed, official statements and scholarship close to the establishment highlight just the opposite. Wang

Jisi, dean of Peking University's School of International Studies and former President Hu Jintao's "chief brains trust" for foreign policy, notes that "a peaceful international environment, an enhanced position for China in the global arena, and China's steady integration into the existing economic order" helps to consolidate the Communist Party's (CCP) power in China. Outlining the various considerations at play in "China's search for a Grand Strategy" (which addresses the three core and often competing interests of sovereignty, security, and development), Wang noted an internal debate over Deng Xiaoping's teaching of *tao guang yang hui*, or "keeping a low profile in international affairs." According to this logic, China should focus on economic development and "hide its capabilities and bide its time." Critics, however, perceive this as too soft in periods of rising nationalism or acute security challenges. Furthermore, keeping a low profile makes sense for China in its relations with the US, but "it might not apply to China's relations with many other countries or to economic issues and those non-traditional security issues that have become essential in recent years, such as climate change, public health, and energy security."[50]

Of particular relevance to this study on China's Arctic interests, Wang outlines four ongoing changes in China's strategic thinking that might indicate the foundations of a new grand strategy. First, he notes "the Chinese government's adoption of a comprehensive understanding of security, which incorporates economic and nontraditional concerns with traditional military and political interests."[51] China's principal interests in the Arctic (scientific research, climate change, resources, and shipping)[52] fit within this expanded concept of security, which also acknowledges that China's integration into the global economic system makes it hard to separate friends from foes. In addition, China's interests have become far more diffuse; it is now interacting with a wider array of countries on a more diverse set of issues than ever before.

Second, Wang explains that China is becoming less country-oriented and more multilateral and issue-oriented. "This shift toward functional focuses – counterterrorism, nuclear nonproliferation, environmental protection, energy security, food safety, post-disaster reconstruction – has complicated China's bilateral relationships, regardless of how friendly other states are toward it." China's Arctic interests connect to several of these issue areas, including environmental protection, food safety/security, and energy security.[53]

Third, Wang notes changes in the mode of China's economic development, with "Beijing's preoccupation with GDP growth ... slowly giving way to concerns about economic efficiency, product quality, environmental protection, the creation of a social safety net, and technological innovation." This may indicate growing support for environmental stewardship, a key prong in most Arctic states' development strategies.[54]

Fourth, Wang suggests that "soft power influence requires China to seek common values in the global arena such as good governance and transparency." China's growing interest in participating in Arctic governance, particularly through the Arctic Council, and its desire to uphold rights to the "common heritage of mankind," fit with this logic.[55] In short, despite substantial fears among the public, pundits, and policymakers, there seems to be little that China can achieve in the Arctic by adopting a coercive or revisionist policy posture. Indeed, an assertive push in the Arctic may undermine China's bilateral relations with Arctic states, countries that can facilitate China's rise in a number of ways including cooperative resource development and support at international institutions.[56]

A final consideration that Wang outlines is also relevant to the Arctic. In order to form and implement its own grand strategy, China will need to overcome internal challenges related to decision-making. "Almost all institutions in the central leadership and local governments are involved in foreign relations to varying degrees," he notes, "and it is virtually impossible for them to see China's national interest the same way or to speak with one voice. These differences confuse outsiders as well as the Chinese people." Furthermore, arriving at a coherent strategy requires careful management of "the diversity of views among China's political elite and the general public, at a time when the value system in China is changing rapidly."[57] Indeed, the International Crisis Group outlined how competing bureaucratic interests and domestic political considerations led to a more heavy-handed Chinese posture towards the South China Sea in 2010–11.[58] In this context it is important to consider the organizations that make China's Arctic policy.

Major Chinese Government Actors Interested in Arctic Affairs[59]

While there is a tendency to treat China's Arctic ambitions as monolithic and coherent, particularly among those who assign nefarious motives to its Arctic activities, China's Arctic decision-making framework, within its broader grand strategic considerations, is not straightforward. Chen observes that:

Whereas past Chinese debates were principally internal deliberations among a narrow elite, current research increasingly highlights a more public dimension with multiple inputs from actors not commonly involved in these traditionally insular processes. It is true that China's foreign policy-making process to a large extent is still vertically organised, with the core figure of each division of CCP leadership having the last word on all vital issues. However, as final arbiters of foreign policy-making, the paramount leaders tend to become more consultative and consensual than their predecessors due to their decreasing authority within the Politburo in the post-Mao era. Meanwhile, facing a much more complicated external and internal context, the core leader today has many other responsibilities and depends on others to help plan and implement Chinese foreign policy, which further reduces personal influence while magnifying institutional and pluralistic impacts upon the whole process.[60]

Although final decision-making power rests with the Politburo Standing Committee (PSC), led by President Xi Jinping, the pluralization, decentralization, and fragmentation of Chinese foreign policy-making means that influence over the policymaking process is no longer exclusive to the Ministry of Foreign Affairs, the Ministry of Commerce, and the PLA. It now involves "universities, research organisations and military academies, chief executives of oil companies and other enterprises, bank directors, local government officials and leading media representatives [who] operate on the margins outside the traditional centralised confines of the party state."[61]

Nevertheless, policy makers and policy shapers in China must be situated within the government machinery with specific competency in Arctic affairs (which is usually clustered with the Antarctic into Polar affairs more generally). The Ministry of Foreign Affairs (MFA) is the lead organization in managing China's international relations with the Arctic states, including Canada. The Department of Law and Treaty in particular prepares China's official statements in the Arctic and coordinates Chinese representation at Arctic Council meetings.[62] This is usually led by an assistant foreign minister who oversees Arctic affairs. As Chen notes, the MFA will remain "a significant player in the Arctic policy-making, as the strategic priority at the current stage is to dispel suspicion and burnish its credentials as a non-threatening, unobtrusive 'joiner' in the Arctic politics, which is synchronous with the axioms of 'avoiding confrontation' and 'advancing incrementally' that guide its national grand strategy before it has fully risen as a global power."[63] Indeed, despite its role as China's face in the Arctic region, the MFA remains a weak institution. For instance, neither the foreign minister – currently Wang Yi but also his predecessor Yang Jiechi – sit on the Politburo. Indeed, the Chinese foreign minister is not the country's leading foreign affairs official. Rather, this falls to the State Councillor that directs the Central Foreign Affairs Office, currently Yang Jiechi and formerly Dai Bingguo. Even this influence is not formalized. For instance, President Xi Jinping has reportedly tasked Vice-President Li Yuanchao with some responsibility for foreign affairs and Li, unlike Yang, Wang, or Dai, is a member of the Politburo and therefore has considerably more say over the numerous organs that influence foreign policy.[64]

Chen notes that other entities within the Chinese state – or state-owned enterprises connected to it – are more aggressive in pursuing their interests:

> With China's Ministry of Foreign Affairs still hoping to keep low profile [sic] and follow the principle of sovereignty so as not to provoke other Arctic powers, other institutional players, like the State Oceanic Administration (SOA), the Ministry of Commerce and state-owned behemoths like the three national oil companies and China Ocean Shipping (Group) Company (COSCO), are expected to take more pushy stands in the making and implementation of China's Arctic strategy. CAA's [Chinese Arctic and Antarctic Administration] budgetary requirement will demand more research and development activities there, and also a considerable deviation from the previous docile diplomatic positions. As part of the SOA, which is working on China's maritime strategy (*haiyang zhanlue*), the CAA plans to put the Arctic strategy as a component of this marine strategy to be included in the national grand strategy.[65]

The SOA, which reports to the Ministry of Land and Resources, is the main government institution that manages all polar issues. Its mandate is to regulate marine activities including patrols in disputed waters in the Yellow Sea, the East China Sea, and the South China Sea using the newly unified

China Coast Guard, draft China's maritime-related laws and regulations, and facilitate China's participation in international maritime treaties.[66] The SOA also sponsors annual seminars and invites government personnel to conduct studies on polar issues, geopolitics, political science, economics, and the Arctic legal regime.[67] In addition, it oversees the China Arctic and Antarctic Administration, which organizes Chinese Arctic and Antarctic expeditions and administers related polar affairs, and heads the Chinese Advisory Committee for Polar Research (CACPR, *Zhongguo jidi kaocha gongzuo zixun weiyuanhui*), which serves as a government coordinating body on polar issues.[68]

The China Institute for Marine Affairs (CIMA) is currently drafting China's maritime strategy, which "will be an important component of China's grand strategy that aims to preserve long-term global interests through the integration of its overall political, economic, military, and technological capabilities." In turn, this strategy will frame the country's future activities in the Arctic.[69] Indeed, it was in the context of China's broader maritime strategy that some analysts misinterpreted a remark by retired Chinese Admiral Yin Zhou, who noted that the Arctic Ocean was the common heritage of all mankind.[70] Most likely, the admiral was speaking of the waters and seabed beyond the jurisdiction of the Arctic states, an area understood by all parties to be international. In this regard, his choice of words clearly reflected existing law in that the UN Convention on the Law of the Sea (1982) states that "the sea-bed and ocean floor, and the subsoil thereof, beyond the limits of national jurisdiction ... as well as the resources of the area, are the common heritage of mankind."[71]

Maritime issues, particularly economic, have grown in prominence in China in recent years. Growing China's maritime economy was addressed in both the 11th and the 12th Five Year Plans, with the latter calling for the rational use of maritime resources and greater resource development.[72] According to the 2011 *China National Offshore Development Report*, the country's marine economy grew at 13.5 per cent in 2010 and amounted to 9.6 per cent of China's total gross domestic product.[73] It is thus unsurprising that the working report for the 18th Party Congress called for China to become a maritime power.[74] However, there are considerable limits to China's ability to adopt a strategy in the Arctic similar to that in its "near seas."[75]

Conclusion

Much as is the case for Western commentators on China, the manner in which Chinese commentators view Arctic affairs is also coloured by their general perceptions of Western interests. Li Zhenfu of Dalian Maritime University, for example, decries China's position in multilateral institutions, "guided and established by a minority of great Western powers and reflect[ing] the imperatives of their own self-interests." His recommendations that China must assert its interests and rights in the Arctic more forcefully is a clear reflection of his desire for China to perform "as a responsible major power in the international arena, and [hasten] the rationalization and democratization of international relations." He explains at length that:

> The theories of the international mechanisms the world now has were all formulated under the guidance of developed Western countries. The theoretical bases for these formulations are freedom, equality, democracy, and other such Western rational concepts [*linian*]. Because of this, in their fundamental nature all international mechanisms currently in effect are, along with their theories, heavily colored by liberalism. There are obvious discrepancies between the theories of international mechanisms formulated in accordance with freedom, equality, democracy, and other Western rational concepts on the one hand and the basic social system and mainstream ideology of China on the other. As a result, China's participation in international mechanisms is restrained, and this in turn has led to China's shortcomings in international mechanism theory and has created China's current failure at formulating an international mechanism theoretical system which has rigorous logic and strong interpretive capabilities.

In short, he fears that through apathy or inaction in Arctic affairs China may lose its "right to speak up" (*huayu quan*) on behalf of humanity and miss an opportunity to enhance its stature in global affairs through "theoretical prestige."[76] As an emerging global power, China clearly feels it must assert itself into emerging areas of global importance, like the Arctic. It does so not only for the practical gains (either real or theoretical) to be had, but on the principled belief that its interests must be taken into account.[77]

This chapter has shown, however, that "Chinese interests" in the Arctic must be disaggregated to reflect the plurality and diversity of relevant interested actors, as well as the absence of a formal or coherent foreign policy position on Arctic affairs. We have noted that the MFA, for example, has placed its emphasis on burnishing China's credentials as an unobtrusive, non-confrontational, and incremental joiner, and dispelling suspicion about Chinese intentions – precisely the type of suspicion that Zhenfu's call could presumably arise. Indeed, this push for a more activist agenda is but one side of the coin. Linda Jakobson observed in 2010 that:

> To date China has adopted a wait-and-see approach to Arctic developments, wary that active overtures would cause alarm in other countries due to China's size and status as a rising global power. Chinese officials are therefore very cautious when formulating their views on China's interests in the Arctic. They stress that China's Arctic research activities remain primarily focused on the climatic and environmental consequences of the ice melting in the Arctic. However, in recent years Chinese officials and researchers have started to also assess the commercial, political and security implications for China of a seasonally ice-free Arctic region.[78]

Her analysis is equally applicable today. China's declared policy objectives are to promote and maintain peace, stability, cooperation, and sustainable development in the Arctic region.[79] Its official activities to date reflect the traditional Five Principles of Peaceful Coexistence: mutual respect for sovereignty and territorial integrity, mutual non-aggression, non-interference in each other's internal affairs, equality and mutual benefit, and peaceful coexistence.[80]

Whether this will hold beyond the next decade is open to debate. In 2008, the National Intelligence Council published "Global Trends: A Transformed World" which concluded that, by 2025, the current US-dominated global system will yield to a multipolar world in which China and India exercise decisive influence on global economics and geopolitics. In the Arctic, it suggested, "the greatest strategic consequence over the next couple of decades may be that relatively large, resource-deficient trading states such as China, Japan, and Korea will benefit from increased energy resources provided by any Arctic opening and shorter shipping distances."[81] To ensure access to these resources and shipping routes, China has already begun to forge economic and diplomatic relations with Arctic countries (particularly in northern Europe). Still, it remains unclear how much relative emphasis it places on the Arctic compared to the rest of the world, and how much it will over the coming decades. Xi Jinping's policy agenda is crowded and is overwhelmingly focused on domestic issues.

Reflecting on the Arctic's place in China's emerging global ambitions, Chen summarizes that:

> Besides its massive presence that has been growing tremendously in Asia, Africa and Latin America, the continental power's growing interest in the remote Arctic region embodied by intense diplomatic, economic and research manoeuvres in the core and surrounding area presents another evidence for the existence of a global grand strategy employed by China. In fact, if the Middle Kingdom's ultimate strategic goal is to win a smokeless war without fighting for supremacy in the world, then the melting Arctic region that will provide abundant natural resources and shorter navigable sea routes may emerge as one of the battlefields that demand tactics and sub-strategies.[82]

Whether or how China's Arctic strategy will reflect the general axioms summarized by Aaron Friedberg – avoid confrontation, build comprehensive national power, and advance incrementally – remains to be seen.[83] Nevertheless, analysts should beware of many Western alarmist narratives about China's Arctic interests, intentions, and capabilities that oversimplify the issues, reinforce outdated perspectives on China's rise and, in some cases, even obscure more pressing challenges that stem from the growing outsider interest in Arctic affairs. By exploring China's Arctic interests, intentions, and capabilities in more detail, the chapters that follow cast these largely unspecified narratives in further doubt.

The Snow Dragon:
China, Polar Science, and the Environment

With its unique geographic location and natural environment,
the Arctic has great scientific value as an indicator of global
climate change and a "laboratory" for global scientific research.
As of today, mankind's exploration and understanding of the
Arctic is still limited. This makes it necessary for governments,
social organizations, academia and business community to
work together, further strengthen cooperation, and explore and
understand the Arctic in a comprehensive way.

VICE FOREIGN MINISTER ZHANG MING,
Third Arctic Circle Assembly (2015)[1]

Science forms an important foundation for Canada's Northern Strategy across all four of its pillars, a fact demonstrated by Canada's world-leading $150 million investment in the International Polar Year (2007–09).[2] Arctic research initiatives emphasize Canada's international obligation to contribute to knowledge about the "nature, mechanisms and extent" of connections between the Arctic and the rest of the globe.[3] The federal government is carrying through on its promise to create new research infrastructure, particularly a world-class Canadian High Arctic Research Station (CHARS) in Cambridge Bay, Nunavut, and Canadian granting councils are encouraging researchers to coordinate their efforts across relevant topic areas (such as resource development, transportation, community sustainability, health, and the environment) so that they can translate their findings into concrete policy recommendations.[4]

This emphasis dovetails with Chinese priorities and capabilities. Viewed through the lens of official statements, China's primary Arctic concern relates to climate change and associated scientific research efforts.[5] Speaking to Norway's High North Study Tour in 2010, Assistant Foreign Minister Liu Zhenmin argued that, by virtue of China's geographic location, it is exposed to Arctic weather patterns, with impacts on the country's agriculture and economic development. The melting of the ice cap also affects the country's continental and ocean environment. Dr. Huigen Yang, the chief scientist of the IPY China program and the director of the Polar Research Institute of China at Shanghai, explained that:

> The Chinese public has understood the linkage between the unprecedented sea ice retreat in the Arctic Ocean in September 2007 and the heavy snow disasters that happened in southern China in January of 2008. Many Chinese have also realized that if all Arctic and Antarctic ice sheets melt, the consequent sea level rise would affect China's coastline and the most populated and prosperous regions such as Guangzhou, Shanghai and Tianjin would be totally under water. Chinese scientists have attached great importance to the Arctic and Antarctic regions in understanding the earth system and its global changes and in pursuit of sustainable developments on this planet.[6]

The report of the Second Sino-Canadian Exchange on the Arctic provides a tidy summary of Canada's situation:

> Canada has an extensive coastal archipelago with complex navigable and non-navigable channels in the Arctic. It claims the full range of maritime zones permitted by the United Nations Convention on the Law of the Sea, 1982 including a claim of historic internal waters over the interconnecting waters of its Arctic archipelago. Like other Arctic Ocean coastal States, Canada is in the process of preparing a submission regarding the outer limits of its extended continental shelf in accordance with the LOS Convention. Pursuant to its Northern Strategy Canada has

active programmes to support indigenous and other communities in the region, resource exploration, marine scientific and climate research, development of infrastructures, maintenance of navigation aids and services and building of polar capable vessels. It has bilateral agreements for scientific and climate research, navigation areas and meteorological information services, search and rescue, oil pollution response and other matters with its neighbours.[7]

Although Canada is a global trading nation, its perspective on the Arctic is unambiguously that of a coastal state with all the rights and responsibilities that that entails.

China's interests in the Arctic are best conceptualized as those of a "maritime state" rather than those of a coastal state (the lens which dominates its regional maritime interests). During the First Sino-Canadian Workshop on the Arctic, held in Beijing in February 2010, Dr. Gao Zhiguo (then a sitting member of the International Tribunal for the Law of the Sea) explained that while China does not border the Arctic Ocean, it has significant economic and maritime interests in the region.[8] In particular, China is interested in enhanced navigational access to Arctic waters and the economic potential of the region, particularly with regards to offshore oil and gas. As a major shipping power and oil importer, China would expect to benefit or be affected by the opening of new sea routes and the exploitation of oil and gas and other natural resources in the Arctic Ocean. Furthermore, as a party to both the LOSC and the Svalbard Treaty (as well as other international instruments applicable to the Arctic), China is actively engaged in multilateral discussions about Arctic issues and is concerned about the potential loss of access to open ocean and deep seabed areas.[9]

From a research perspective, China can be conceptualized as a polar state, rather than an Arctic state. Its interests in Antarctic research predate its Arctic interests and the China Arctic Administration/China Institute for Marine Affairs budget still reflects an 80/20 per cent split in favour of the southern pole. The Chinese Arctic and Antarctic Administration's website is telling:

[The Chinese Arctic and Antarctic Administration] has been playing an active role in the scientific research and international cooperation activities in the Antarctic continent and the Southern Ocean within the principles and the framework of the Antarctic Treaty System. China has done 27 national Antarctic expedi-. tions until 2011 with the operating of two year-round Stations, namely the Great Wall Station located in King George Island, west Antarctica and the Zhongshan Station located in the Larsemann Hills, east Antarctica, and one inner land summer station, namely the Kunlun Station ... Within the framework of related conventions, treaties and other legal obligations, China is making her contribution to the scientific research and peaceful development both in the Antarctic and Arctic.[10]

When discussing polar science, China clearly emphasizes its accom-plishments and contributions in the Antarctic above those in the Arctic. Accordingly, China's interest in Arctic scientific research must be situated within its broader polar research program. New Zealand political scientist Anne-Marie Brady notes that Beijing's annual spending on polar expeditions has trebled over the last decade and it has made huge investments in polar-related infrastructure. She quotes the Deputy Head of the China Arctic and Antarctic Administration Chen Lianzeng, who stated in June 2011 that the overall goal of China's five-year plan for polar research was to increase China's "status and influence" in polar affairs to better protect its "polar rights." Brady astutely observes, however, that "for all the attention it receives, China is not putting a lot of money into its Arctic program" and, "compared to China's budgeting elsewhere, the polar budget receives very little funding. On the Arctic, Beijing produces a lot of smoke, mirrors and big talk, which disguises their small investment."[11]

Nevertheless, Brady acknowledges that China's increased polar science expenditures and activities in recent years "reflect the country's growing economic and political power and international ambitions."[12] With its growing economy and expanding global interests, China certainly has the resources and capacity to enhance its polar research profile. As Rob Huebert and other commentators emphasize, the substantial investment that China has made in polar sciences over the last decade has dramatically expanded its pool of experienced polar scientists and its network of polar research centres, including a new surge of interest in circumpolar political and legal issues.[13] Still, to suggest that China invests more in Arctic science than Canada is erroneous.

This chapter explores the substance of China's research interests, activities, and capacities, and shows them to be poor fodder for alarmist narratives.

The Arctic and Climate Change

A more sober analysis suggests that much of China's interest in the region relates to changing climate. Of all the regions in the world, the Arctic has had the greatest influence on climate change over the past century. Many studies and climate models[14] indicate that increasing levels of atmospheric greenhouse gases will bring intensifying large-scale change in the Arctic during this century, including a general scientific consensus that the region will warm between three and four degrees by 2050.[15] Indeed, the Governing Council of the United Nations Environment Programme (UNEP) characterized the Arctic as the world's barometer of environmental change. Its February 2008 resolution on "Sustainable Development of the Arctic Region" urged better cooperation between states and non-governmental stakeholders to ensure sustainable development,[16] given that the root causes of climate change are intrinsically global.

The impacts are also regional and local. The effects of climate change on the Arctic ecosystem have been widely documented, including rising temperatures, melting icecaps, glaciers and permafrost, and changes in flora and fauna.[17] The decline in Arctic sea ice levels is a tangible indicator that the world's cryosphere – comprising that part of the earth's surface where frozen water is present – is fundamentally changing. The landmark report of the Arctic Climate Impact Assessment (ACIA) in 2004 noted a rate of sea ice reduction from 1972–2002 of approximately 300,000 km^2 per decade.[18] Satellite data reveal that, in the Arctic Basin north of 65°N and between 50°E and 290°E, the open water area has increased at the rate of 23 per cent per decade while sea surface temperature has increased at 0.7 degrees per decade.[19] According to the ACIA report, the rate of warming in the Arctic is more than twice the global average.[20]

Based on recent forecasts, some zealous commentators predict that the decomposition of this ice will leave the Arctic Ocean similar to the Baltic Sea, reportedly covered by only a thin layer of seasonal ice in the winter and therefore fully navigable year-round.[21] In addition, while the timelines are hotly contested, many observers do predict that the Arctic Ocean will be completely ice-free during the summer in the coming decades,[22] with some indicating that this may even occur within the next decade.[23]

Although commentators tend to emphasize climate change as a "threat multiplier which exacerbates existing trends, tensions and instability,"[24] the challenge in the Arctic will likely relate to humanitarian and ecological issues, not a heightened danger of military conflict over the next decade. Thomas Homer-Dixon asserts that:

> the most common "state-centric" concerns about the effect of climate change on the Arctic ... are exaggerated. These concerns are grounded in a set of assumptions that may have been appropriate for 19th and 20th century world affairs but are entirely inappropriate as a basis for addressing the 21st century's challenges. Indeed, these state-centric concerns divert policy attention away from far more critical issues, including the larger climate consequences of Arctic ice loss, such as more rapid melting of the Greenland icecap, invigoration of carbon-cycle positive feedbacks, and potentially dramatic changes in precipitation patterns much farther south affecting global food production ... Access to the Northwest Passage and to reserves of oil and natural gas in the Arctic Basin will seem trivial in a world whip-sawed by climate change shifts resulting from loss of Arctic sea ice. Policymakers need to focus on what is really important, not what fits their 20th century worldview.[25]

Potential security and sovereignty threats must be considered alongside issues of food security, cultural survival, physical health, threats to settlements on the coast or built on permafrost, and the vulnerability of critical infrastructure. By extension, both preventing and adapting to climate change are abiding concerns for Indigenous groups. These groups recognize that global action is needed to reduce greenhouse gas emissions and slow the pace of change to provide northern residents with time to adapt to changing conditions – to the extent that such adaptation is possible.[26]

However defined, Canada's climate change strategy must be global in its aspirations for mitigation while sensitive to the needs for – and limits of – local adaptation. After all, overwhelming scientific data indicates that anthropogenic pollution is the leading cause of climate change. Over two centuries of industrial activity has elevated atmospheric greenhouse gas concentrations and air pollution (i.e. persistent organic pollutants) over time, with the Arctic's climate catching a disproportionate share of such pollutants in a "cold trap."[27] The melting of the sea ice, receding glaciers, changing weather patterns, and the thawing of the permafrost are all signs of and contributors to global warming. Scientists have discovered that the modest thawing of the permafrost occurring can trigger a warming cycle as methane gas is released. Although methane is present in the atmosphere at a smaller volume than carbon dioxide, it can absorb twenty-five times more heat from the sun than carbon dioxide. If all of the existing Arctic permafrost melted, this would release approximately ten times more methane into the atmosphere than the current annual rate of global greenhouse gas emissions.[28]

Reduced ice cover has also produced more erosion along Arctic shorelines, which directly affects some Arctic communities. Furthermore, some air pollutants – notably black carbon[29] – darken the ice caps, changing the reflective surface to absorb more sunlight and exacerbating a positive feedback, a dynamic that creates a melting cycle known as the ice-albedo feedback loop. This effect is playing out on a large scale as reflective glaciers and sea ice are replaced by dark, heat-absorbing land and open water.[30] These changes help to explain the consistent trend toward warmer and less icy conditions. Increased blending of tropical air and polar air has also produced larger and more intense weather systems and regional climatic changes, including severe tropical storms, winter storms in Eastern Canada and the United States, and the overall trend of warmer winters. Even if worldwide emissions were to stop today, atmospheric greenhouse gas concentrations would remain elevated. Scientists debate if the world will soon reach a "tipping point" when the effects of climate change cannot be slowed – or if this point has already been passed.[31]

Drastic changes to the ecology and biodiversity of the Arctic directly affect human habitats. Indigenous communities have adapted to the Arctic climate and its related stresses over millennia, but emerging climate-related stresses are occurring over an unprecedentedly short time-scale, and have added a new set of challenges and sense of urgency that is likely to accelerate over the next decade and beyond. The Arctic Climate Impact Assessment noted that, "for Inuit, warming is likely to disrupt or even destroy their hunting and food sharing culture as reduced sea ice causes the animals on which they depend to decline, become less accessible, and possibly become extinct."[32] This statement raises core questions about the future of Arctic societies and the limits of adaptation. Author Alun Anderson tidily summarized that: "the Arctic is ever more entangled with the south and ever more at the mercy of decisions made elsewhere, often without the slightest consideration for the top of the world."[33]

This discussion highlights what most scientists have known for decades: climate change is not simply a regional issue but a global one. Joshua Ho, a senior fellow at Nanyang Technological University in Singapore, notes the implications for Asia. According to a November 2009 World Wildlife Fund (WWF) report on the impacts of climate change on major urban centres, Asia is the most vulnerable continent to changing precipitation patterns, rising sea levels, and extreme weather events. He cites another analysis, conducted by the Tyndall Centre for Climate Change Research at the University of Oxford, which estimates that an increase of one metre in sea level by the end of this century will displace more than 100 million people and flood more than 900,000 square kilometres of land in Asia. This will affect major cities in China such as Guangzhou, Shanghai, Tianjin, and Ningbo.[34] Studies also indicate that the Arctic air stream generates extreme weather in China.[35] According to recent ICPP reports, Asia will overwhelmingly bear the brunt of the natural, and consequently social, consequences of climate change.[36]

The Chinese public acknowledges climate change and its consequences.[37] Given that the long-term effects of global warming have an obvious bearing on Asian interests, it is small wonder that China and other Asian states wish to take an active role in polar research, conduct Arctic studies, and increase their involvement in international institutions and conferences.[38]

China's Polar Research Program

Although media commentators often perceive China's scientific interest in the Arctic as a very recent phenomenon, China has been doing research in the Arctic for several years, the organizational foundations for which were established some time ago.[39] China has been a party to the 1920 Treaty Concerning the Archipelago of Spitzbergen (also known as the Svalbard Treaty) since 1925,[40] though China did not show much direct interest in polar research until it created the Office of the National Antarctic Expedition Committee in 1981. Although China amassed field research experience in the Antarctic in the 1980s,[41] its polar research capabilities only expanded significantly during the 1990s.[42]

China began strengthening those programs with the founding of the Polar Research Institute of China (PRIC) in 1989 and the renaming of the Office of the National Antarctic Expedition Committee as the Chinese Arctic and Antarctic Administration (CAA).[43] Falling under the State Oceanic Administration, the CAA directly manages polar affairs and is administratively in charge of China's National Arctic/Antarctic Research Expeditions (CHINARE).[44] Its primary functions are:

1. Drawing up the national strategies, policies, and plans for Chinese Arctic and Antarctic expeditions, and organizing the studies on the major polar issues.

2. Formulating the laws, regulations, relevant standards, and rules concerning polar expeditions and other polar activities, and administering relevant Arctic and Antarctic affairs in accordance with laws and regulations.

3. Being responsible for the organization, coordination, and supervision of the Chinese National Arctic and Antarctic expeditions, and organizing the scientific research activities within the polar area.

4. Being responsible for the organization, coordination, and supervision of the infrastructures and capacity constructions for Chinese National Arctic and Antarctic expeditions.

5. Organizing and coordinating the manning for Chinese polar expeditions, and administering the Chinese polar expedition winter training base and the representative offices abroad.

6. Organizing and participating in the international affairs and organizations in the area of polar research. Cooperating with the overseas national polar programs.

7. Undertaking the science popularization and promotional work in the area of polar expedition.

8. Undertaking the other tasks assigned by SOA.[45]

The PRIC, located in Shanghai, is the other primary Arctic-focused institution.[46] In February 2010, Dr. Yang Huigen, the Institute's director, explained its missions: to carry out scientific, technological, and strategic studies in the Polar regions; to conduct polar environmental monitoring and detection; and to operate polar vessels, stations, and logistical support. Its dedicated labs and facilities provide Chinese researchers with the means to organize polar expeditions, with a research focus on subjects including glaciology, oceanographic science, upper atmospheric physics, biological science, and polar information platforms. Yang also outlined the PRIC's future plans, which includes new facilities in Shanghai, an expansion in personnel (from 144 to 229), and capacity-building investments such as new Antarctic and Arctic research facilities, and laboratory upgrades.[47] In a move that reflects China's increasing awareness of the Arctic's geopolitical and strategic importance, Zhang Xia, who published the first Chinese report on Arctic geopolitics, established an Arctic strategic research department at the PRIC in July 2009.[48]

The PRIC also oversees China's Polar Information Centre, created in 1995. It has become a national repository for polar archives with nearly 1,000 volumes of polar scientific and technological sources, more than 1,000 photographs, twenty records of audio-visual materials, and 1,000 digital discs. The Polar Research Library contains approximately 20,000 brochures, 270 reference books, and over 4,000 technical studies. China also created a digital database system in 2002 that now includes over 2,000 datasets covering polar oceanography, solar-terrestrial physics, and glaciology, with about 80GB of data available online, and hopes that this may serve as the basis for an international database on polar science.[49] It also seeks to participate in a spatial data infrastructure (SDI) initiative with the Arctic states, where Arctic data, information, and services are shared and integrated in a seamless manner.[50]

Other Chinese organizations and institutions engaged in polar research include the Shanghai Institutes of International Studies (SIIS), one of the most prestigious Chinese research institutions in the area of international affairs, and the China Institute for Marine Affairs (CIMA), which was established within the SOA in 1987 to conduct research on marine policy, legislation, economics, and interests. The SOA also has particular competency on Arctic legal issues. Meanwhile, the Chinese Academy of Sciences conducts scientific studies about the Arctic environment and climate change, mostly through the Institute of Oceanology (a multidisciplinary forum for marine science research and development).[51]

Academic "institution-building" also indicates rising Chinese academic interest in Arctic affairs in recent years. In 2010, the Ocean University of China established the Polar Law and Politics Research Institute as the first institute in China dedicated explicitly to polar social science research. The China-Nordic Research Center was founded in 2013 in Shanghai as a joint Chinese-European centre for cooperative research.[52] In 2016, the Russian Far Eastern Federal University established a Polar Engineering Research Centre with the Chinese University of Ha'er Bing, with a focus on the industrial exploitation of the polar regions.[53] Other polar research institutes have also been established at Shanghai Jiaotong University, Fudan University, and Wuhan University.[54]

China's physical assets have likewise been expanding. In 1993 Beijing purchased a Russian-made icebreaker from Ukraine, which it christened *Xue Long* [雪龙] (the Snow Dragon). This 167-metre-long vessel has an icebreaking capacity of up to 1.2 meters and is equipped with advanced self-contained navigation and weather observation systems, along with a data processing centre and seven laboratories.[55] Its complement also includes three boats and a helicopter. In October 2009 the State Council (the Chinese Cabinet) decided that *Xue Long* alone no longer met the country's expanding polar research needs and required "brothers and sisters." After months of deliberating between purchasing a second-hand foreign vessel and building domestically, Beijing approved the building of a new high-tech polar expedition research ice-breaker. Preliminary plans peg the cost at two billion yuan ($300 million) and work has been under way within the CAA since at least early 2009.[56] This new icebreaker, with a displacement of 8,000 tonnes and a 20,000 nm endurance, will be smaller than the *Xue Long* but still a substantial vessel, specifically designed as a platform for scientific research. Designed in cooperation with an international company and built in a Chinese shipyard, it should be delivered in 2019.[57]

Cumulatively, these organizations, institutions, and assets signal China's interest in conducting multidisciplinary studies that integrate the interests of government and non-governmental institutions. They also illustrate China's limitations in coordinating efforts. Funding, for example, flows from various sources administered by the State Council. Obtaining a decision can be laborious and lengthy, given bureaucratic red tape and competition for resources, authority, funding, and attention. This helps to explain ambiguity about

"China's" position on Arctic issues and why it is unlikely to issue an official policy towards the Arctic region.

China and the Antarctic

While China's Arctic activities get a lot of attention in alarmist narratives, they are better framed as a small component of a significant polar research program. In recent years, the Chinese government announced significant increases in its Antarctic research program. The past two Five Year Plans (2006–10 and 2011–15), for instance, increased the country's Antarctic research budget from $23 million in 2003 to about $55 million per annum, in addition to significant new investments in infrastructure. Anne-Marie Brady provides a concise summary of these historical and contemporary activities: "Beijing acceded to the Treaty in 1983, launched the first Chinese expedition to the Antarctic continent in 1984 and rapidly built two bases, first Changcheng Station on the Antarctic Peninsula (1985), then Zhongshan Station (1989) on the Australian Antarctic claim. All along China's engagement in Antarctica has focused on establishing a significant presence, which would enable to it to assert rights to be involved in decision-making." In 2008, it built Kunlun Station at Dome A (including telescopes for deep space research), with Chinese scientists declaring that "the research done here may lead to China's first Nobel Prize for science." Officials have also indicated plans to establish a fourth Antarctic base. Compared to these infrastructure expenditures, however, Brady notes that actual scientific research funding is modest, and China has no dedicated fund for polar science.[58]

Brady estimates Beijing's annual spending on polar affairs at roughly $60 million – about the same as India and South Korea. Although these are modest expenditures compared to "established players" like the United States and Australia in the Antarctic (see figure 2.1) and the United States and Canada in the Arctic, China's "massive investments in polar hardware in the last five years" set it apart. The US, for example, "capped polar spending in 2008 and is desperately in need of a new icebreaker. By contrast, Beijing recently spent $60 million to refurbish its Antarctic research bases and upgrade its national polar facilities in Shanghai. It also found $300 million for a new icebreaker and plans a new ice-capable plane, a new polar campus in Shanghai, and a rapid expansion of the numbers of Chinese polar scientists from 200 to up to 1,000." Brady soberly observes, however, that this dramatic expansion of China's polar infrastructure does not correlate to a strong impact on polar science:

> With the successful completion of the current five-year plan's objectives in 2015, China will have caught up with most of the developed states' Antarctic operational capabilities with two ice-fitted ships operational, ice-suitable long-range aircraft, and state-of-the art facilities at its polar bases. Beijing will not be spending as much, because it simply does not engage in as much science. In the 2011–2012 austral summer, China sent only 17 scientists to work at Changcheng Station while a mere six scientists worked at Zhongshan Station that year. In the Arctic, China is even more of a bit-player when it comes to science, but any activities there are promoted heavily in Chinese media reports targeted at both domestic and foreign audiences.[59]

Some Western scholars warn that it is simply a matter of time before Chinese researchers and scholars take a stronger position in Arctic studies and use this as leverage to influence Arctic affairs,[60] but they have succumbed to symbolism rather than substance in heralding China's ascendency to the top rank in polar science.

China's scientific engagement in the Antarctic has brought diplomatic benefits with various countries. International collaborations with countries such as Canada, Chile, France, Germany, Norway, Japan, New Zealand, South Korea, Romania, Russia, the United Kingdom, and the United States since the 1980s have "not only been profitable from a scientific point of view, they have also been a useful platform for track-two diplomacy." Scientific activities bring a country legitimate influence in decision-making about governance and resource management on the continent, so Brady notes that "it is only natural that Antarctic diplomacy is also frequently conducted via scientific cooperation." Given that "these scientific exchanges almost always continue regardless of other disagreements between the cooperating countries … they can serve as a useful confidence-building exercise" in addition to their scientific contributions.[61]

It is reasonable to assume that China is applying a similar logic to the Arctic. Trends in Antarctic research may also indicate China's approach to balancing scientific interests with sovereignty concerns. For instance, in

2.1 Investments in Antarctic Research in millions of USD, Anne-Marie Brady, "The Emerging Economies of Asia and Antarctica: Challenges and Opportunities," in *Australia's Antarctica: Proceedings of the Symposium to Mark 75 Years of the Australian Antarctic Territory*, Julia Jabour, Marcus Haward, and Tony Press eds. (Institute for Marine and Antarctic Studies, Occasional Paper no. 2, February 2012.)

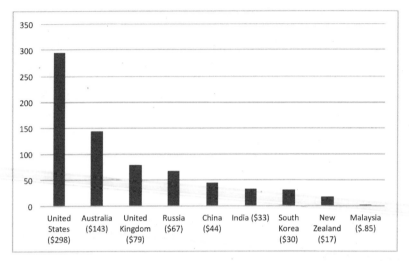

recent years China has offered "generous research and funding opportunities to Australian scientists" to appease concerns about research activities in the Australian Antarctica claim area.[62]

China and Arctic Research

In February 2010, Dr. Chen Liqi provided participants in the First Sino-Canadian Workshop on the Arctic with a review of Chinese priorities for Arctic scientific research, emphasizing Chinese scientists' interest in the impact of climate change in the Arctic and how these changes will affect other ecosystems around the world. He reviewed scientific observations about atmospheric and climate systems, ocean waters and systems, sea ice, environmental processes, and ecology. He explained that CHINARE had conducted three scientific cruises on the *Xue Long* in the Arctic Ocean since 1999. In addition, China established the Yellow River (Huanghe River) research station on Svalbard in 2004 – after setting up its own section at Ny-Ålesund in 2003 – and carried out annual research expeditions there. Research findings from these expeditions relate to physical changes in the Arctic Ocean (such as halocline structure, ocean currents, sea level, and biogeochemistry) and their impacts on global climate change; atmospheric-ocean-sea ice interactions and its influence on climate and ecosystems; and Arctic environmental processes and ecological evolution.[63] Chinese publications on polar science reflect this emphasis on the natural sciences.[64]

China has completed seven Arctic science missions (compared to thirty-two Antarctic science missions) through to the end of 2016. Using the *Xue Long*, it completed its first Arctic expedition in 1999 where it conducted scientific programs in the Bering Sea, Chukchi Sea, and the Canadian Basin in an attempt to better understand:

1. the role of the "Arctic in the global change and its impact on the climate in China";

2. the variable impact of the water mass exchange between the Arctic Ocean and North Pacific on the North Pacific circulation; and

3. the ecosystems and living resources in the sea area adjacent to the Arctic Ocean on the development of China's fishery.[65]

Although the Chinese authorities notified Ottawa that the *Xue Long* intended to sail into Canadian waters, and the Canadian Ice Service used Radarsat data to help the icebreaker navigate through thick ice north of the Alaskan coast, the ship's arrival in Tuktoyaktuk, Northwest Territories surprised local officials. Defence scholar Nancy Teeple notes that:

> The unannounced arrival at Tuktoyaktuk was apparently the result of miscommunication between agencies in Canada, as sources report that the Canadian embassy in Beijing had been notified by the crew of their intentions to sail into Canadian waters. Assuming that the ship intended to sail north, away from Canadian waters, the Canadian Ice Service did not communicate the seemingly unannounced presence of the Chinese ship to Canadian authorities – i.e., the CCRA, CIC and Transport

Canada. In addition, Beijing would have informed Foreign Affairs, whose role would have been to inform the RCMP and relevant agencies that the Chinese had requested permission to sail into Canadian waters.[66]

The Standing Senate Committee on National Security and Defence later concluded that the Chinese had provided advanced notification and had received the requisite approvals; still, this episode exposed the lack of interdepartmental communication among Canadian federal stakeholders and raised questions about intelligence, law enforcement, and potential espionage. The alleged discovery of "excessive" weapons and ammunition aboard the icebreaker[67] further served to make the case an oft-cited example of the potential security threat emanating from the North and Canada's need to invest in Arctic surveillance and enforcement capabilities.[68]

Sébastien Pelletier and Frédéric Lasserre concluded in their recent study of the affair, based upon a series of Access to Information requests submitted between 2010 and 2012, that they had no reason to suspect bad intentions on the part of China in connection with the *Xue Long*'s 1999 visit or that the ship posed a real security threat. They also question the idea that the vessel arrived unannounced or that its appearance was a surprise to Canadian authorities, given that the RCMP was aware in advance that the Canadian consulate in Shanghai had issued eighty one-day visas to the Chinese prior to the visit. Two immigration officers had to be flown from Edmonton, Alberta, as well as a customs officer from Inuvik, NWT, in order to complete the process required to first allow the ship to enter Canadian waters and then allow passengers to go ashore. They found no record of evidence suggesting an "excessive" amount of weapons (never mind the "criminal intent" intimated by Teeple), and the RCMP corporal cleared the ship after "minor problems" (a failure to follow normal procedures by Vancouver-based organizers of the visit) were resolved. In the end, they suggest that the Canadian media made "much ado about nothing" and that the exaggerated treatment of the visit by scholars such as Rob Huebert, Michael Byers, and Teeple served to misrepresent a rather "trivial" incident as a serious security or sovereignty concern.[69]

According to the CAA, China's second expedition in 2003 focused on the following subjects:

1. Variability mechanism of Arctic circulation, water structure, and exchange.

2. Process of Arctic sea ice change and its influence to the air/sea exchange.

3. Carbon flux in the upper Arctic Ocean and the land-source matters influence to the Arctic Ocean.

4. Interaction between the north Pacific and the Arctic Oceans.

5. Mechanism of Arctic climate variability and its influence to the climate in China.

6. The geobiochemical processes and past environment survey in the Arctic Ocean.

7. Interactions between biological and physical processes of the oceans in the north high latitudes.[70]

These expeditions also gave China the confidence and experience necessary to open their first Arctic station at Ny-Ålesund on Svalbard in 2003, which Chinese officials hold up as an example of the country's growing status as a major polar research country.[71]

The International Polar Year from 2007–09 also helped China's polar research to mature. It raised public awareness of the importance of the Polar regions, provided fresh data for analysis, led to plans for further observation networks, and promoted international collaboration.[72] The Chinese government launched the IPY China program, consisting of two projects. The Antarctic project, named PANDA, carried out observations and investigations in the changes of and interaction among the ocean, ice shelves, and high plateaus of the ice sheet. The Arctic project, coded ARCTML (for the study of Arctic Change and its Tele-impacts on Mid-Latitudes), involved two Arctic expeditions (the third and fourth CHINARE expeditions in 2008 and 2010) in which scientists from Canada, Finland, France, Norway, and United States participated. In summarizing the achievements, Huigen Yang noted:

IPY 2007–2008 provided China with a great opportunity to explore polar science frontiers and to raise public polar awareness through international cooperation. By participating in IPY with a national program, China achieved multidimensional polar linkages, increased its understanding of the earth's system and climate change, raised public awareness of polar environmental conservation and protection, and advanced polar science, technology and culture. In the coming decades, a more comprehensive development of polar linkages will be achieved for the benefit of mankind. And a more creative and harmonious polar culture will be cultivated for a sustainable planet.[73]

The fourth CHINARE expedition, conducted between July and September 2010, lasted eighty-five days and recorded changes in the ice surface related environmental effects in the Bering Sea, Bering Strait, Chukchi Sea, Beaufort Sea, Canada Basin, and the Alpha-Mendeleev Sea Ridge. It was China's largest expedition to date, and included 120 scientists, logistical staff, and media persons from China (including one scientist from Taiwan), as well as seven scientists from Estonia, Finland, France, South Korea, and the United States. It did not enter Canadian waters.[74]

In 2012, China launched its fifth Arctic scientific expedition, with *Xue Long* completing an unprecedented trip through the Northern Sea Route, after leaving Qingdao port in July. During these expeditions, scientific research included systematic geographical surveys, installation of an automatic meteorological station, and investigations on oceanic turbulence and methane content in Arctic waters.[75] Expedition leader Huigen Yang, the head of the PRIC, was surprised at the lack of ice along the route at this time of the year: "To our astonishment ... most part of the Northern Sea Route is open," he told Reuters TV. The major difference with this voyage in comparison to China's prior Arctic expeditions was that the news was global.[76] On a return journey to China from an official visit to Iceland in August 2012, the *Xue Long* took advantage of the largest summer sea ice retreat on record and attempted to cross the Arctic Ocean via the North Pole – a route that some Western observers quickly identified as a future shipping lane for Chinese exports and cargo.[77] China's sixth research expedition took place in July 2014 and saw the *Xue Long* transit the Bering Sea into the Arctic Basin north of Canada. The seventh, undertaken in the summer 2016, saw the icebreaker travel 13,000 nm to the Bering and Chukchi Sea and through the Canada Basin. Scientists studied marine meteorology, geology, and chemistry, and surveyed seven ice stations while laying several observation buoys along the way.[78] Upon its return one scientist interviewed by the *Chinese Scientific Newspaper* emphasized the importance of these missions for understanding climate change and potential opportunities for Arctic shipping. "China should not be left behind," the scientist was quoted, "but we don't need a fight."[79]

All told, China aspires to become a significant player in Arctic polar science. It considers the Arctic an "important area for China to enhance its sense of national pride and cohesion," given that most of the countries conducting Arctic scientific research are developed countries. Accordingly, it seeks to deepen research cooperation with key Arctic stakeholders. It joined the International Arctic Science Committee, a non-governmental organization, in 1996, and has reached out bilaterally to foster links with Arctic states. As one Chinese official noted in 2012, "to strengthen dialogue, enhance understanding, promote scientific exchange, and expand cooperation with Arctic states, is very important for the further development of China's polar research capabilities."[80] As China expands these capabilities it naturally carves out a place for itself in scientific discussions about the Arctic and ensures that it cannot be excluded from some of the larger discussions taking place concerning the Arctic and climate change more generally. One official from the Polar Affairs section of the Norwegian foreign ministry noted that China's involvement in climate science was now too significant for it to be excluded.[81]

Social Science Research

Dr. Xinjun Zhang, Associate Professor of Public International Law at Tsinghua University, told participants in the First Sino-Canadian Workshop on the Arctic that Chinese academic interest in the Arctic has expanded significantly since Russia planted its flag on the seafloor at the North Pole in 2007. Subsequently, Chinese social science journals began publishing articles on Arctic issues (with much of the research sponsored by the Chinese government) including the status of the land, continental shelf, water, and ice in the Arctic Ocean Basin; the international legal status of the Northern Sea Route and the Northwest Passage; environmental protection and scientific research in the Arctic; and international cooperation in governance and dispute settlement in the Arctic region. Most of this research focused on treaty interpretation of the relevant articles in the LOSC and the Svalbard Treaty, while some proposed or indicated preferences for the international legal regime in the Arctic.[82]

Li Zhenfu of Dalian Maritime University has criticized Chinese research for "fail[ing] to provide fundamental information and scientific references for China to map out its Arctic strategy," therefore inhibiting China's ability to protect its rights in the international arena. Linda Jakobson notes that "this kind of criticism of the government's approach by Chinese scholars is rare in Arctic-related publications," but Li's 2009 article appeared in a national journal administered by the prestigious China Association for Science and Technology (CAST).[83] Similarly, Jakobson notes that Chinese scholar Guo Peiqing of the Ocean University of China expressed disapproval in media interviews with China's natural sciences-dominated Arctic research and said "it is not in China's interests to remain neutral and 'stay clear of Arctic affairs.'" Guo asserts that "any country that lacks comprehensive research on Polar politics will be excluded from being a decisive power in the management of the Arctic and therefore be forced into a passive position."[84]

Recent indications suggest that China has paid heed to this advice. Yang Huigen explains that: "Realizing that the Arctic is a region where natural and social developments are closely coupled, a new research division on polar social and human sciences was established in the Polar Research Institute of China. This research division has fostered a national network with more than 40 social scientists and 16 research universities and institutes. Topics on Arctic passages, law, economics, governance, geopolitics and international Arctic cooperation have been examined intensively and internationally."[85]

Chinese scholar Kai Sun noted in a recent paper that the project topics suggested by the Chinese Social Science Fund (the top ranked funding agency in China) serve as a barometer of China's governmental focus. In 2013, its list included both Arctic Studies and "Russia's Arctic Policy and Its Regional Impacts." Furthermore, the CAA serves as another major source for natural and social science research through its Polar Strategic Fund (established in 2006), and Kai observes that the funded projects in recent years include more research from social science disciplines.[86]

The first Sino-Canadian Exchange on the Arctic, which brought together senior Canadian and Chinese academics and experts for exchanges of viewpoints and dialogue on international law, policy, and governance issues, confirmed China's growing interests in social science research. At the opening session, Dr. Gao Zhiguo emphasized that China has maintained an active scientific research program since the 1990s, and highlighted the importance of climate change, maritime shipping, environmental protection, regional inter-governmental cooperation, and scientific research exchange and cooperation. During the Shanghai session, Yang Huigen emphasized China's cooperative approach to polar research, as well as correlations between changes in the Arctic Ocean and climate changes observed in China itself.[87]

During the second workshop, hosted by Dalhousie University in Halifax in 2012, Chinese officials reaffirmed the need for cooperation in scientific research, emphasizing the importance of scientific agreements with countries such as Canada, Iceland, and Norway.[88] One Chinese presenter from the PRIC provided a comprehensive overview of China's position on a range of scientific, political, economic, defence, and legal issues. This individual's concluding remarks are worth citing completely, to give a sense of China's understanding of policy issues:

- The importance of the Arctic region in international affairs has increased considerably in recent years on account of debate about climate change, natural resources, continental shelf claims, and new shipping routes.

- The Arctic Policy Rush on the one hand predicts more competition will occur in the Arctic, on the other hand, through these policies, we can know each country's interests and concerns on the Arctic Issue well, which will facilitate the identification of fields for future cooperation.

- Transparency of National Arctic Policy is important for a peaceful and stable Arctic.

- China's past activities in the Arctic mainly focused on the scientific research issues, and China does not have a specific Arctic policy ...

- China does need to formulate a comprehensive Arctic Policy to guide its future activities in the Arctic and to reduce international concerns and misconceptions against China.

- China needs to enhance relevant research on the Arctic issue, so as to discern its national interests in the Arctic.

- China needs internal coordination with a view to formulate a common policy on the Arctic and to take up concrete and concerted positions.

- China needs to seek more participation in the Arctic Governance, particularly through international and regional regimes, in order to play a constructive role in the Arctic.

To finish, the presenter indicated that China's launching of the five-year "Chinese Polar Environment Comprehensive Investigation and Assessment Programs" in February 2012 – its largest program ever – might facilitate the development of an official state policy. The main focus would remain on environmental research into climate change in the polar regions and corresponding effects on China, but it would also more specifically identify "China's national interest in the polar region."[89]

Marine Scientific Research and International Law

Scientists have long recognized the importance of the Arctic for marine scientific research (MSR). This awareness explains the creation of the Svalbard Treaty, 1920, as well as the extensive international rules codified in Part XIII of the Law of the Sea Convention (LOSC) on MSR. The first section of the convention on general provisions notes that "all States, irrespective of their geographical location, and competent international organizations have the right to conduct marine scientific research subject to the rights and duties of other States as provided for in this Convention" and that states and competent international organizations "shall promote and facilitate the conduct of marine scientific research."[90] Article 240 of the LOSC lays out the general principles that activities must be conducted for peaceful purposes, must employ appropriate scientific methods – "shall not unjustifiably interfere with other legitimate uses of the sea" – and must conform with international law, including "the protection and preservation of the marine environment."[91] Within this framework, the convention also promotes international cooperation within the conduct of research activities.[92]

Accordingly, China's research activities in Canadian waters and on its continental shelf are clearly constrained, but not prohibited, by international law. Canada retains significant regulatory controls as a coastal state and there is no reason to believe that China does not abide by these rules.[93] In spite of this, China remains a maritime state (at least in its outlook on the Arctic) and has argued that it would like to see the Arctic coastal states adopt a more uniform and consistent application of these research provisions, including streamlined procedures for requesting permission to conduct research work that transcends coastal state boundaries. Chinese officials also expressed concern that once the Arctic coastal states defined their continental shelves beyond their 200 nautical mile Exclusive Economic Zones, this would reduce the areas open for research. As such, Chinese commentators have highlighted China's need to press their rights (as they exist in the LOSC) to ensure maximum benefit from any development on the sea floor.[94] Chinese experts have also suggested that some aspects of the regime for scientific research in the Antarctic Treaty System might be useful to inform those research regimes in the Arctic.[95]

Conclusions

Given that long-term investments in physical, human, and social scientific research are needed to avoid the "feast and famine" cycle that has marked Canadian Arctic research,[96] Canadian stakeholders may mobilize concerns about losing ground to China as a justification for continued investment in Canadian science. On the other hand, as a global leader in Arctic science, Canada might seek opportunities to enhance its research relationships with China and use this as a means of sharing best practices and of shaping and monitoring China's evolving interests in Arctic research.

Indeed, science can serve as a conduit for international collaboration, influence, and confidence building across a range of issues and areas. In an article in *Jingji Cankao Bao* (*Economic Information Daily*), Liu Huirong of the School of Law and Political Science, Ocean University of China, Qingdao, argued that an ongoing focus on climate change offered China the best opportunity for engagement on Arctic issues, serving as a conduit to raise issues related to biodiversity, shipping, fishery management, and indigenous rights.[97] Given the complexity of local-global linkages, "the problematic nature of sovereignty as a framework for addressing problems of global ecology," and the critical role of science in informing debates related to "planetary politics,"[98] this is an appropriate and shrewd approach for China to pursue. Jakobson

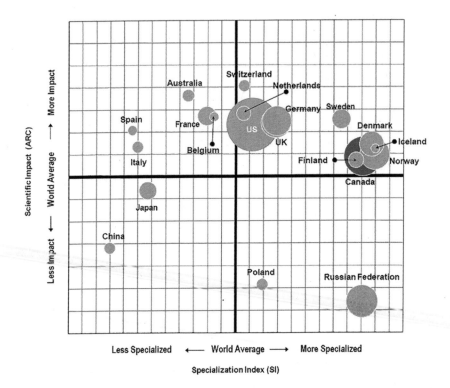

2.2 Positional analysis of leading countries in Arctic science, 1996-2007. *Calculated by Science-Métrix Using the Scopus Database for Aboriginal Affairs and Northern Development Canada (2010).*

and Jingchao astutely note that prominent Chinese researchers and commentators recommend that China prioritize climate change in its public agenda to generate a "new public narrative" through which Chinese scholars can "strive to circumvent the sensitivity of Arctic resources and sovereignty issues, and to calm outsiders' jitters about China as a rising power. Cooperation on climate change is one of those ways that China can partner with other states on the Arctic agenda."[99]

Rather than succumbing to media rhetoric about Canada's need to match East Asian states in a "polar icebreaker race"[100] or accepting unfounded claims that China spends more on Arctic research than Canada, Canada should shake its insecurity complex in the scientific domain. The Canadian government spent approximately $152 million on Arctic science and technology in 2007–08 (including both federal programs and granting councils). Canada also made the largest national contribution to International Polar Year, supporting fifty-two natural science, social science, and health research projects, with more than 1,750 Canadian scientists conducting research at over 100 study sites across the Canadian North and aboard Canadian Coast Guard icebreakers. The federal government has also invested $85 million through its Arctic research infrastructure fund, as well as $46 million in 2003 and an additional $67.3 million to the Network of Centres of Excellence ArcticNet program. Furthermore, the "impact factor" of Canadian Arctic scientific research is second only to that of the United States and is far higher than Asian research.[101] In short, Canada need not feel insecure in its Arctic research, and China better represents a potential partner on specific projects – rather than a nefarious rival deploying science as a Trojan horse.

3

Sovereignty and Shipping

Once this route [the Northwest Passage] is commonly used, it will directly change global maritime transportation and have a profound influence on international trade, the world economy, capital flow and resource exploitation.

China's Maritime Safety Administration (2016)

It is a curious irony that, for the better part of four centuries, British explorers plied the waters of the North American Arctic seeking a northwest passage to China – yet in the twenty-first century, as the polar ice recedes, Canadians seem concerned that China may soon use the Northwest Passage as a route to Europe and the eastern United States. This chapter explores Chinese shipping interests in the region, and places concerns about them in the context of the international legal regime that governs the Arctic waters, Chinese foreign policy interests, and the relative viability of different prospective sea routes. Contrary to many of the fears expressed in recent years about the threat Chinese shipping may pose to Canada, we find that neither the viability of the Northwest Passage nor the alleged threat to Canadian sovereignty live up to their hype. In the short to medium term, China is much more likely to pursue whatever Arctic shipping interests it has through Russia's Northern Sea Route (NSR), which is better supported and more easily navigable. What's more, what little Chinese shipping that does take place through the Northwest Passage is likely to be in compliance with Canadian rules and regulations, and more likely to strengthen Canada's sovereignty than to threaten it.

3.1 Distances between Major Ports. Dark grey indicates the shortest routes, light grey indicates those that are nearly as short.

Origin–Destination	Panama	Northwest Passage	Northeast Passage	Suez and Malacca
Rotterdam–Shanghai	25,588	16,100	15,793	19,550
Bordeaux–Shanghai	24,980	16,100	16,750	19,030
Marseilles–Shanghai	26,038	19,160	19,718	16,460
Gioia Tauro (Italy)–Hong Kong	25,934	20,230	20,950	14,093
Barcelona–Hong Kong	25,044	18,950	20,090	14,693
New York–Shanghai	20,880	17,030	19,893	22,930
New York–Hong Kong	21,260	18,140	20,985	21,570
Rotterdam–Los Angeles	14,490	15,120	15,552	29,750
Lisbon–Los Angeles	14,165	14,940	16,150	27,225

China's shipping interests are a product of its position as the world's leading trading nation. China achieved this distinction in 2012, when the country exported $3.87 trillion worth of goods – most of which travelled by sea.[1] Roughly 46 per cent of China's GDP comes from international trade and the country continues to develop its maritime infrastructure at a break-neck pace.[2] Accordingly, China's interest in the Northwest Passage, and in Arctic waters more generally, are an extension of these broader trade concerns. Beijing closely monitors any change to global trade routes that might affect shipping, given the inevitable impacts on the Chinese economy.[3] The emergence of new Polar routes – either through the Northwest Passage, the Russian Northern Sea Route, or even the Transpolar route across the Arctic Ocean itself which the *Xue Long* navigated on its return trip from Iceland to China in 2012 – would naturally qualify as such a change.

From a strictly geographic perspective the Arctic routes seem to offer significant advantages over the traditional sea lanes around the Cape of Good Hope, Cape Horn, or through the Suez or Panama Canals (see figure 3.1). The NSR would be particularly appealing for traffic between China and northern

3.2 The Arctic from a Chinese Perspective, Linda Jakobson, *China Prepares for an Ice-Free Arctic* (Stockholm, Sweden: Stockholm International Peace Research Institute, March 2010).

Europe, while the Northwest Passage would (at least at first glance) seem to offer a better alternative for ships travelling from China to the American eastern seaboard. Shorter routes, presumably, mean shorter transit times and therefore reduced crew and fuel expenses, as well as the ability to maintain a trade route with fewer ships. One Chinese academic approximates that a viable Northern Sea Route could yield $60–120 billion in savings a year for Chinese shipping firms.[4] Shou Jianmin and Feng Yuan, of Shanghai Maritime University, estimate that use of the route would lead to savings of 10 per cent in fuel and 25 per cent in overall costs.[5] Estimates by the Polar Research Institute of China, which envision 5–15 per cent of Chinese international trade travelling through the NSR by 2050, seem to support this supposition. In September 2012, an official from the National Development and Reform Commission, attending the 15th EU-China Summit, asserted that 30 per cent of the cargo between China and Europe is expected to transit via the NSR "in the future." He even argued that, by 2030, about 50 per cent of the container traffic from traditional routes along Suez and Panama would be diverted to Arctic routes - a figure used by Chinese scholars.[6]

In addition to the economic benefits, new shipping routes might also be of strategic benefit to China. Its existing trade routes pass through a series of canals and chokepoints which could conceivably be closed by either criminal activity or a hostile foreign state. An upsurge in piracy in the Gulf of Aden, for instance, increased the cost of insurance for ships travelling through the Arabian Sea to the Suez Canal by more than 1,000 per cent in the short period between September 2008 and March 2009.[7] More generally, piracy has increased both the dangers and costs of operating along some of the world's most travelled sea lanes. The worldwide cost to shipping companies from such attacks has been estimated at $7–12 billion a year in insurance premiums, ransoms, and disruption.[8] While Chinese shipping has been affected by piracy off the Horn of Africa, such attacks are also a regular occurrence closer to home – in and around the vital Strait of Malacca. Although the frequency of these attacks has fallen considerably in recent years (owing to better cooperation between Indonesia, Malaysia, and Singapore) it remains a persistent problem facing Southeast Asia.[9]

For China, viable Arctic routes could offer important alternatives and/or redundancies. In the event that one or more other straits were closed to its shipping, the Arctic might provide an outlet for Chinese manufactures as well as an import route for the oil and raw materials that the country relies upon to fuel its economy. As mentioned in the first chapter, Chinese officials have cited the security of their country's oil supply as a particular concern. With 50 per cent of its oil coming from the increasingly unstable Middle East and 85 per cent through the Strait of Malacca, a blockade or closure of that route during a conflict could prove both economically and strategically disastrous.[10] Chinese officials and the media have dubbed this danger the "Malacca dilemma." In November 2003 President Hu Jintao declared that "certain major powers" were bent on controlling the strait, and called for the adoption of new strategies to mitigate the perceived vulnerability.[11] Under these circumstances, the prospect of an alternate route (or a number of alternate routes) through the Arctic is particularly appealing.[12]

In 2010, for instance, Guo Peiqing, a professor of polar politics and law at the Ocean University of China, told an interviewer that he foresaw the Arctic becoming "a new energy corridor that would be safer than the Indian Ocean where piracy is such a plague on the world's shippers, including China."[13] Li Zhenfu, a professor at Dalian Maritime University, together with a team of specialists, has been looking closely at the benefits that polar shipping might provide. Referring both to the shortened shipping routes between East Asia and Europe or North America and to abundant Arctic oil, gas, mineral, and fishery resources, Li concluded that "whoever has control over the Arctic route will control the new passage of world economics and international strategies."[14] Thus, while China does not have an official Arctic strategy related to shipping, academics and government officials have indicated that more attention should be paid to the region.[15] However, neither this awareness of the potential value of northern shipping routes, nor the occasionally aggressive statements of its academics should be mistaken as evidence of a Chinese plot to take control. As scholar Timothy Wright points out, both Admiral Zhuo and Li Zhenfu – whose provocative statements are widely quoted by Western analysts as demonstrating nefarious intentions – have decided to stop (or been told to stop) their impolitic statements. Meanwhile, today's scholarly work in China is more grounded and conservative.[16] Moreover, China's foreign policy orientation and its polar and maritime interests, combined with robust international legal norms, are more likely to position it in support of Canada's sovereignty position and push it towards increased regional cooperation – rather than the reverse.

The Northwest Passage: A Convenient Shipping Route?

The idea of a Northwest Passage connecting Europe to the "Orient" and opening new trade opportunities has fired the imagination of navigators, trading companies, and states for more than five centuries. The map of the Arctic Archipelago is replete with the names of explorers who attempted to twist their way through the maze of islands and channels that comprise the Northwest Passage (which is really a series of routes through Canada's Arctic). During the early Cold War, security considerations produced an increased tempo of Canadian and American maritime activity in these waters to build and resupply weather and radar stations. Concurrently, the voyages of the Eastern Arctic Patrol continued to "show the flag" for Canada by resupplying Arctic settlements. Apart from submarine transits through these waters, the vast majority of maritime activity was therefore in the form of destinational shipping, with few vessels actually passing through the Northwest Passage.[17]

In 1969 the voyages of the American oil tanker *Manhattan* rekindled popular interest in the commercial possibilities of transpolar-shipping through the Archipelago. While the supertanker's dramatic transit stimulated

Canadian sovereignty and environmental concerns, it ultimately proved the route uneconomical.[18] In recent years a renewed interest in mining and oil and gas development has generated new interest in using the Northwest Passage as a route in and out of the region, however the shipping industry is does not consider it as a viable passage through the region at this time.[19]

In Canada, however, discussions of Arctic shipping naturally gravitate to the potential opening of the Northwest Passage to this kind of through traffic. There have been commentaries in Chinese newspapers and political journals implying that China should enjoy rights of passage through the Arctic straits; however what that "right" actually entails is rarely spelled out and is often considered as part of China's acceptance of recognized maritime law.[20] Equally important, most Chinese scholars writing about potential transit are equally interested in Canadian or Russian regulations as an important enabling factor – indicating an implied respect for an Arctic coastal state's rights to apply regulations.[21]

The idea that the Canadian Arctic may turn into a transit route was given new life in April 2016 with the publication of a manual on navigation through the Northwest Passage by China's Maritime Safety Administration. Ministry spokesman Liu Pengfei was widely quoted in the Canadian media saying that Chinese ships will sail through the Northwest Passage "in the future," and "once this route is commonly used, it will directly change global maritime transport and have a profound influence on international trade, the world economy, capital flow and resource exploitation."[22]

While the publication of this shipping guide highlights China's continued interest in Arctic shipping it does not represent the threat to Canadian sovereignty as alleged by some media commentators.[23] This report, like China's shipping instructions for the Northern Sea Route (published in 2014), consists of chapters addressing the following:

1. General Arctic ice terminology

2. Navigation routes and maps

3. An introduction to coastal state rules, ports, meteorological information, and ice distribution

4. Northwest Passage navigation practices

5. Navigational aids in the Northwest Passage (including telecommunication services)

6. Hydrographic information and ice data

7. Northwest Passage rules concerning ship inspection, risk assessment, and crew requirements

8. Arctic shipping risks response guidelines and environmental protection

9. A case study of the *Nunavik*'s 2015 transit of the Northwest Passage[24]

This guide offers nothing new or particularly threatening. There is no information on the economics of Arctic shipping that might be useful for planning a voyage, nor is there anything that could be seen as a challenge to Canada's legal position or its jurisdictional control over any portion of the Northwest Passage. If anything, this report actually supports Canadian sovereignty. When addressing regulation, for instance, the Ministry authors write: "The Canadian government considers the Northwest Passage as internal waters, and foreign ships are obliged to apply for a permit and to pay relevant fees. Foreign ships should obey the 'Canada Shipping Act, 2001' and the 'Northern Canada Vessel Traffic Services Zone Regulations 2010' [translated from the original Mandarin]."[25] In a later chapter the authors remind ship owners that they are required to report into NORDREG (Canada's northern vessel reporting system), that vessels carrying dangerous goods must apply for approval, and that "foreign ships should submit a sailing plan (SP) to Marine Communications and Traffic Services."[26] What emerges from this report is an implicit acceptance of Canadian sovereignty, as the Northwest Passage is clearly being treated as waters over which Canada enjoys full jurisdiction – rather than as an international strait, which would not require this level of reporting to transit.

Canadian waters offer only one of the potential transpolar routes and, by almost every consideration, the least attractive one.[27] From a Chinese perspective the NSR appears to hold the greatest appeal. Because of its geographical characteristics and position, coupled with its more advanced level of infrastructure, select but regular shipping through Russia's northern waters is a near-term possibility.[28] Meanwhile, the use of Canadian waters for transit shipping remains a distant hypothetical.[29] A note from the Chinese Ministry of Commerce, dated September 11, 2013,[30] underlines these differences and clearly highlights Chinese interest in the NSR over the Northwest Passage.

In terms of distance from China to the major European and North American ports, the NSR is superior to the Northwest Passage in all but one case: travel from China to Canadian or American ports in the North Atlantic. From Shanghai to New York, for instance, travel through Canadian waters would cut nearly 3,000 km from the voyage compared to the NSR, or roughly 3,700 km compared to the Panama Canal. This reduction in travel time would eliminate roughly five days from the voyage, assuming an average speed of 13.3 knots.[31] While this reduction might result in cost savings under ideal conditions, it is unlikely to induce any shipping company to move into the Canadian Arctic in the foreseeable future, since any distance advantage could easily be nullified by difficult and unpredictable ice conditions, adverse weather, and a lack of supporting infrastructure.[32] This fact is recognized in China where some commentators have pointed to Canada's unwillingness to invest in northern shipping infrastructure – or at least on the same scale as Russia – as a limiting factor.[33] This is particularly the case in the age of just-in-time inventory management where shipping schedules are precisely calculated and late arrivals are unacceptable.[34]

The melting of the Arctic ice has generally been opening the region as a whole to increased activity, while also increasing certain hazards in the Canadian Arctic. Specifically, the melting of first-year ice in the western Arctic allows winds and ocean currents to drive more old ice from the Arctic Ocean into the narrow channels of the Archipelago. As such, some of the more important areas (from a shipping perspective) have actually exhibited an increase in hazardous ice levels. This shift is largely the result of an ocean current pattern called the Beaufort Gyre, which regularly shifts multi-year ice from farther north into the western channels of the Archipelago.[35] Accordingly, most experts predict that even as overall ice cover in the Arctic Basin recedes, conditions in Canada's Arctic shipping channels will continue to remain extremely dangerous.[36] As young ice in large segments of the passage melts during the summer shipping season, old ice from farther north moves south and the result is an increase in dangerous ice conditions exactly when ships might otherwise have been able to move through the passage.

Compounding the dangers posed by ice are the draft requirements for many of the passages within the Arctic Archipelago. The easiest and most travelled routes through the Northwest Passage have always been through Peel Sound and M'Clintock Channel; yet both of these passages restrict the draft of a ship, meaning that the economies-of-scale provided by the world's biggest cargo vessels cannot be realized. The deep-draft routes through Prince of Wales and M'Clure Strait could handle even the 25-metre draft of an ultra large crude or cargo carrier, but these are the areas with the most extreme ice conditions in the Canadian Arctic and, even in the summer months, are currently limited to Arctic Class 3 vessels.[37]

The Arctic Maritime Shipping Assessment (AMSA), a four-year, multi-national project undertaken by the Arctic Council's Protection of the Arctic Marine Environment working group, concluded that the Northwest Passage is highly unlikely to become a viable trans-Arctic route before 2020.[38] For the environmental, economic, and administrative reasons already listed, the models that the AMSA used to gauge the future viability of Arctic sea routes indicate that the last regions of the Arctic Ocean to safely open to shipping would be northern waterways of the Canadian Archipelago and the northern coast of Greenland.[39] A 2013 report by the US National Academy of Sciences reached a similar verdict. Under none of their simulations did shipping through Canadian waters emerge as a viable option before 2040–59.[40]

To demonstrate this point on the operational level, Lasserre has gone beyond the theoretical ice melt calculations and in 2008 contacted sixty-five of the shipping firms that might have been interested in Arctic operations. He found that few of them had any interest in shipping through the Northwest Passage and that most of those that did were already involved in the annual sealift of bulk supplies to northern communities. Of the major Chinese firms contacted then, neither Orient Overseas Container Line (OOCL), China Ocean Shipping Company (COSCO), nor China Shipping Container Lines (CSCL) expressed an interest in opening Arctic shipping routes in the short or medium term, largely because of the slower speeds across these routes, the higher insurance costs, the high probability of delays, and the serious risks of damage to the ships and cargo.[41] A second, more extensive survey in 2009 yielded similar results, with only six out of forty-six container shippers willing to state that they would even consider an Arctic route.[42] A third survey of 125 firms, conducted between 2009 and 2010, led to the conclusion that, among the ninety-eight answering firms, there was still very little serious interest[43] (see figures 3.3 and 3.4).

Lasserre updated these numbers in September 2013 after a series of direct interviews with twenty-three Chinese shipping and forwarding companies.

3.3 Overview of Responses According to Company's Main Sector of Activity.

	Container	RoRo	Container and Bulk	Bulk	General Cargo	Special Project	Total
			Sector of Activity				Total
Yes			2	9	5	1	17
No	35	2	5	25	4		71
Maybe	3		1	6			10
Total	38	2	8	40	9	1	98

3.4 Overview of Responses According to Company's Home Region.

	Europe	Asia	North America	Total
		Home Region		Total
Yes	10		7	17
No	32	25	14	71
Maybe	5	3	2	10
Total	47	28	23	98

The pattern remained the same, with few industry representatives expressing any real interest for Arctic shipping (see figure 3.4).[44] Only two companies admitted to even considering Arctic operations: the first thought it a possibility but still questioned the profitability, while the second displayed an interest in transporting Arctic natural resources, but only from Siberia to China. COSCO did send a ship, the *Yongsheng*, across the NSR in 2013, but some officials from the company recognize that the profitability of large-scale shipping in the Arctic remains to be ascertained – and remains questionable.

While several interviewees expressed a belief in the *potential* of Arctic shipping, none had yet undertaken an extensive cost/benefit or "SWOT" analysis of that potential.[45] Chinese companies cited various problems with Arctic operations, including the high investment necessary to buy ice-strengthened ships; market constraints surrounding schedules and ship sizes limiting economies of scale; an Arctic market too small to build a profitable route and, therefore, a longer return on investment on costly ice-strengthened ships; as well as physical risks and high insurance costs.

3.5 Overview of Responses According to Type of Shipping – Question: "Are You Considering Developing Operations in the Arctic?" (2013).

	Container and bulk	Container	Bulk	Multipurpose	Charterer/ forwarder/ broker	Total
Yes	1		1			2
No	1	1	5	6	5	18

The most recent such survey – undertaken in 2016 by Leah Beveridge, Mélanie Fournier, Frédéric Lasserre, Linyan Huang, and Pierre-Louis Têtu – demonstrated the general continuity of this trend, though with a noticeable uptick in interest when companies were asked to speak of potential for the industry as a whole. Of those companies asked about the commercial potential of Arctic shipping, twenty-eight saw potential for the industry; fourteen saw none "yet," and three saw no potential ever emerging. When asked about their company's interest (rather than the industry's writ large) only two saw real potential, with nineteen responding that their company had none and three saying that they were unsure. In short, while Chinese companies remain pessimistic about their individual corporate futures in the Far North, the generally positive response when asked about the industry as a whole does show a trend towards the possibility of Arctic shipping – at least when speaking in the hypothetical.[46]

This survey also expanded upon why these companies continued to express limited interest in the North. As figure 3.5 illustrates, shipping companies see the risk in Arctic activities as being ice, weather, the remoteness of the region, timetable uncertainty and variability, and the heightened potential for accidents.[47] Reasons for potential interest (either for their company or the industry in general) revealed nothing surprising; most companies surveyed saw the shorter distances and potential for resource shipping as the most attractive aspects of Arctic operations. Somewhat surprisingly, only three responses out of forty-seven (6 per cent) mentioned the melting sea-ice, which is ironic given the level of attention this factor receives in Western media and scholarly literature.[48] Overall, these results reinforced the conclusions of previous surveys in demonstrating little concrete interest on the part of Chinese shipping companies in Arctic operations. What interest exists remains in certain niche markets, or as speculation on future potential.

3.6 Risks of Arctic Shipping, Leagh Beveridge et al., "Interest of Asian Shipping Companies in Navigating the Arctic," *Polar Science* 10, no. 3 (2016).

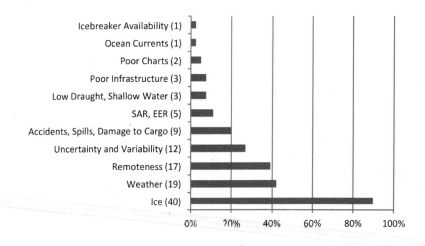

3.7 Interests in Arctic Shipping, Leagh Beveridge et al., "Interest of Asian Shipping Companies in Navigating the Arctic," *Polar Science* 10, no. 3 (2016).

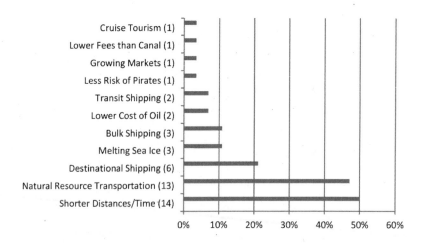

This analysis of shipowners' intentions reveals a different, and much more restrained, picture from the often repeated news media image of a future Arctic shipping highway. Although marine traffic in the Russian and Canadian Arctic is increasing, it is far from representing an "explosion" in new activity. The constraints of just-in-time planning and schedule creation, as well as collision/grounding risks, are simply too great when placed against the relatively modest savings in time and fuel. Furthermore, while many Chinese shipowners have ties to the Chinese government, there is no indication that they are acting as strategic actors to execute a nefarious government policy; instead, they appear to be operating along the same economic principles as the rest of the international shipping industry.[49]

Rather than international shipping, which has the choice of various different routes, current trends point to destinational shipping as the most likely user of the Arctic sea routes (and particularly the Northwest Passage). Destinational traffic, which is defined by vessels travelling into or out of the Arctic, includes ships servicing local communities and natural resource exploitation activities from Arctic sites like Deception Bay, Kirkenes, Vitino, or Murmansk. This scenario assumes heightened resource development in the region, itself a proposition dependent on many variables: from global resource prices to permitting and support from local populations. Nevertheless, as new mines come online in the Canadian Arctic the process will only accelerate. Fednav, a Canadian-owned shipping company, moved the first cargo of nickel concentrate from Deception Bay, Quebec to China via the Northwest Passage in September 2014 and began shipping iron ore from the Mary River Mine on Baffin Island in 2015.[50] Tourism remains a major source of activity as well, with seventeen voyages in Canadian Arctic waters in 2013, eleven in 2014, and eighteen in 2015.[51] Meanwhile, community resupply missions will continue to increase as Canada's northern population expands (the current rate of population growth in Nunavut is 3.2 per cent versus Canada's 1.2 per cent).[52]

Even if Chinese ships are involved in this destinational traffic, that activity is unlikely to damage Canadian sovereignty in any way. Because their stopover in a Canadian port immediately triggers the regulations of the state (Canada) that owns the port, the ships involved would have to obey Canadian law and shipping regulations. In fact, China has never shown any intention of challenging Canadian sovereignty. In a March 2013 meeting of Canadian researchers (including Lasserre) and representatives of the Canadian Embassy with Chinese researchers and officials from the Polar Research Institute of

3.8 The Fednav vessel *Nunavik* in the Prince of Wales Strait, courtesy of Fednav.

China (PRIC), the official Chinese scientific leaders stressed that China intends to seek permission to transit through the Northwest Passage for its research icebreaker, thus expressly recognizing the Canadian position.[53]

From a practical perspective there would also seem to be little possibility of an implicit challenge from Chinese ships since these ships involved would have to obey Canadian law and shipping regulations, thus reinforcing Canada's position that the Northwest Passage constitutes internal Canadian waters. Any refusal to do so would jeopardize that company's rights to continue mining on Canadian soil. After investing many hundreds of millions of dollars developing a mine, it seems unlikely that any company, Chinese or otherwise, would feel the need to risk its investment with an aggressive political stand against Canadian sovereignty.[54]

China and the Northern Sea Route

While systematic studies have downplayed the Northwest Passage as a viable shipping route in the foreseeable future, studies such as the landmark AMSA 2009 Report recognize the emerging potential of the Northern Sea Route, particularly as Chinese manufacturers seek to open new markets in the European Union.[55] The NSR not only offers significantly shorter routes to Europe but a level of maritime infrastructure and navigational support that is absent in the Canadian North.

The NSR was first developed by the Russian czars in the early twentieth century and expanded considerably during the Soviet era, both as an export route for Siberian raw materials as well as a strategic link with the Russian Far East. At its height in 1987, the route carried almost seven million tons of cargo.[56] The NSR's infrastructure, which includes icebreaking support and navigational and port infrastructure, fell into disrepair after the collapse of the USSR, but it has received renewed attention as reduced sea ice makes international traffic along the route increasingly viable. Over the last decade, the Russians have invested heavily to develop the NSR as a fully integrated "national transportation route" connecting Europe and Asia – a project that requires modern harbours, new icebreakers, air support, and enhanced search and rescue capabilities.[57] Indeed, Russia recently opened the first of ten search and rescue centers planned to operate along the route by 2015.[58]

Cargo transported along the NSR reached a post-Cold War record in 2011 at 820,789 tons.[59] By 2013 it had grown to 1,355,897 tons.[60] Most of this was destinational rather than through traffic, but the route's potential for international shipping has caught Chinese attention. In May 2014 Vladimir Putin and Chinese President Xi Jinping formalized this interest, issuing a joint statement on Russian-Chinese cooperation that, among other things, included a Russian promise to facilitate Chinese shipping along the route. Two months later, China released a sailing guide to the NSR that included nautical charts, sailing methods, ice-breaking instructions, as well as information on the laws and regulations of countries along the route.

Commenting on the successful test voyages from South Korea to the Netherlands via the NSR by two German commercial vessels in the summer of 2009, Chen Xulong of the China Institute of International Studies wrote that "the opening of the Arctic route will advance the development of China's north-east region and eastern coastal area. It is of importance to East

Asian cooperation as well." Chen continues on to say that, for these reasons, China should develop a long-term vision regarding Arctic shipping.[61]

Other commercial voyages have transited the route since that time. In 2012, the LNG carrier *Ob River* completed the westbound voyage in ballast in only six days and, after loading LNG at the port of Hammerfest, made its return voyage to Tobata, Japan without incident. The Russian gas giant Gazprom has held this transit up as proof that the NSR can be developed as a viable trade route linking the northern Russian gas fields to Asian markets.[62]

Calls to exploit this new route are now coalescing in China. State media has reportedly praised the NSR as the "most economical solution" for shipping between Chinese and European ports, while paraphrasing Yu Cheng of the Chinese maritime industry[63] who referred to it as the "Golden Waterway."[64] Recent developments attest to the possibility of a nascent economic niche for certain cargoes. Taking advantage of accelerating ice decline along the Siberian coast, the first attempt at transporting hydrocarbons from Russia to China by the NSR was undertaken in August 2010 when the *Baltica*, escorted by a Russian icebreaker, took twenty-seven days to deliver natural gas condensate from Murmansk to Ningbo (Zhejiang). This trial was followed by a commercial agreement on long-term cooperation on Arctic shipping along the NSR between the Russian sea shipping company *Sovcomflot* and China National Petroleum Corporation (CNPC) that was concluded on November 22, 2010. This agreement, declared to be part of the Russia-China energy cooperation strategy, was signed in presence of the Russian Federation vice-prime minister Igor Setchin (who is also president of the board of the oil company *Rosneft*, the second largest oil producer in Russia), and of Wang Qishan, vice premier of the People's Republic of China.[65] In 2014, plans were also set in motion to construct sixteen new icebreaking tankers to operate along the route, supplying Russian gas from the Yamal project to Asian customers. Six of these vessels were already being built for China LNG Shipping when Western credit for the project dried up with the imposition of sanctions in the summer of 2014. Consequently, project operator Novatek turned to Chinese banks for $10 billion in additional funding.[66]

Huigen Yang, director general of the Polar Research Institute of China, proclaimed at a conference in Oslo in March 2013 that fully 15 per cent of the country's international trade could travel through the Arctic by 2020.[67] These ambitious goals should, however, be viewed with a healthy degree of skepticism. While the NSR is better supported and more easily navigable than the Northwest Passage, its use remains subject to constraints that are similar, if less severe, than those of its Canadian counterpart. These include harsh environmental conditions, a brief window of operation, and high icebreaker fees. In the summer of 2016, Chinese captain Wu Weibing transited the route aboard the COSCO vessel *Yong Sheng*, and his report of the voyage after the fact highlighted these difficulties. In an article published by the Chinese journal *Marine Technology*, Weibing noted real "challenges and inconveniences," ranging from a lack of detailed navigational information, a language barrier working with Russian officials, and hydrographic charts that were sometimes off by ten metres. Ice-reporting was, likewise, sparse and inconsistent while communications were limited by the high latitude.[68] Still, Weibing notes that the route holds great potential value. At 3,500 nm (and eleven days) shorter than the Suez route, the ship likely saved $210,000 in charter and fuel savings.[69]

The Northern Sea Route also faces competition from new transportation corridors further south. In September 2013, Chinese president Xi Jinping announced his country's plans to construct the "Silk Road Economic Belt," a series of high-speed rail, freeways, and pipelines that will criss-cross lands once traversed by caravans in the first millennium, backed by a $40 billion development fund. Theoretically, this route will enable shipments between China and Europe to move faster than they would through the NSR, while avoiding the dangers and uncertainties of the Arctic environment.[70] While megaprojects of this nature often fail to live up to their initial promise, an efficient cross-Asia land route would siphon off some of the NSR's expected business.

The most likely scenario for Chinese shipping (with or without a new silk road) is that the NSR will remain a niche route for select cargoes – at least for the foreseeable future. Indeed, some of the enthusiasm surrounding the NSR began to deflate in 2014 when traffic was roughly halved compared to its 2013 levels and cargo levels fell a stunning 80 per cent, in spite of a longer shipping season.[71] The NSR administration blamed this decline on shipping decisions made by two of its largest users, EvroKhim and Novatek, indicating that the reduced tempo may be temporary but also demonstrating how concentrated NSR traffic is in a few local shippers.[72]

As with the Northwest Passage, most of the traffic using the NSR will continue to be destinational – with supplies flowing into northern communities and resources flowing out. Until significant new resource projects come online requiring shipping to Chinese (or other Asian) ports, usage of the NSR will continue to be both light and extremely variable. Few stories of China's growing Arctic interest address how small this interest actually is, relative to China's massive and ever-expanding shipping interests elsewhere in the world. Rather than actively preparing for the opening of the Northwest Passage, Chinese companies have invested heavily in modern non-ice-strengthened cargo ships to serve their overseas markets. Along these lines, Chinese firms are investing in port terminals along the classical routes through Panama (or potentially a new canal through Nicaragua) and the Suez/Malacca route.

Chinese port management companies, like Hutchison Port Holdings (HPH) in Hong Kong, have acquired major stakes in Panamanian ports and in other canal operators. HPH has stakes in several ports near or along the Suez-Malacca route: Tanjung Priok (Indonesia), Port Klang (Malaysia), Yangon (Myanmar), Sohar (Oman), Alexandria (Egypt), Taranto (Italy), and Barcelona (Spain).[73] In 2008, COSCO Container Lines launched a multimodal service to the Panamanian port of Balboa that links Asian markets with Mexico, Panama, and the Caribbean.[74] Between 2009 and 2013, COSCO also invested €340 million taking over terminals II and III at the Greek port of Piraeus, an important hub close to the Suez Canal.[75] COSCO Pacific now also owns 49 per cent of the COSCO-PSA Terminal Private in Singapore and 20 per cent of Suez Canal Container Terminal (in Port Said, Egypt).[76] While there may be Chinese interest in Arctic routes, these investments elsewhere help to keep it in perspective. China remains overwhelmingly wedded to the classical global sea routes through Malacca, Suez, and Panama. The Arctic routes may evolve into something more in the future, but for the moment they are defined by their potentiality rather than their actual utility.

Are the Chinese a Threat to Canada's Sovereignty in the Northwest Passage?

The first and foremost pillar of Canada's foreign policy is "the exercise of our sovereignty over the Far North." The statement highlights that "protecting national sovereignty, and the integrity of our borders, is the first and foremost responsibility of a national government. We are resolved to protect Canadian sovereignty throughout our Arctic."[77] The "hard security" message that had figured prominently in earlier statements by the Harper Government is muted in recent Canadian policy documents, however, and the tone of cooperation with circumpolar neighbours and northerners rings loudest. Accordingly, Canada's *Statement on Arctic Foreign Policy* commits it to "seek to resolve boundary issues in the Arctic region, in accordance with international law." While these well-managed disputes pose no acute sovereignty or security concerns to Canada, most commentators continue to see them as a political liability.

Although it is not a "boundary dispute," Canada's legal position that the Northwest Passage constitutes internal waters is not universally embraced. While the United States has taken a public position suggesting that the passage constitutes an international strait (although it has never been used as such in functional terms), most countries have remained silent on the issue. Canadian commentators often assume that, given their interests as maritime nations, East Asian states must naturally oppose Canada's position. David Wright, for instance, observes that "some Chinese scholars are carefully examining Canada's claims of historical sovereignty over the Arctic in general and the Northwest Passage in particular," indicating that "Beijing does not want to affirm the accuracy or appropriateness of Canada's historical claims." Although he concedes that "the small number of scholars in China who consider these claims in detail seem largely to end up sympathetic with, and supportive of," the Canadian position, he reiterates that "the Chinese government itself does not seem ready to affirm Canadian Arctic sovereignty." Accordingly, he stresses that "Canada needs to be on its guard against Chinese attempts to water down Canada's Arctic sovereignty and should strengthen cooperation with democratic Arctic states for the security and stability of the region."[78] Ironically, a closer look at some of the Chinese statements that Canadian scholars point to as questioning Canadian sovereignty suggests that Chinese commentators are often simply citing the work of those same Canadian scholars in making their case. Accordingly, there is a circular logic at work when commentators point to vulnerabilities in Canada's position and then, when others reference these potential vulnerabilities, use this as proof that their concerns are warranted.

Contrary to these hawkish perspectives, China is unlikely to challenge either Canada's assertion that the waters of its Arctic Archipelago constitute historic internal waters or the validity of its straight baselines. In the first instance, despite China's interests in Arctic shipping lanes, these are secondary to its broader interests as a coastal state. In particular, its perspective on the Qiongzhou Strait separating Hainan Island from the Chinese mainland is similar to Canada's perspective on the Northwest Passage. Furthermore,

China (and indeed all East Asian states) have made straight baseline claims based on a liberal interpretation of article VII of the LOSC.[79] China's claim to the South China Sea is particularly contentious. Marked by the "nine-dashed line," China has implied that these waters are territorial, although what Beijing means by "territorial" does not appear to conform to any standard maritime regime under international law.[80]

As Lincoln Flake points out, American and Chinese navigational interests in the Arctic are unlikely to combine to challenge the Canadian position. Not only would such a challenge call into question China's own maritime position, it would also conflict too starkly with the overall anti-US narrative developing in Sino-Russian relations. Similarly, US support for its Asian allies on navigation in the South China Sea precludes cooperation with Beijing on the issue in the Arctic.[81] As such, China is unlikely to challenge Canada's position, unless Canada joined the United States in its comprehensive opposition to China's own maritime claims. Conversations with Chinese academics support this perspective and reinforce the probability that China will respect well established maritime claims in the Arctic. Even Guo Peiqing, who has argued for a robust assertion of China's rights in the Arctic, emphasizes that China will conduct its research in compliance with Arctic state jurisdictions.[82]

Concerns about China's desire for influence and potential for revisionist action in the Arctic must ultimately be weighed against one of its overriding diplomatic imperatives: its absolute respect for a state's right to manage its affairs within its own jurisdiction. China has long been wary of foreign powers meddling in its own internal affairs and has often spoken out against foreign intervention in what it sees as either internal conflicts or issues (see for example its positions regarding the Syrian and Libyan civil wars). This strongly Westphalian position on state sovereignty would therefore make it awkward for China to question Canadian activity within an area over which Canada claims complete jurisdiction. In the 2012 edition of the *Arctic Yearbook*, Yang Jian, the vice president of the Shanghai Institutes for International Studies, explained China's position as follows: "For China, Arctic affairs can be divided into those of a regional nature and those of global implications. It has been China's position that the former should be properly resolved through negotiation between countries of the region China respects the sovereignty and sovereign rights of Arctic countries, and hopes that they can collaborate with each other and peacefully resolve their disputes over territory and sovereignty."[83] This reflects what Linda Jakobson and Jingchao Peng described as the more "subdued" public messaging from Chinese Arctic scholars since 2011, which also fits with China's "preoccupation with staunchly defending its perceived rights in the South and East China seas."[84] Thus while China's aggressive stance in its own backyard is sometimes held up as a reason to worry about the country's activities in the Arctic, a more grounded appreciation of Beijing's foreign policy orientation suggests just the opposite. The same sovereignty concerns that motivate belligerence in the South and in East China seas predict accommodation of Canada's sovereignty interests in the Arctic.

While wide-scale, transit shipping is unlikely in the foreseeable future, and China is unlikely to challenge or undermine Canadian sovereignty, the question should be asked: might an increase in Chinese Arctic activity inadvertently damage the Canadian legal position? In a 2003 article in the *International Journal*, Rob Huebert theorized that even a single ship moving through Canadian waters without permission could create a precedent that would seriously damage Canada's legal position by demonstrating that the Northwest Passage can be used as an international strait.[85] A conflict with a vessel refusing to request such permission might quickly expand if that ship's flag country were forced to support its right to transit those waters and therefore to challenge Canada's legal position.[86] Huebert's argument was made in response to a 2003 article by Franklyn Griffiths in which Griffiths downplayed the potential danger posed by Arctic shipping.[87]

In the decade since this debate began in earnest, the evidence indicates that Griffiths' evaluation of the danger was the more prescient. There have been no rogue transits of the Northwest Passage and those ships that have made the passage have complied with Canadian laws and regulations or else have been seized by the RCMP. Commercial operators, unlike certain governments (in particular the United States), gain nothing from refusing to recognize Canadian sovereignty. To this point they have followed the path of least resistance when operating in Canadian waters – namely, accepting Canadian jurisdiction – and there is every indication that they will continue to do so.[88]

With respect to Chinese vessels, Huebert's fearful scenario that a state government will feel the need to back a ship carrying its flag in a dispute with Canada seems unlikely to materialize. China's own maritime claims make it unlikely that Beijing would see any advantage to disputing Canada's sovereignty position in the Arctic. As such, it is difficult to see the Chinese government challenging that sovereignty on behalf of a Chinese flagged merchant vessel.

Even if the Chinese government were to deem the Northwest Passage a vital shipping route, conflict is hard to envisage. Canada has long declared its support for shipping through the Arctic Archipelago, as long as it complies with Canadian laws and regulations.[89] The Canadian government provides search and rescue support, ice and weather reporting services, and other assistance to foreign vessels. There is no reason for the Chinese government to challenge Canadian sovereignty when Canada is prepared to encourage and assist shipping that complies with its reasonable regulatory regime.

Furthermore, in the event that Chinese ships begin to ply the waters of the Northwest Passage, either regularly or sporadically, these voyages may in fact support Canada's sovereignty position. Even if the companies involved are not asked to explicitly recognize Canadian sovereignty, but merely to comply with pollution control regulations, mandatory reporting regimes, and other Canadian regulations, the net effect would be the same. While the United States may persist in viewing the Northwest Passage as an international strait in principle, if the passage becomes viable as a transpolar route, the use of those waters by US government vessels will be substantially less than the commercial transits by Chinese and other international shippers. China, for reasons discussed and for simple convenience, is more likely to accept Canadian sovereignty and jurisdiction than to officially side with the Americans.[90]

China's Role in the Development of International Arctic Shipping

In the future, the governance of Arctic shipping will require an internationalist approach. While the Arctic states have the right to exercise jurisdiction within their internal and territorial waters, that control does not extend into the Polar Basin where shipping routes may also emerge.[91] It is clearly in Canada's interest to see uniform shipping standards adhered to by all ships operating in the circumpolar Arctic, and this means Chinese cooperation. Canada has spent more than two decades spearheading an effort by a group of countries, classification societies, and industry experts seeking to establish and implement a harmonious set of rules for the construction and operation of ships transiting ice-covered waters.[92] In November 2014, these years of effort culminated in the establishment of the Polar Code, a set of rules

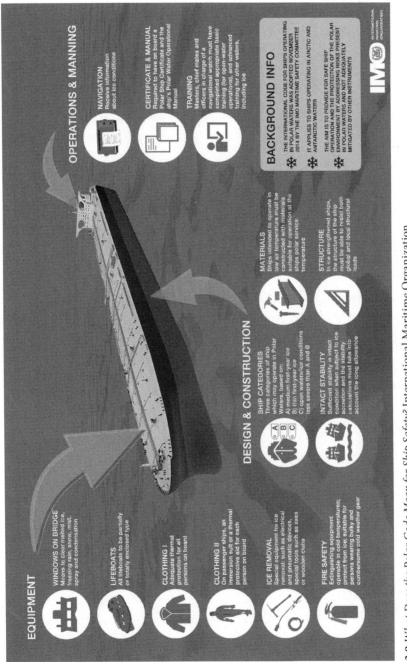

3.9 *What Does the Polar Code Mean for Ship Safety?* International Maritime Organization.

promulgated by the International Maritime Organization covering certification, design, equipment systems, operations, environmental protection, and training for Arctic navigation. These rules provide an added layer of environmental protection and safety in Arctic waters outside of state jurisdiction and simplify requirements for shippers moving between Arctic jurisdictions.[93] As a major shipping nation, China's adherence to the Polar Code is vital to preserving the Arctic marine environment. As such, working with China and the broader international community to develop and regulate Arctic shipping is, and will continue to be, essential.

Developing this cooperative approach should be possible, given China's stated intention to participate in the cooperative promotion of Arctic shipping. Speaking in Norway in February 2013, for instance, Ambassador Zhao Jun highlighted his country's keen interest in building cooperation between the Barents Region and non-Arctic states as Arctic waterways open.[94] Chinese scholars and officials have expressed similar sentiments in the understanding that cooperation will be necessary for China to obtain a position in Arctic affairs. Zhao continued to say that "it is natural for China to participate in discussions on Arctic issues, as a potential user of Arctic waterways ... Cooperation is the key to dealing with Arctic issues."[95]

Provided that Chinese shipping is not unfairly discriminated against or denied access to emerging sea routes without reasonable grounds, Beijing is likely to accept international safety standards for Arctic vessels. Professor Guo Peiqing sums up China's preferred view of the Arctic, saying that "circumpolar nations have to understand that Arctic affairs are not only regional issues but also international ones."[96] That China accepts circumpolar affairs as international should naturally lead to a greater willingness to accept and encourage others to accept the sort of global approach to Arctic safety represented by the IMO Polar Code. By extension, this logic supports indications that China recognizes that "Arctic countries, with a larger stake in Arctic-related issues, should play a more important role in Arctic affairs, such as marine environment protection, and marine search and rescue."[97]

Conclusions

Over the next decade, China will continue to express interest in the possibility of new Arctic shipping routes. In the distant future, this may even mean the use of the Northwest Passage. In the short to medium term, however, environmental conditions and a dearth of infrastructure are likely to keep these options "on ice." Instead, the Northern Sea Route will almost certainly elicit the most Chinese attention over the next decade – yet even that traffic is likely to be relatively limited.

It is possible that Chinese shipping companies will seek to use the Northwest Passage for irregular transits, possibly in support of local resource exploration or export, and, while China has not publically accepted the Canadian government's position that the waters of the Arctic Archipelago constitute historic internal waters, it has not denied this position either. Given Chinese claims to the Qiongzhou Strait and the entire South China Sea, it is simply not in Beijing's interest to challenge the Canadian claim. If Chinese shipping plies Canada's Arctic waters it is likely to be destinational, and proceed in compliance with Canadian rules and regulations. Far from damaging Canadian sovereignty, such voyages could strengthen it by building an important precedent of foreign flagged ships operating in the Arctic Archipelago and accepting them as internal waters. As a major shipbuilder and commercial maritime power, China will certainly play an important role in the future of Arctic shipping. All signs indicate that it is ready and willing to cooperate with the international community to ensure that potential polar sea lanes are managed and operated with respect to international law.[98]

4

Arctic Resources and China's Rising Demand

Speaking about the North Pole, it's obvious that its significance is not limited by scientific research only. Now it is called a "global construction site." What does this mean? It means that economic activities there are not clearly described by the international agreements. So, the one who starts first will most likely ensure one's advantages for the future. As we know, the planet's resources are limited. This means it's impossible to turn a blind eye to the natural deposits in the area of the North Pole. One can say, it's the [Middle East] of the future or the second [Middle East].

COLONEL LE LI,
PRC Army (2012)[1]

With the possible exception of Russia, there is no country whose Arctic ambitions are viewed with more apprehension in the Western world than China. Wealthy and increasingly assertive, China's interest in the region's resources is growing, raising the spectre of a powerful communist dictatorship controlling strategically vital elements of the circumpolar economy. Since the early 1990s, the rapid growth of Chinese industry has transformed the country from a net exporter of raw materials into the world's largest importer, a transition that resulted in the formation of some of the world's largest state-owned mining and oil companies, which were sent overseas to secure new reserves. Over the past decade, these state-owned enterprises (SOEs) have spent billions establishing themselves as leaders in global resource extraction. In 2013 alone, China's overseas resource investments soared to $53.3 billion, up from $8.2 billion in 2005, and a rapidly growing percentage of this investment is being funnelled into the Arctic.[2] The attraction is obvious: the circumpolar region is one of the last, largely undeveloped regions in the world and is purported to hold a significant share of the planet's remaining minerals, oil, and gas.[3] In the years to come this investment will almost certainly increase and China's role in northern development will become even more pronounced. In spite of this, China's role in Arctic resource development should not be exaggerated. China has been cautious in moving forward on risky Arctic ventures and many of Chinese-owned projects have stalled in the face of low resource prices. This chapter examines China's growing interest and investment in Arctic resources and places these activities into context to show the role and intent of Chinese companies, and to demonstrate that popular fears of a "resource grab" are largely unfounded.

Canadian Policy and Chinese Resources

One of the most prominent aspects of China's resource strategy, and one that reinforces its Arctic interests, is its effort to diversify the geographical source of its imports so as to mitigate the risks associated with supply disruption.[4] China thus has a natural interest in developing the Arctic and has been particularly active in cultivating new economic ties with Greenland, Iceland, and Russia.[5] This is not to say that China's aim is to control these nations' resources per se, but rather to play a role in bringing them online (or at the very least to have that option). A Chinese-owned mine in the Arctic may not necessarily export its product to China; nevertheless, controlling world-class Arctic resource deposits will strengthen Chinese companies by increasing revenue and reserve life. From a broader Chinese national perspective, Arctic production will increase supply, thereby lowering commodity prices, reducing capital outflows, and positively affecting China's balance of payments.

According to Taiwanese scholar Wang Kuan-Hsung, China's "nightmare scenario" is one in which the Arctic coastal states divide the region's resources among themselves and exclude Chinese companies.[6] In the West this approach has some supporters – commentators who point to the participation of a communist dictatorship in circumpolar development as a potential threat.[7] Yet, in spite of its history of caution when it comes to China, Canada's federal government has recognized that foreign (including Chinese) investment is an essential part of its development strategy in the Arctic. Canada's *Northern*

Strategy and its *Statement on Arctic Foreign Policy* both uphold resource development as a main conduit to "unleashing the true potential of Canada's North."[8] Likewise, it is recognized that this development hinges on foreign capital and that these new economic ties will improve Canada's trade relations "not only with our immediate Northern neighbours but also with other states such as those in central Asia and Eastern Europe."[9] Details are scant on how this might play out in practical terms, but a desire to attract foreign capital is clear.

While Canadian policy does not single out China as a partner in Arctic development, the fact that Chinese SOEs are some of the best funded in the resource industry makes the connection inevitable. China is now Canada's second largest trading partner[10] after the United States, and has shown keen interest in the Canadian energy and resource sector. Public opinion polls also indicate that a solid majority of Canadians view Asian economies as vital to Canada's economic well-being, and that a majority believe Canada will benefit from increased Asian investment. Polls also suggest that, while many Canadians view China with suspicion, they also consider it important to Canada's prosperity (second only to the United States and far ahead of other Asian countries).[11]

China is clearly an important customer and investment partner – but do its Arctic interests present a risk to Canada and other circumpolar states? The evidence suggests that fears of a Chinese resource grab are unfounded, at least in the short to medium term. The simple fact remains that, at present, all of the Arctic's commercially viable resources are either onshore or (in the case of oil and gas) in waters well within Arctic coastal states' respective jurisdictions.[12] Chinese participation will thus occur under the laws of the Arctic states – unless of course China aspires to conquer one of these states, which are all either armed with nuclear weapons, members of NATO, or both.

Arctic Resources: Speculation and Anticipation

The theoretical resource potential of the Arctic is huge. The US Geological Survey estimated in July 2008 that 90 billion barrels of oil, 1,670 trillion cubic feet of natural gas, and 44 billion barrels of natural gas liquids may remain undiscovered in the Arctic, with 84 per cent lying in offshore areas.[13] The region also contains virtually every strategic or commercially important mineral, including iron ore, zinc, rare earth elements, gold, base metals, and diamonds. Interest in northern fisheries, tourism, and freshwater are also expected to expand as global warming opens up easier access to the region. As a result, the notion that this treasure-laden frontier may hold the key to Canada's future prosperity has reentered the popular consciousness.

Development issues are intrinsically both domestic and international. As the wild price fluctuations of 2014 demonstrated, oil and gas exploration and production is driven by international energy supply and demand, as well as issues of energy security and diversity of supply. Mineral prices are likewise determined by volatile international markets, leaving the North susceptible to the same "boom and bust" cycles that have short-circuited past attempts at development.[14] Adding to this uncertainty is the Arctic's position as a high-cost environment, where operations are difficult and infrastructure is either poor or non-existent. Investment in the region requires a great deal of capital, a long timeframe, and comfort with risk. While resource prices have been unpredictable in recent years, longer-term international demand for energy and raw materials will likely continue to rise as China, India, and many of the world's developing countries industrialize and aspire to higher standards of living. Meanwhile, traditional resource bases remain unstable. The rise of the Islamic State in Syria and Iraq (and a host of other militant groups) has put Middle Eastern oil supplies in jeopardy while the Russian invasion of Ukraine, and the subsequent Western sanctions, has called into question the long-term viability of relying on Russian oil and gas. In the midst of Middle-Eastern civil wars and broader geopolitical strife, Canada (and much of the Arctic) remains a safe haven for resource investment; as former NWT Premier Floyd Roland noted, "the bottom line is that Canada's Arctic remains one of the last politically stable places on Earth with abundant energy resources."[15]

China and the Mining Sector

Over the past thirty-five years China's resource consumption has risen in tandem with its massive industrial growth. In the twenty-first century, the country became a major importer of raw materials and Chinese overseas investment skyrocketed as its SOEs financed new mines and purchased existing operations around the world. Canada has been the recipient of $3.3 billion of this investment in the past decade – a substantial sum, but a tiny percentage of China's broader investment program. Chinese companies have spent the lion's share of their raw materials capital in Australia ($31.9 billion), South

America ($23.51 billion), and Africa ($26.73 billion). In Canada, Chinese investment has been directed at the energy sector (and the oil sands in particular), where these SOEs have invested over $34 billion in the past decade.[16] This investment history has built a certain level of comfort operating in Canada, and Chinese mining companies are beginning to pay attention to the long-term potential of the Canadian Arctic. In April 2011 Patricia Moore, a commodity specialist with Scotiabank, told the Nunavut Mining Symposium that she saw "no end" to the "tsunami" of Chinese money flowing into Canada's energy and mining sectors, with Chinese investors "eyeing Nunavut with far more interest than before."[17]

Complicating the picture for Western nations, Chinese investment has not only been growing, but replacing that of the world's private mining companies. The recession of 2008 and the soft recovery that followed severely damaged many mining companies, slowing merger and acquisition activity, deferring major capital expenditures, and limiting companies' ability to finance on good terms.[18] As a result, many firms have entered a period of retrenchment and consolidation. In a 2013 survey of mining companies undertaken by the Fraser Institute, over 90 per cent responded that they found it more difficult to raise capital for new projects.[19] Consequently, only 46 per cent of companies surveyed planned to increase their exploration budgets in 2013 – down from 68 per cent in 2012 and 82 per cent in 2011.[20] North America's junior exploration firms have been hit the hardest. These companies have long relied on the multinationals to acquire them or on private investors to fund them. With capital being held back, many now face bankruptcy.[21] In a response to the Fraser Institute survey, the manager of one exploration company stated that, while there is money in the West to develop new mines, it simply is not flowing to the companies that need it. "Eastern countries," meanwhile, "have a more optimistic outlook and hence dominate investment in the mining industry."[22] When asked about Chinese money replacing European or American funds, Jens-Erik Kirkegaard, Greenland's minister of industry and minerals, likewise noted that there were simply no Western investors coming forward to support Arctic projects and that "the more risk-friendly money is in Asia."[23] Chinese money is, therefore, not only coming to the Arctic, it is moving in when many of the private sector mining firms are limiting their own expansion.

In Canada this trend has led to a greater Chinese presence in the north. Quebec, for instance, is looking to China for investment to realize its Plan

Nord (an $80-billion, twenty-five-year plan). China's third largest steel company is already involved in a joint venture with a Canadian company to build an iron mine at Lac Otelnuk in Nunavik (northern Quebec).[24] In the Raglan District on the Ungava Peninsula, Jilin Jien Nickel Industry Co. spent $735 million building a mine and the accompanying infrastructure to produce nickel, copper, platinum, and palladium.[25] In September 2014, the first shipment from this mine moved through the Northwest Passage to China.[26] In the Yukon, Yunnan Chihong Zinc and Germanium have finalized a $100 million joint venture proposal with Selwyn Resources to develop the Selwyn lead and zinc project.[27] And, in the northern reaches of the territory, the Wolverine zinc and silver mine is in operation after being taken private by Jinduicheng Molybdenum Group Co. Ltd. and Northwest Nonferrous International Investment Company Ltd.[28]

The most significant Chinese mining investment remains on the drawing board: the Izok Lake (or Corridor) project, proposed by MMG Minerals – an Australian company that is 75 per cent owned by Chinese state enterprise Minmetals Resources Ltd. The project includes plans for two mines in Nunavut and several joint ventures between the Wuhan Iron and Steel Group Corporation and Century Iron Ore in northern Quebec.[29] In 2012, MMG submitted its project description to the Nunavut Impact Review Board (NIRB) to initiate the environmental review and permitting process for the project. The proposed plan includes a mine and mill at Izok Lake, a mine at High Lake, and a port at Grays Bay. Infrastructure to service the project will include a 350-kilometre all-weather road, with seventy bridges stretching from Izok Lake to Grays Bay on the central Arctic coast. MMG also plans to construct a processing plant able to handle 6,000 tonnes of ore a day, tank farms for 35 million litres of diesel, two permanent camps totalling 1,000 beds, airstrips, and a port that could accommodate ships that would make sixteen round trips annually (both east and west) through the Northwest Passage during an eighty-day window from mid-July to October.[30]

The company originally planned to submit a revised project description to the NIRB in late 2013, but has requested that the review be halted in the wake of declining resource prices. Since that time, low resource prices have placed the project in limbo as MMG seeks alternate financing for the infrastructure needed to develop the mine. In an attempt to restart the process, the government of Nunavut has pushed for a federal contribution. Nunavut Senator Dennis Patterson has called the plan a "nation-building project" and has asked for $34 million from Ottawa in order to complete the permitting and engineering process."[31] If MMG secures government assistance the Nunavut Resources Corp. – a wholly-owned subsidiary of the Kitikmeot Inuit Association – would build and own the road and port in a partnership with the Government of Nunavut. The Kitikmeot, thanks to a change in federal policy in 2015, is now eligible for large amounts of federal infrastructure money through the P3 Canada Fund and the New Building Canada Fund.[32] If the territorial and federal governments became involved it would represent not only a major Canadian gamble on the economics of the project but also the largest and closest tie-up between the public sector and a Chinese SOE in Canadian history.

For MMG the payoff from the project would be one of the largest copper and zinc mines it the world, capable of producing 180,000 tonnes of zinc and 50,000 tonnes of copper in concentrate per year. The quality of the resource is as significant as quantity: the reserve's 12 per cent zinc and 2.5 per cent copper grade make it twice as rich as other major projects now going forward around the world. As the world's largest consumer of zinc (a key ingredient in making galvanized steel), China is anxious to see large new deposits brought online. For MMG, Izok Lake could also be the large hole in production that will be left when the company winds down its massive Century mine in northern Australia.[33]

Mining in Greenland

Canada's eastern neighbour, Greenland (population 57,000), is also looking to resource development as a way to transform its economy. Dozens of international mining companies – including several Chinese – are exploring the island for minerals they hope will become more accessible as the ice cover retreats on both Greenland and its surrounding waters. In 2009, Jiangxi Zhongrun Mining joined Britain's Nordic Mining to search for gold on the island's south. That same year Jiangxi Union Mining became the first Chinese mining concern with operations inside the Arctic Circle. In 2014 China Non-Ferrous Metal Industry's Foreign Engineering and Construction Co. Ltd. entered into two memoranda of understanding, with Ironbark Zinc to finance 70 per cent of the Citronen Zinc project in northern Greenland, and with Greenland Minerals and Energy Limited to develop its massive Kvanefjeld rare earths deposit, and to ship those raw materials to China for processing.[34]

These developments are particularly interesting in light of the 2009 Act on Greenland Self-Government, the preamble of which recognizes Greenlanders (who are predominantly Inuit) as a people with rights to self-determination under international law. "A principal objective of introducing self-government has been to facilitate the transfer of additional authority, and thus responsibility, to Greenlandic authorities in fields where this is constitutionally possible and based on the principle of accordance between rights and obligations," the Danish Statsministeriet notes. Although foreign, security, and defence policy remains with Copenhagen, the Greenlandic government will assume greater responsibility for law enforcement and transportation. Most significantly, the act has "radically changed" Danish-Greenlandic relations regarding mineral resource activities. The Greenland Self-Government authorities assumed the right to use the mineral resources found in the subsoil effective January 1, 2010, and will accrue revenues from these activities.[35]

In their study on new strategic dynamics in the Arctic, Charles M. Perry and Bobby Andersen note that most commentators believe that full Greenlandic independence remains decades away. Most Greenlanders take a long view as well and assume that "the long-term objective of independence relies almost mechanically on harnessing the region's enormous mineral potential on land and at sea."[36] When Ove Karl Berthelsen, Greenland's minister of industry and mineral resources, led a delegation of Greenlanders to the China International Mining Conference in November 2011 in search of Chinese investment, he indicated that mining was key to the island's economic development and to realizing its desire to "shake off its Danish dependency." Berthelsen told Chinese reporters that "our goal is to change Greenland into a land of mining resources."

In recent years China and Greenland/Denmark have made every effort to strengthen relations. In April 2014, Queen Margrethe II of Denmark paid a state visit to China and was received by President Xi Jinping. During the visit the two states signed maritime technology and energy conservation agreements to strengthen ties.[37] In a sign of how highly China values this developing relationship, Denmark was also offered a loan of two pandas. "It's the ultimate symbol of the friendship" said Danish Foreign Minister Martin Lidegaard, "and something that only happens on very rare occasions."[38] Chinese "panda diplomacy" is often used to mark important occasions or cement strategically important ties; Mao Tse-tung offered bears to North Korea and the Soviet Union in the 1950s, and Premier Zhou Enali presented two to Richard Nixon as a symbol of China's Cold War rapprochement with the US. While this remained unspoken, China's interest in Denmark likely has more to do with Greenlandic resources than with securing strategic supplies of LEGO and wooden shoes.

As with Canada, Denmark and Greenland see this relationship as mutually beneficial. Greenland is resource rich but capital poor and China is the obvious suitor. For many in Greenland, however, the fear is that Chinese investment will overwhelm this tiny aspiring nation. With less than half the population of Prince Edward Island, Greenland will not be able to provide the necessary labour for this new industry. Foreign companies have, therefore, accepted the need for imported workers (including Chinese labour crews) to operate the mines. Although the Greenlandic government has "stressed that mining projects should provide jobs for the nation's workers," Greenland's population primarily consists of Inuit hunters, fishers, and educated professionals – making local labour hard to come by.[39]

Greenland is no longer subject to the European Union's labour laws and, in 2012, its parliament passed a law facilitating the opening of large mines, including procedures to permit migrant workers. London Mining, a British company now operating in administration, spent years trying to develop one of the most promising greenfield sites on the island and was the first to include foreign workers in its plans. The company began negotiations in 2011 with Sichuan Xinye Mining Investment Co., a company owned by a provincial mining bureau, to finance its Isua iron ore project. Sichuan Xinye estimated that it would need 700 workers for the project – and as many as 3,000 during the peak construction period. Even when this financing agreement fell apart, London Mining maintained its foreign-worker requirement, estimating that only 10 per cent of the construction jobs and 55 per cent of the mining positions would go to Greenlanders (and this only after five years of operations). The remainder of the positions would go to foreign employees of as yet undisclosed nationality.[40] Broader estimates for all of Greenland's future projects put the island's requirement at a staggering 10–20,000 imported labourers.[41]

Greenland's March 2013 parliamentary elections reaffirmed the controversial nature of this issue. The *Guardian* reported that "voters in Greenland feared that ministers were surrendering their country's interests to China and foreign multinationals and called an end this week to the government of Kuupik Kleist."[42] The pro-development Kleist was replaced as premier by Aleqa Hammond and her center-left Siumut party who promised a more careful scrutiny of foreign investment and its impact on Greenlandic lifestyles and human rights.[43] Hammond's victory reaffirmed the controversial nature of the resource issue and demonstrated how uneasy many Greenlanders remain with major resource projects. Still, Hammond's election did not represent a decisive change in direction. In October 2013, the Siumut government took the critical step of removing Greenland's long-standing ban on uranium mining. This move not only allows the construction of uranium mines but smoothes the way for mines like Kvanefjeld, where uranium is produced as a by-product.

This pro-development stance was reaffirmed in another Greenlandic general election in 2014. The Inuit Ataqatigiit, Greenland's leading opposition party, campaigned against uranium production and pledged to reinstate the ban.[44] The victory of Simut, which formed a government with the support of pro-mining parties Demokraatit and Atassut, represents a significant vote of confidence in resource development.[45] While the island's course is not decisively set, this position will help to attract foreign investment. Still, it is recognized that a more concrete regulatory framework will eventually have to be put in place. Interim Premier Kim Kielsen expressed these concerns in October 2014, saying: "If we change the policy every time a new government takes office, then we lose all foreign investment. We need a stable arrangement."[46]

In spite of China's obvious interest in Greenlandic resources, and the reciprocal Greenlandic interest in Chinese money, fears of a flood of Chinese workers and influence into Greenland are unwarranted thus far. While Chinese companies have financed some projects, the vast majority of investment in the island still comes from North American and European sources. In 2013, for instance, the Greenlandic government approved over 120 requests for permission to undertake oil, gas, and mineral exploration – and none went to Chinese companies.[47]

Dampening the Optimism

In both Canada and Greenland, optimistic projections of resource growth have been tempered by the costs and difficulties of Arctic operations, as well as by the changing dynamics of global supply and demand. In 2011 Jorn Skov Nielson, Greenland's deputy resources minister, predicted that full-scale mining operations could begin as early as 2012, and "five or six mature projects for extracting iron, zinc, and rare earths" might be under way within five years.[48] In retrospect, such assumptions can only be called wildly ambitious.

In 2014, iron ore prices fell from roughly $140 to $74/ton, and then by early 2016 to $50, with few analysts projecting a strong recovery in the near future. In large part this drop was caused by an oversupply in ore production and a build-up of stocks in China, as well as a move away from infrastructure investment towards consumption, reducing demand for steel.[49] Analysts at Wood Mackenzie also point to new environmental controls in China and the fear that these will negatively impact steel production.[50] This has resulted in iron and other mineral prices that are low enough to cancel or delay most of the major Arctic mining projects in both Canada and Greenland.

In Canada, Baffinland's $4 billion Mary River iron mine opened in September 2014 – though at only 20 per cent of its initially planned capacity. Elsewhere in Nunavut, the Izok Lake mine remains in limbo while West Melville Metals cancelled its Fraser Bay iron project in December 2014.[51] Cliffs Natural Resources is also shutting down its Bloom Lake mine in northern Quebec (jointly owned with Chinese steelmaker Wuhan Iron and Steel) and its Wabush mine in Labrador. The closure of Bloom Lake, one of the larger operations in the region, has even called into question the viability of Plan Nord.[52] In Greenland, development has been slow to materialize for the same reasons. The island's flagship project, the Isua mine, is now stalled after its original owner, London Mining, entered bankruptcy protection and was forced by creditors to sell off its only producing asset in Sierra Leone.[53] In January 2015, the Isua project was taken over by the General Nice Group, a private Chinese trading company. The buy-out has been estimated at $2 billion though the group has not yet released any detailed plans to develop the mine.[54]

The reality is that none of these mines have moved forward because both Western and Chinese companies operate to make a profit. Without high mineral prices, developing the Arctic remains an unattractive proposition. Mining and shipping costs at Isua, for instance, are estimated at roughly $80 per ton of concentrate.[55] Cliffs' Bloom Lake mine faces similar costs.[56] While Arctic reserves are often world-class, extraction costs are now higher than the price of the resource. They are also uncompetitive when compared to rapidly expanding production from other mining jurisdictions – principally Brazil and Australia. Operating costs for BHP Billiton's iron ore mines average less than $20, Rio Tinto produces at $20.40, and Vale SA at $24.71 per ton of concentrate.[57]

In spite of these hurdles, it should be kept in mind that delays and cancellations in the wake of price fluctuations are common for resource projects in high-cost jurisdictions and developing the Arctic has always been a long-term enterprise. Over the long term, the advantage possessed by many of these deposits is their purity and size. Mineral concentrations at Mary River, Izok Lake, Isua, Kvanefjeld, and others are world-class and, with better infrastructure, can present excellent economies of scale. When resource prices justify activity, many of these projects will almost certainly be revisited.

The quality of certain Arctic resources may even expedite development if China chooses to aggressively push new environmental reforms. In March 2014, Chinese Premier Li Keqiang "declare[d] war" on pollution, saying it was "nature's red-light warning against the model of inefficient and blind development."[58] China's major industrial cities are choked by smog, often containing airborne particulate matter at high enough levels to cause serious health problems; Li cited particulate matter known as PM 2.5 and PM 10 as a special concern.[59] As part of this fight, steel plants (the country's main producer of PM 2.5/10 emissions) were targeted and more stringent emission controls are being imposed. Mills in China's key steel-making provinces of Hebei and Jiangsu are under particular pressure to lower emissions and, although this move has created concern for future iron ore demand, it has also increased the premium for high-quality feed for China's smelters.[60] Sintering, the process of agglomerating low-quality iron ore fines to create a product that can be used in a blast furnace, is the most polluting process within a steel plant, responsible for 80–90 per cent of total dust and soot emissions and more than 60 per cent of total sulphur emissions from the industry.[61] A newfound concern for air quality means that many plants will look to replace sintering with more expensive, higher quality, and environmentally friendly ore – like that found in the Arctic. Already, premiums for higher quality iron are rising – sometimes reaching $40 per dry metric tonne[62]

From the second quarter of 2013 to the second quarter of 2014, as iron ore fines prices fell 22 per cent, the higher quality pellets fell only eight per cent.[63] London Mining's initial plans for the Isua mine involved production of 70 per cent iron content (FE) pellets, significantly better than the baseline high-grade 62 per cent FE currently favoured by Chinese buyers.[64] Mary River produces lump iron, another form of high grade product that can be used without sintering. If pollution becomes a big enough problem, domestically mined Chinese ore (which averages only 21 per cent FE)[65] may be slowly phased out, thereby increasing demand for foreign supplies. It is far from certain that China will remove a significant amount of domestic, low-quality ore from the market, or that its environmental regulations will drive premiums for the Arctic's higher quality ores high enough to justify development. As air pollution worsens, however, it is conceivable that the political pressure to act will have an effect that will trickle down (or up) to the Arctic.

While the largest of China's overseas mining projects are base metals like iron ore, the resources that have garnered the most attention (and raised the most concern) are rare earth elements (REEs). This basket of metals consists of seventeen chemical elements in the periodic table, specifically the fifteen lanthanides plus scandium and yttrium, that are essential components in modern technology – in everything from solar panels and wind turbines to smartphones, hybrid cars, and smart weapons. Contrary to what their name implies, rare earths are not particularly rare, but they are seldom found in concentrations great enough to justify extraction. A common concern in the West has been that China enjoys a near monopoly on their production. After closing most of its REE mines in the 1990s because environmental regulations made their production cheaper in China, North American and European countries found themselves hostage to Beijing, which has occasionally used its monopoly as a political weapon.

In September 2012, for instance, China halted shipments of REEs to Japan during a heated dispute over Japan's detention of a Chinese fishing trawler that rammed two Japanese coast guard vessels near disputed islands.[66] In October 2010, China also halted some shipments of raw rare earths to the United States and Europe after the Obama administration opened an investigation into Chinese violations of international free trade rules, including China's restrictions on rare earth exports. These restrictions caused a dramatic spike in REE prices from mid-2010 to 2012.[67]

Given the importance of rare earths to Western industry, many commentators have pointed to Greenland's major REE deposit at Kvanefjeld as a "diplomatic flashpoint."[68] In February 2013, Paula Briscoe, the national intelligence fellow at the Council on Foreign Relations in Washington, highlighted a European Union request to Greenland to restrict Chinese access to Greenlandic rare earths for strategic reasons. The premier of Greenland Kupik Kleist rejected this overture, proclaiming that "Greenland is open for investments from the whole world."[69] In 2016 the state controlled mining company Shenghe Mining purchased a 12.5 per cent share of Greenland Minerals and Energy Limited, with the option to acquire up to 60 per cent of the Greenlandic company if it so desires in the future. Coupled with a 2014 strategic partnership, signed with China Non-Ferrous Metal Industry's Foreign Engineering and Construction Co. Ltd., it is certain that the island's rare earths will be at least partially Chinese-owned, and will be sent to China for processing.[70]

While this arrangement will strengthen China's hold on global REE supplies, the economic and geopolitical situation has changed significantly from the monopoly scares of 2010–13. Ironically, the fear generated by Chinese export restrictions provided fertile ground for Western companies to finance new mines outside of China, which began coming online in 2012. The two largest, Mt. Weld in Australia and Mountain Pass in the US, together have a production capacity of roughly 41,000 tons/annum – which is almost the entire REE demand of the world outside of China.[71] These mines have never operated at capacity, largely the result of the crash in REE prices following the addition of new supply. In 2014, China's share of REE fell to around 75 per cent and could easily fall further if prices rise again. In fact, any attempt by China to limit access to its domestic supply of REEs (or those it controls in Greenland) will simply erode its position by encouraging Western investors to fund new mines (some of which would be in the Canadian Arctic).[72]

Longer-term issues – related to the defence and security of an independent Greenland, its alliance commitments, and the increased tempo of Chinese development activities on its territory or in its waters – are beyond the scope of this study. Given the geographical proximity of Greenland to Canada, and the relationship between Canadian and Greenlandic Inuit, the situation should at least be monitored. As Briscoe notes, "if Greenland manages the development properly and takes the time needed to ensure it can effectively oversee development, then the people of Greenland will be on the road to a prosperous future where many native Greenlanders are better educated, more skilled, and generally better off than they are now." On the other hand, Chinese influence in Greenland "could help buy Beijing a proxy vote in Arctic matters … If Greenland, lured by the promise of investments and earlier autonomy from Denmark, allows itself to be overwhelmed by foreign companies, then China could use its influence to Beijing's advantage."[73]

Chinese Activities in Iceland

China's relationship with Iceland is an oft-cited example in the Western media of Beijing's growing geopolitical interest in the circumpolar world. Icelandic officials recognize that should the central Arctic Ocean ever open to transpolar shipping, their small island holds a strategically significant location as a potential hub – and this position would clearly be of interest to major trading nations like China. President Ólafur Ragnar Grímsson noted in June 2011 that China had sent high-level delegations to the island during each of the previous six years – and not a single such delegation to the United States.[74] Likewise, reports in the Icelandic and Western news media circulated after 2012 that China's "super-embassy" in Reykjavik staffed 500 diplomats (while its embassy in the US was staffed by seventy).[75] Although less than ten full-time Chinese embassy staff actually occupy the massive building,[76] the persistence of this alleged example of China's incomparable interest in Iceland – a myth with no empirical grounding – is telling.

Nevertheless, China has been preparing the ground for a more strategically important Iceland since initiating bilateral free trade talks in 2006. The foreign affairs ministers of both countries discussed options for enhanced Arctic cooperation in 2012,[77] with China indicating its interest in establishing a second Arctic research base in Iceland.[78] The two states signed a free trade agreement the following April, and in March 2014 China's largest oil company (CNOOC) partnered with Iceland's Eykon Energy to explore for oil in a large block of Iceland's northeastern coast.[79] Meanwhile, Iceland's aluminum industry is receiving Chinese financing while Orka Energy of Iceland and China's Xianyang Municipal People's Government and Sinpoec Star Petroleum have signed an agreement to develop the island's geothermal resources. Preliminary discussions are also ongoing between Icelandic and Chinese shipping companies about trans-Arctic partnerships.[80]

These strengthening ties between China and Iceland have worried some Western officials. "Nobody knows what the devil they are up to," said Einar Benediktsson, Iceland's former ambassador to Washington and a critic of his country's expanding ties with Beijing. "All we know is that it is very important to China to get a foothold in the Arctic, and Iceland is an easy prey."[81] From a Chinese perspective, this sort of involvement is seen as a cooperative way of allaying suspicion and cementing the nation's position in regional affairs by being a provider of resources or service.[82]

Like Greenland, Iceland is a small country, with a population of only 323,000 (less than that of London, Ontario). Its economy was also disproportionately damaged by the financial crash of 2008, leaving it very receptive to foreign investment. In spite of this, the country maintains a robust and largely corruption free government (rated twelfth of 174 states by Transparency International) that will not be influenced as easily as others in the developing world.[83] Indeed, there are few signs that Chinese investment has led to the sort of strategic penetration feared by some commentators.[84] In September 2011 for instance, Chinese businessman Huang Nubo's plan to purchase Grímsstaðir á Fjöllum (comprising about 30,639 hectares in northeast Iceland) for 1 billion ISK (about $200 billion USD) was rejected by the Icelandic government. Fears that this land might be used for a naval facility or a listening post, and that military personnel might pour in, disguised as hoteliers and golf caddies,[85] were almost certainly exaggerated. Still, despite the generally positive attitude towards China among Icelanders, the idea of selling land remains an uncomfortable one.[86] Icelandic policy is best described as a balancing act, whereby the small island seeks economic benefit from Chinese investment while being careful to avoid surrendering too much influence to a much larger country.[87]

China and Arctic Energy: The Case of Russia

Over the past thirty years, China's consumption of oil has increased as quickly as its consumption of raw materials. As a result, its state-owned oil companies have spent billions buying up assets around the world, and one of the most promising new development regions is the Russian Arctic. The area's potential is huge. In 2008 a US Geological Survey estimate placed sixty per cent of the Arctic's undiscovered oil and gas reserves in Russian territory or its EEZ.[88] Unlike Canada, Greenland, and the US, Russian Arctic exploration is already well advanced. Moscow has spent billions developing the region, which it intends to use as its "foremost strategic base for natural resources" by 2020.[89] Russian state energy producer Gazprom, for instance, plans to start extracting offshore deposits in the Barents, Okhotsk, Kara, and Pechora seas before 2030, while Rosneft drilled its first exploratory well in the Kara Sea in September 2014.[90]

Because Russian state law classifies these reserves as a strategic sector of its economy, foreign ownership is limited to minority status. Accordingly,

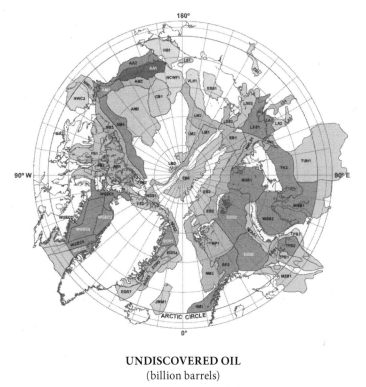

UNDISCOVERED OIL
(billion barrels)

■ >10   ▢ 0.1–1   ▢ Area not quantitatively assessed

■ 1–10   ▢ <0.1   ▢ Area of low petroleum potential

4.1 Undiscovered Oil in the Arctic Basin, US Geological Survey, *Circum Arctic Resource Appraisal*, 2008.

under the existing regulatory framework it is impossible for a Chinese company to operate independently in Russia. In a reversal of longstanding Russian policy, however, Chinese SOEs have recently been allowed to acquire large minority stakes in northern projects operated by Russian companies. This kind of foreign investment is essential to bringing Russian production online. The cost of working in the region is massive and Russia's national oil companies are in no condition to undertake these projects on their own. This fact was laid bare in September 2014 when Rosneft requested $49 billion in government aid to help it cope with its massive debt (which sanctions prevent it from refinancing in the West) and ongoing capital expenses.[91]

Russia's first choice for foreign investment was to partner with Western oil firms. In 2011, Rosneft signed a joint venture with BP to develop the Kara Sea. This deal fell apart but BP was soon replaced by Exxon. Meanwhile, French energy giant Total signed a deal with the Russian company Lukoil to explore shale reserves in northern Siberia, and with Novatek to develop the massive Yamal gas project, and the Italian company ENI also agreed to work with Rosneft in the central Barents. Western drilling and service companies, such as Halliburton, Weatherford, Schlumberger, and Baker Hughes have likewise played an increasingly large role in enabling the operations of the Russian majors and their partners.

This set of corporate alliances was fundamentally upset by the Russian invasion of Ukraine and the resulting Western sanctions targeting the country's oil sector. In the wake of these restrictions, Exxon was forced to pull out of its drilling operations while Shell suspended its work with Gazprom in the Khanty-Mansiysk region and slowed a project in western Siberia. Meanwhile, many other joint operations remain in limbo. The fear of Western finances and drilling technology disappearing is so great that, in October 2014, President Putin announced the creation of a state-owned oil exploration and drilling company to replace the Western services which may be withheld for years to come.[92]

While the outcome and duration of Russia's conflict with the West cannot be predicated with accuracy, it is rapidly propelling China from a supporting player to Russia's premier partner in the North. Since March 2014, Moscow has dramatically tightened its Arctic ties with China, which in turn has announced that it will never support sanctions against Russia.[93] The result has been a torrent of new oil and gas deals. In May 2014, the two countries unveiled a $270 billion agreement to double China's oil imports from Rosneft to more than 620,000 barrels a day. The deal, one of the biggest ever in the history of the global oil industry, should bring cash-strapped Rosneft a $60–70 billion upfront pre-payment from China.[94] The two states also signed an agreement that month worth $456 billion to build a pipeline to ship Russian gas to China.[95] This deal stretches over thirty years, and involves Gazprom supplying China National Petroleum Corp. (CNPC) with 38 billion cubic meters of gas annually beginning in 2018. To complement this arrangement, the two countries signed a follow-on agreement in November 2014 for an additional 30 billion cubic metres of gas (annually). As of 2016, however, there has been little effort to move forward on these deals – most of the expected Chinese loans and prepayments have not been forthcoming, while some talks on further Chinese buy-ins to Russian fields have stalled.[96] Whether this is an indication of cold feet on one or both partners' part, or simply the time required to implement such a large deal, remains to be seen.

Whatever the case, Russia is serious about opening its oil and gas industry to direct Chinese investment. In May 2014, CNPC partnered with Rosneft to explore three offshore fields in the Barents and Pechora Seas, the first such deal Russia has signed with an Asian company. CNPC also purchased a 20 per cent stake in the $27 billion Yamal gas project (on the south coast of the Kara Sea). Once Yamal is operational, gas will be transported along the Northern Sea Route to China in icebreaking LNG tankers.[97] In September 2014, CNPC also paid $1 billion for a 10 per cent stake in the Vankor oil field (currently producing 442,000 barrels per day) south of the Kara Sea.[98] This purchase was widely seen as favouring the Chinese, which paid roughly $2,262 for each producing barrel (compared to the $7,200/barrel that CNPC spent acquiring Nexen in 2013).[99] In November 2014, CNPC was also allowed to purchase a 10 per cent stake in an Eastern Siberian unit of Rosneft.[100]

In the eastern Arctic, Chinese investment has likewise flown into building up Russia's offshore oil and gas. On Sakhalin Island, Sinopec and Rosneft are partners (25.1 per cent and 74.9 per cent) in the Sakhalin-III gas/oil fields. Further west, CNPC and Rosneft have established a joint venture (49 per cent and 51 per cent) to develop the Srednebotuobinskoye oil field – an area with estimated reserves of 134 million tons of oil and 155 bcm of gas.[101] This partnership allows development to proceed without forcing Rosneft to take on much more debt, and with CNPC developing the resource potential of Eastern Siberia and guaranteeing supplies to the Tianjin oil refinery that the company plans to construct by 2020.

In light of Russia's oil and gas companies being cut off from western financial markets, Chinese money is also being used to finance some of Russia's Arctic projects. Total, for instance, has announced that it is looking to finance its share in the Yamal project not in dollars but in a combination euros, yuan, and rubles.[102] Russian state gas giant PAO Gazprom has also secured a €2 billion ($2.17 billion) loan from Bank of China Ltd., the largest single-bank credit in the Russian company's history and a sign of how Western sanctions are increasing Russia's economic reliance on China.[103]

This growing partnership is a new phenomenon. Historically, Russia has preferred to keep China at arm's length in the Arctic. Moscow is already sensitive to China's growing economic and military clout, and the Arctic offers one of the few areas where Russia maintains a clear advantage and has not had to treat China as an equal (or even senior) partner.[104] The rapid expansion of China's role in the Russia Arctic was the product of necessity and will likely continue to expand if Western capital remains out of reach. Nevertheless, Russia remains unlikely to seek any sort of formal strategic Arctic relationship with China. While Chinese money will continue to be essential if Western capital cannot be accessed for development, it cannot provide the technological skill and assets that have been withdrawn by Western sanctions. While there is certainly an interest in China to collaborate with polar nations to develop this capability,[105] for the moment, Arctic offshore drilling and other advanced recovery techniques pioneered by Western firms cannot be duplicated by Chinese SOEs, thus limiting their utility to financing.[106] Given these limitations, and Russia's continued wariness of Chinese strength and intentions, the two nations will likely continue to manage projects and issues on a case by case basis, with Chinese influence in Arctic resource development remaining that of a financier.[107]

China's "Wait-and-See" Energy Policy in the Canadian Arctic

For Canada, this massive Chinese investment in Russia may limit future Chinese investment in the oil sands, or in the Canadian Arctic if energy development proceeds there. It may also limit the potential Chinese market for liquid natural gas exports that companies are planning from fields in Alberta and British Columbia. As the ongoing crisis in Ukraine sours Russian-European relations, Moscow has moved to diversify its customer base. Negotiating from a position of strength, Chinese buyers have used this opportunity to negotiate a favourable long-term price. The $400 billion deal between Gazprom and CNPC, for instance, is rumoured to price gas between $10 and $10.50 per million btu, almost 25 per cent cheaper than the spot price at the time of signing.[108] Estimates for Canadian export prices vary, but North American LNG would likely be from $11–14/Mbtu.[109] In the long term, these deals may also enable Chinese oil companies to develop as competent Arctic operators. This process will take many years, but if China and

Russia can develop the expertise and technology to operate in the Arctic offshore region they will break the monopoly that Western firms currently hold in that area.

While China has invested aggressively in Russian oil and gas, it has refrained from taking a similar stake in the North American Arctic. While underexplored and less developed than the Eurasian North, the potential rewards for drilling in Canada's Arctic may still be substantial. The Mackenzie region is estimated to hold upwards of 2.8 billion barrels of crude oil reserves and more than 60 trillion cubic feet of natural gas.[110] Further east, the Geological Survey of Canada estimates that the Sverdrup basin contains 4.3 billion barrels of oil and 79.8 trillion cubic feet of gas. The region is also one of the least explored in the world, thus offering the possibility of significant new discoveries. During the 1970s and 1980s, exploration in the Beaufort Sea found 1.5 billion barrels of oil.[111] Industry analysts agree that further exploration will certainly yield more.

In spite of promising reserves, drilling in the Canadian Arctic has been inhibited by heavy regulation, protests from environmental groups, and caution in the wake of the catastrophic Deepwater Horizon oil spill. Costs of operating in the harsh Arctic climate are also high, and made worse by Canada's dearth of shipping, pipeline, resupply, and support infrastructure. Operating costs therefore limit activity to the largest multinationals with the resources to undertake expensive long-term projects. These companies would likely be too large for even China's SOEs to acquire, although that has not been Beijing's strategy in the Russian Arctic. Rather, Chinese companies have sought partnership agreements to share risk and minimize political exposure. Evidence of this may be the fact that the one small Chinese investment in northern Canadian gas was a $20 million buy-in by CNOOC to Northern Cross Ltd., a Canadian company developing the Eagle Plain basin of northern Yukon.[112]

In Canada, Chinese investment in oil and gas has been controversial. This investment has been necessary for Canada, but it has also provoked popular concern over the growing influence of the Chinese state in an important sector of the Canadian economy. Such fears peaked in 2013 during the $15-billion takeover of Nexen Energy by China's National Offshore Oil Company.[113] Despite China's clear interest in Canada's energy resources, however, popular fears of a Chinese resource grab in the Arctic are unfounded, particularly in the short to medium term. China cannot simply move into the Arctic and begin exploiting Canadian resources. The only known, commercially viable, Arctic hydrocarbon resources are either onshore or in waters well within national jurisdiction. Chinese participation will thus occur under Canadian law and at the pleasure of the Canadian government. China will also have to partner with Western companies. China bought its stake in the oil sands by acquiring North American companies or purchasing minority shares in projects. This strategy is driven by China's inability to develop unconventional oil reserves on its own. The same holds true in the Arctic, where its SOEs lack cold-water drilling experience and the special skills and equipment that the West's multinationals have been developing since the 1970s.[114] As one Chinese scholar admitted, "there is a rather large gap between Chinese and advanced foreign deep-sea oil extracting technology."[115]

Such partnerships can be envisaged over the next decade. Arctic operations are extremely expensive and Western oil companies currently operating in the region may welcome a Chinese partner to share the costs and risks. Still, Canadian Arctic reserves have not been proven economically viable, and bringing them into production will take at least a decade. They may also fall prey to the sort of regulatory hurdles that plagued the Mackenzie Valley Pipeline or that Shell has experienced working in Alaska.[116] Although China will likely continue to monitor developments in the North American Arctic over the next decade, all indications are that Chinese SOEs will continue to concentrate on parts of the world where reserves are more defined and closer to production.[117]

Arctic Oil at $50?

During the second half of 2014 the world's oil industry suffered a dramatic shock as Brent crude prices fell from over $100 to under $50 in only a few months. A combination of oversupply driven by the surge in American shale production and a refusal by Saudi Arabia (or other OPEC nations) to reduce production has upended industry projections and the economic viability of many oil fields – including those in the Arctic. Facing prices below the lifting costs of many fields, oil companies soon cut more than $150 billion in future projects in an effort to reduce costs and protect their balance sheets.[118] The projects being cut are those with high exploration and production costs – and there is nowhere in the world with higher costs than the Arctic offshore.

In the Canadian Arctic, Chevron has closed its Arctic operations while, in Greenland, the government has chosen to extend its two remaining licenses in an effort to keep companies interested in its offshore region.[119] Dong, a Danish firm with a share of a ConocoPhillips licence in the northern part of Baffin Bay, will retain its licence to explore off the eastern coast while Statoil and GDF Suez are pulling out of a partnership with Cairn Energy, which itself shuttered its Greenlandic office in 2014.[120] In the Chukchi Sea, Shell has also closed down its drilling program which, up to 2016, was the most advanced Arctic exploration program in North America.

In this low-price environment there are serious doubts that development in the region will occur.[121] While many Chinese commentators continue to view the North as a region of enormous future potential, the costs involved will slow that development considerably.[122] If the behaviour of Chinese SOEs in the mining sector is any indication, its oil and gas companies are unlikely to chase a resource whose production cost exceeds its market value. In Canada, Greenland, and the United States this decline means that Arctic oil and gas development will likely be put hold for the foreseeable future as companies conserve or redirect capital to lower-cost assets. In Russia, state-owned energy companies have less room to manoeuver. Many of Russia's traditional reserves are in decline and the state has few options other than to develop its Arctic. Given Moscow's reliance on oil and gas, maintaining production is an existential necessity. Even after the sharp drop in prices, Gazprom Neft's managing director, Alexander Dyukov, reaffirmed the view of the Arctic as "a strategic priority" for the company.[123] Ultimately, the ability of Russia and its SOEs to fund these operations may hinge on its relationship with China and the interest Chinese SOEs show (or can be persuaded to show) in long-term risk.

Arctic Fisheries

At present, there is little certainty regarding governance issues in the central Arctic Ocean beyond national jurisdiction, consisting both of high seas and the international seabed (the common heritage of mankind) – a space that will emerge once the coastal states have determined the outer limits of their continental shelves in the region. Climate change is altering the distribution of fish stocks within both the national and international waters of the region and may soon make new areas attractive to commercial fishing concerns.

Still, reliable information on these trends is virtually non-existent, and scientists of every nationality have been left to their best guesses.[124]

This situation is part of a global crisis in which attempts to exploit increasingly scarce resources may further destabilize ecosystems and undermine a major part of the global food supply. Scientists have expressed concern about this possibility given the absence of any overarching management and conservation regime.[125] Although fishing is partly regulated through the North Atlantic Fisheries Organization, illegal and unreported harvesting still takes place in Canadian waters and there are indications that these pressures may increase in the near future.[126]

Future Arctic fisheries, straddling Canadian and neighbouring waters, must be managed for both ecological and economic reasons.[127] Canada has already joined with the United States and Denmark in placing a moratorium on commercial fishing in the High Arctic while studies are undertaken to improve our comprehension of the region's potential and vulnerabilities.[128] Meanwhile, Northern Canadians have expressed interest in building their own commercial fishery, a move the federal government has tentatively supported with an $8 million investment in a new commercial harbour at Pangnirtung.[129] Asia is already the primary market for the growing Pangnirtung turbot fishery, bringing about $400,000 to the local economy, with most products going directly to China.[130]

China, which is one of the world's leading fisheries nations, has not expressed any immediate interest in fishing Arctic waters – but it has conducted research on marine sea life in the region and views scientific research as part of its effort to develop a greater understanding of the potential viability of a commercial fishery. In this context, Chinese scholars reiterate their concerns about being excluded from discussions on fisheries management issues. While the Chinese are quick to point to the tragedy of other unregulated high seas fisheries areas, they are wary of efforts to have fisheries management regimes forced on their industry in the absence of transparent information sharing and consultation.[131] As evidence of this, China (and Russia) blocked the creation of an Antarctic wildlife reserve in 2014 over fears that it might limit access to fish stocks in the south polar region.[132]

Securing International Recognition for the Full Extent of Canada's Extended Continental Shelf

Article 76 of the UN Law of the Sea Convention (LOSC) defines the rights and responsibilities of states in using the oceans and lays out a process for states to claim continental shelves beyond the 200 nautical mile EEZ. Each of the five Arctic Ocean basin states (including the United States, which is not a party to the LOSC) have indicated that they will claim an area of shelf over which they have exclusive sovereign rights regarding the resources of the shelf. To that end, the coastal states have been undertaking scientific work to determine the full extent of their shelf areas and both Denmark and Russia have already filed submissions.

For its part, Canada has made significant investments to ensure that it "secures international recognition for the full extent of its continental shelf" in the Arctic.[133] It ratified the LOSC in November 2003 and began submitting evidence for its extended continental shelf to the Commission on the Limits of the Continental Shelf (a body of scientists established by the LOSC to examine the information presented by coastal states) in December 2013. While Canada's claim will likely overlap with those of the Danes and Russians, the countries involved have emphasized that the division of the shelf will be peaceful.[134] The Arctic coastal states made this pledge at Illulissat, Greenland in 2008 and, in April 2010, Russia and Norway resolved a forty-year disagreement over the division of the Barents Sea.[135] Cajoling Canada to take note of this landmark resolution, Sergei Lavorv and Jonas Gahr Støre (the Russian and Norwegian foreign ministers respectively) noted that "the Law of the Sea provided a framework that allowed us to overcome the zero-sum logic of competition and replace it with a process focused on finding a win-win solution."[136]

While the Arctic coastal states appear to have the matter well in hand, fears have been expressed that China (and other non-Arctic states) might object to the Arctic powers dividing up so much territory among themselves. Yang Xiao of Beijing International Studies University dubbed the exclusion of non-Arctic powers the "Monroe Doctrine of the Arctic Council."[137] In writing about Chinese ambitions to break that monopoly or power, commentators often cite statements made in March 2010 by Vice-Admiral Yin Zhou – a member of the Chinese People's Political Consultative Conference – that "the Arctic belongs to all the people around the world as no nation has sovereignty over it," and that "China must play an indispensable role in Arctic exploration as we have one-fifth of the world's population."[138] Gordon Chang, writing in the influential foreign affairs magazine *Foreign Policy*, argued that "Yin's comments on the Arctic are at the very least an indication of the direction of Chinese thinking on the subject, and a reflection of a hardened attitude in Beijing."[139] Furthermore, Chang claimed that the comments rendered obsolete a more balanced assessment of China's Arctic strategy released the week prior by the Stockholm International Peace Research Institute (SIPRI).[140]

Yin, however, was speaking in the context of China's broader maritime strategy and referring to the area in the central Arctic Ocean that is beyond national jurisdiction.[141] Dr. Gao Zhiguo, a Chinese representative on the International Tribunal for the Law of the Sea, is more judicious in his explanation of the situation. After reviewing the maritime boundaries and potential continental shelf claims beyond 200 nautical miles of the littoral states, he notes that there will be a limited area subject to the international management under the United Nations Convention of the Law of the Sea. Accordingly, China – together with other members of the international community – is increasingly interested in exploring options for international governance that balance national sovereignty with the rights of the international community to the Arctic and its resources.[142] Chinese commentators expect that there will be (or should be) an area of seafloor in the Arctic Ocean basin that is beyond the limits of national jurisdiction of any adjacent state when all the shelf claims have been resolved. The mineral resources of this area will be subject to the "common heritage of mankind" and the authority of the International Seabed Authority, as per the LOSC.

With this in mind, various Chinese commentators have expressed concern about potentially excessive shelf claims by the Arctic coastal states that could impinge upon their perceived rights and those of the global community.[143] International lawyer Aldo Chircop of Dalhousie University notes that:

> China has spoken for the global commons in ways that no other major state has done in recent times. Clearly there is self-interest in reminding Arctic states that extended continental shelf claims, while permitted to coastal states under UNCLOS, should not trench on the international seabed area. In doing so, however, it is also playing the role of advocate for the common heritage

of mankind and interests of developing countries, which no other Arctic state is doing. It has given itself a voice for developing countries. Considering its substantial official development assistance in all developing regions, this is a role which many developing countries are likely to endorse.[144]

Indeed, this narrative is consistent with China's foreign policy tradition outlined in chapter two; it sees itself as a developing country with ever greater global interests. China's concerns in the Arctic relate to the possibility that coastal states' claims to extended continental shelves may erode the size of the area that remains beyond coastal state jurisdiction, but in which China has taken an active interest as an extension of its interests in the Area worldwide.

Chapter four suggests that China is unlikely to challenge Canada's position on the Northwest Passage. But what if China does not agree with an extended continental shelf claim submitted by Canada or another Arctic littoral state to the Commission on the Limits of the Continental Shelf? The CLCS will make recommendations that are "final and binding" on the basis of Law of the Sea criteria and the data submitted by the coastal state related to its extended continental shelf. Accordingly, it is unclear how the recommendations can be "final and binding" if another state objects to the Commission's recommendation.[145] Indeed, there is ample precedent of this. Various states – including Canada, Denmark, Norway, and Japan – protested Russia's first submission to the CLCS. There is also a precedent for third party states, that do not share the border concerned, to file protests. Indonesia availed itself of this option against China when Beijing submitted its infamous U-line map in protest to a Vietnamese-Malaysian submission to the CLCS.[146] China could file protests of excessive claims, but there is no legal mechanism within the CLCS process to address outside intervention. In practice, such claims are frozen until the parties involved can negotiate an acceptable solution. Furthermore, and perhaps most importantly, China has no claim to the Arctic shelf (despite vague comments by one Chinese expert that it could make one).[147] On balance therefore, China could interfere with Canada's submission to the CLCS, though the benefits of doing so remain unclear.

Conclusions

This chapter has outlined several challenges that have arisen from the world's growing interest in Arctic resources and, on balance, has made the case for heightened awareness rather than panic about China's intentions on the part of Arctic states. Chinese interest in these resources is based on its continuing need for oil, gas, and minerals. Despite a slowing economy and decreasing emphasis on heavy industry, China will remain the world's largest importer of raw materials for the foreseeable future. Even thought it has earned a reputation as a voracious consumer with an unquenchable appetite for resources, the country's overseas investments have become increasingly strategic and market-driven. Chinese SOEs have demonstrated a willingness to forego or delay projects if the economics are not enticing, and to concentrate resources where they are. As such, there appears to be no Chinese rush into the Arctic.

China's North American Arctic projects are moderate in scale or still in the formative stages. In Greenland and Iceland, its SOEs are building their positions from the ground up by financing small local (or Western) companies with promising projects. Only in Russian has China jumped into the Arctic with both feet. Western sanctions on the Russian oil industry fundamentally altered Moscow's approach to development and China seems poised to replace Western companies as Russia's partners of choice. China has seized on the opportunity to secure long-term access to some of the world's last untapped hydrocarbon resources. It has also leveraged its position as financier and consumer to secure these resources at an excellent price.

Chinese interest in North American Arctic oil, however, is minimal. In part this is because Chinese oil companies have investment opportunities in other, more readily available, oil reserves. Alberta's oil sands are still open to foreign investment, even after the Canadian government placed restrictions on foreign ownership in the wake of CNOOC's purchase of Nexen.[148] In recent years, however, Chinese companies have been reconsidering their strategy in North America. After paying high prices for resources and facing repeated delays in moving some projects to production, some SOEs are regretting their headlong rush into the area.[149] Moving forward with large oil sands projects (like Sinopec's Northern Lights or CNOP's Dover) has proven more costly and difficult than expected. CNOOC is even having difficulty integrating Nexen into its corporate structure, with its new acquisition's return on equity trailing the company average by a considerable margin.[150] In light of these frustrations, it is unsurprising that appetite is lacking for North American Arctic resources – where costs and timescales are greater and regulations even more stringent and uncertain.

Chinese political influence, which often follows its economic investments in the developing world, is unlikely to present a serious problem in Arctic countries. Even if Chinese investment is scaled up considerably and major projects, such as Izok Lake, do go forward, it is difficult to conceive of a scenario by which this investment translates into the political influence feared by some Western commentators.[151] Corruption in western Arctic countries is simply too uncommon, and the rule of law too strong. It is also illustrative to highlight that China's $34 billion investment in Canadian resources over the past decade did not stop Prime Minister Harper from highlighting China's poor human rights record.[152] Accordingly, there is little chance that the negative side effects of Chinese resource investment found in African and other developing countries, including job loss due to labour disruption and associated social unrest due to growing resentment, will occur in the Canadian Arctic.

The one possible exception to this general outlook is Greenland, which, if it achieves full independence from Denmark, may lack the regulatory oversight of a developed state. With weak institutions in place, a "resource curse" could make the island ripe for Chinese exploitation.[153] An over-reliance on a narrow band of resource development activities would make a nascent Greenlandic state vulnerable to price volatility, which has led some Greenlanders to express concern about implications for political autonomy.[154] "Instead of relying on the Danish state, which is highly regulated, we may end up relying on oil companies over which we have no influence," warns Birger Poppel, a professor at the University of Greenland, the former chief statistician for the Greenland Home Rule Government, and the project chief for the Arctic Council's Survey of Living Conditions in the Arctic (SLiCA) initiative.[155] Greenland's continuing experiment with developing a resource economy has caused considerable political turmoil, brought down governments, and remains an uncertain proposition. The economics and politics of resource development on the island remain highly uncertain, however, and any fear of Chinese influence is premature.

Resource development in Greenland will continue to attract significant transnational attention – particularly from Inuit who will compare developments there with their experiences in Nunavut and other settlement regions. Inuit assert that "sovereignty begins at home," which has a unique meaning to a transnational people.[156] Along these lines, international Inuit leaders signed the Circumpolar Inuit Declaration on Resource Development Principles in Inuit Nunaat in Nuuk in May 2011, which lays out conditions for sustainable development. Invoking the United Nations Declaration on the Rights of Indigenous Peoples as well as the Circumpolar Inuit Declaration on Sovereignty in the Arctic, the statement emphasizes that "Inuit must be active and equal partners in policy-making and decision-making affecting Inuit Nunaat." Mary Simon, president of Inuit Tapiriit Kanatami, put "the world ... on notice that while Inuit look forward to new forms and levels of economic development, the use of resources in the Arctic must be conducted in a sustainable and environmentally responsible way, and must deliver direct and substantial benefits to Inuit."[157]

The Declaration on Resource Development Principles recognizes the importance of resource development, but it stresses that it must happen "at a rate sufficient to provide durable and diversified economic growth, but constrained enough to forestall environmental degradation and an overwhelming influx of outside labor." This may have an impact on the form and pace of development in Canada, given the shortage of skilled labour in the northern territories to fill the positions required by large-scale mining or oil and gas projects. Furthermore, the Inuit declaration states that "all resource development must contribute actively and significantly to improving Inuit living standards and social conditions, and non-renewable resource development, in particular, must promote economic diversification through contributions to education and other forms of social development, physical infrastructure, and non-extractive industries."[158]

Inuit perceive these principles to be transnational; thus investment in an independent Greenland would likely enforce them as well. Any Chinese attempt to act inconsistently with these principles would send a warning to Inuit in Canada and Alaska about the nature of Chinese SOE behaviour in the Arctic. In any event, Greenland has been working with Canada's National Energy Board to strengthen its own regulatory processes ahead of anticipated resource development. There are regulatory challenges, such as insuring local employment when partnering with companies that prefer to import labour, but these can be addressed.

The statement by Vice Foreign Minister Zhang Ming at the China Country Session of the Third Arctic Circle Assembly, suggests that China is in agreement with these responsibilities and requirements. There, Ming stated that: "China supports proper and orderly development of the Arctic. At the same time, relevant activities should be pursued in accordance with international rules and domestic laws of Arctic countries, with due respect to the rights and concerns of the indigenous population, and in an eco-friendly and sustainable manner ... With respect to the indigenous community in the Arctic region, China respects their traditions and culture and take seriously their concerns and needs."[159] On balance, therefore, there is little reason, based on the evidence presented here, to get caught up in much of the hyperbole that has surrounded the public debate about Chinese resource interests in the Arctic. Chinese interest in Arctic resources will continue and may even present new regulatory or geopolitical challenges in the future. Thus far, however, China's development activities have proceeded in full compliance with local laws and regulations and have yet to present the kinds of subversive or disruptive political threats that some speculators have foreseen.

China and Arctic Governance: Uncertainty and Potential Friction

As the Arctic bears on human survival and development, countries share common responsibilities for the Arctic. The challenges in the Arctic require joint contribution of all stakeholders, including the expertise, technology, capital and market that non-Arctic countries may offer. China proposes that all sides further strengthen communication and coordination to build a cooperation framework at the global, regional and national levels, expand channels for governmental and non-governmental cooperation and seek win-win results through cooperation.

VICE FOREIGN MINISTER ZHANG MING,
Third Arctic Circle Assembly (2015)[1]

Under the rubric of Canada's "sovereignty agenda," the Canadian *Arctic Foreign Policy Statement* addresses Arctic governance and public safety issues. It notes that:

Increasingly, the world is turning its attention northward, with many players far removed from the region itself seeking a role and in some cases calling into question the governance of the Arctic. While many of these players could have a contribution to make in the development of the North, Canada does not accept the premise that the Arctic requires a fundamentally new governance structure or legal framework. Nor does Canada accept that the Arctic nation states are unable to appropriately manage the North as it undergoes fundamental change.[2]

The statement reiterates that an extensive international legal framework applies to the Arctic Ocean, but that new challenges will emerge alongside increased shipping, tourism, and economic development. Placing a clear priority on "regional solutions, supported by robust domestic legislation in Arctic states," Canada emphasizes collaboration with "other Arctic nations through the Arctic Council (the primary forum for collaboration among the eight Arctic states), with the five Arctic Ocean coastal states (on issues of particular relevance to the Arctic Ocean), and bilaterally with key Arctic partners – particularly the United States."[3]

Canada's official position indicates that it prefers a regional governance regime dominated by the Arctic states. In response to the Arctic foreign policy statement, a *Toronto Star* editorial indicated that Ottawa "insists the Arctic Council eight are 'best placed to exercise leadership in the management of the region,' at a time when China and others are showing interest in the North. At root, Ottawa seems to be pushing for Arctic issues to be sorted out by as few interested players as possible, while keeping the rest of the world at a distance."[4] This perspective was forcefully reiterated by Prime Minister Stephen Harper himself.[5] Given that Canadian commentators drew this conclusion, it is not surprising that China might perceive the same intent on Canada's part.

Rob Huebert, for example, has told Chinese audiences that complexity and change are the hallmarks of the twenty-first century Arctic, and that climate change, natural resource development, technological development, and geopolitical dynamics are fundamentally transforming the region. Although the Arctic states have indicated their commitment to the LOSC and international law, science-based decision-making, peaceful resolution of Arctic disputes, and cooperation, he suggests that the current governance regime is nevertheless characterized by unilateral actions by Arctic states, increasing defence expenditures, and a refusal by the circumpolar states to embrace global governance options. Although the Arctic coastal states may voice their interest in cooperative initiatives, Huebert doubts that the existing governance regime can manage with the web of emerging challenges that face the circumpolar states and the international community more generally.[6]

A growing number of Chinese political and academic commentators have expressed their view that the international community (and China in particular) has an important interest in the Arctic region. Accordingly, the Arctic Ocean cannot be considered the private and exclusive preserve of the Arctic coastal states.[7] In the earliest official Chinese statement on the Arctic, Assistant Minister of Foreign Affairs Hu Zhenyue stated in June 2009 that "Arctic countries should protect the balance between the interests of states with shorelines in the Arctic Ocean and the shared interests of the international community."[8] Also consistent with China's perceptions as a maritime state, Yang Jian, the vice president of the Shanghai Institute for International Studies, suggests that China views Arctic affairs in two broad categories: (1) as regional issues that are appropriately managed by the Arctic states, given China's respect for the sovereignty and sovereign rights of the Arctic countries; and (2) those with global implications. In the latter case, he argues:

> China maintains that global Arctic affairs need to be handled through global governance and multi-party participation, because such trans-continental issues as climate change, ice melting, environmental pollution and ecological crisis all pose serious challenges to humankind as a whole and cannot be solved by any single country or region. Instead, solving them requires that all nations work together to provide the necessary public goods that Arctic governance entails. Certainly, countries of the region bear more responsibilities in Arctic affairs, yet non-Arctic countries also have their interests and responsibilities to assume. As an important international body leading the governance of Arctic issues, the Arctic Council should provide *an inclusive and open platform* that can bring in all the positive forces to facilitate good governance for the Arctic and for the planet. Such is the rationale behind China's bid for permanent observer status in the Arctic Council.[9]

While most Chinese commentators and officials acknowledge that "Arctic countries, with a larger stake in Arctic-related issues, should play a more important role in Arctic affairs,"[10] this does not preclude China from likewise seeking a more direct role in Arctic governance. As we have seen thus far, there is considerable anxiety within China that it will be excluded from

Arctic governance discussions that it feels it, as a maritime state and as a "Polar state," has a right to be involved in – with all the implications that such governance may have for future resource development and access.[11]

Despite Chinese officials' recent identification of their country as a "near Arctic state," China has neither an Arctic coastline (and thus no claim to a continental shelf in the Arctic Ocean) nor territory above the Arctic Circle. Yet, as Linda Jakobson and Jingchao Peng note:

> China already has a stake in the general framework of Arctic governance: it is represented in numerous international organizations and is party to several international agreements that pertain directly or indirectly to Arctic governance. Most importantly, China is a veto-wielding member of the United Nations Security Council, the ultimate authority of the 1982 UN Convention on the Law of the Sea (UNCLOS). China is, along with 41 other countries, a signatory of the 1920 Svalbard Treaty, which grants all members equal rights to access Svalbard while recognizing Norway's absolute sovereignty. It is also a member in the International Maritime Organization (IMO), a UN agency responsible for adopting measures to secure international shipping and to prevent marine pollution from ships.[12]

By extension, these authors observe that "China's present Arctic policies and research agenda are based on the premise that the more the Arctic states recognize the potentially lucrative implications of a melting Arctic, leading them to adopt policies to maximize their interests in the region, the more China, as a non-Arctic state, should look after its own interests and what it perceives as its rights."[13]

Chinese scholars have often depicted Arctic states – and the Arctic Council as an institution – as self-interested actors seeking to exclude "user state" perspectives from Arctic governance. David Wright points out that "the Chinese nightmare scenario for the Arctic is that the European and North American Arctic powers will more or less gang up and 'carve up the Arctic melon' and its natural resources among themselves, to the exclusion of everyone else;"[14] a concern found in Chinese academic and news pieces as well.[15] Based upon an extensive reading of Chinese sources from 2009–11, Wright suggests that:

Even though China is currently climbing the Arctic learning curve, it seems reluctant to acknowledge that it being a non-Arctic country, its influence in the Arctic and in Arctic affairs might be somewhat limited. This hesitance arises, however, not from pride or haughtiness but from concern over the multivalent implications of such an acknowledgement: China does not want to lose any ground in its campaign to become a major player in the world in general, and increasingly for Beijing that means being a player in the Arctic. China wants, as the term in Chinese goes, to "insert its hands" *(chashou)* into Arctic affairs but finds it inconvenient to indicate this directly, because that would be infelicitous diplomatically. So instead, China engages in unctuous and circumlocutory diplomatic language about respecting the sovereignty of Arctic countries, hoping that the Arctic countries can resolve their differences quickly and anticipating that Arctic issues can ultimately be worked out through negotiation to the satisfaction of both the Arctic and international communities. But the gentlemanly bows and matronly curtsies and bouquets of Chinese diplomatic gesturing should not be confused for acquiescence or lack of resolve on China's part. Despite its status as a non-Arctic country, China seems bound and determined to have a voice, perhaps even a say-so, in Arctic affairs.

Some Chinese commentators, such as Li Zhenfu of Dalian Maritime University and Guo Peiqing from the School of Law and Political Science at the Ocean University of China, urge China to adopt a proactive campaign to protect its rights.[16] Other scholars preach restraint, suggesting that China should avoid provoking Arctic states by asserting views on topics such as resources and shipping. Indian polar expert Sanjay Chaturvedi notes that "China's much pronounced official foreign policy stand on supporting state sovereignty in its classical-territorial sense could come in the way of articulating the vision of a more inclusive and democratic 'regional' (perhaps even global) governance for the circumpolar Arctic."[17]

That Chinese commentators raise questions about the current Arctic governance regime and call for change should come as no surprise given that Canadian commentators have raised serious questions about the capacity of existing arrangements to ensure regional security and stability. For example,

Huebert suggests that the soft-law approach currently in place will prove ineffective in managing challenges related to climate change, resource development, and increased shipping in the region. He has advocated strong regional institutions with legal powers and even an ambitious new Arctic treaty architecture modeled on the Antarctic Treaty – in obvious opposition to the Ilulissat Declaration.[18] Others have avoided the treaty road while still suggesting that the current regime needs fundamental reform. The Arctic Governance Project issued a report in April 2010 declaring that the Arctic Council needed a "big makeover" because it had become outdated owing to "cascades of change" in the Arctic. Although it did not envisage an Arctic Council with regulatory powers, the project team did recommend that the Council expand its mandate and open its doors to more non-Arctic observers, including China.[19]

China and the Arctic Council[20]

Canada considers the Arctic Council to be "the primary forum for collaboration among the eight Arctic states."[21] Created through the Ottawa Declaration of 1996 (rather than a treaty), this high-level "discussional and catalytic" forum serves as "a means for promoting cooperation, coordination and interaction among the Arctic states, with the involvement of the Arctic Indigenous communities and other Arctic inhabitants on common Arctic issues, in particular issues of sustainable development and environmental protection in the Arctic." Rooted in "soft law," it is not a political decision-making body.[22] Nevertheless, the Council "does excellent technical work and informs and enables states to adopt progressive and environmentally and socially responsible policies."[23] It also plays an important generative role in framing and highlighting issues on the Arctic agenda.[24]

Decisions at all levels in the Arctic Council are the exclusive right and responsibility of the eight Arctic states with the involvement of the permanent participants. The member states – Canada, the Kingdom of Denmark (including Greenland and the Faroe Islands), Finland, Iceland, Norway, Russia, Sweden, and the United States – are the only voting parties. Six international organizations representing Arctic indigenous peoples have permanent participant status, giving them full consultation rights in connection with the Council's negotiations and decisions (but not votes). This indigenous involvement is a unique feature in international organizations.

As a forum for discussion and information sharing based on a non-binding declaration, the Council has established a series of working groups that undertake non-regulatory initiatives (such as assessments, projects, action plans, and programs) on a broad range of environmental and sustainable development issues. In addition to publication of scientific reports, this work has contributed to international scientific negotiations and initiatives concerning environmental impacts in the Arctic region.[25] There are currently six working groups:

- Arctic Contaminants Action Program (ACAP)
- Arctic Monitoring and Assessment Programme (AMAP)
- Conservation of Arctic Flora and Fauna (CAFF)
- Emergency Prevention, Preparedness and Response (EPPR)
- Protection of the Arctic Marine Environment (PAME)
- Sustainable Development Working Group (SDWG)

Each working group operates under a specific mandate, and is overseen by a chair and a management board or steering committee typically comprised of representatives of governmental agencies from the Arctic states as well as representatives from the permanent participants. In operation, these working groups execute the programs and projects mandated by Arctic Council Ministerial Declarations and the official documents produced from Ministerial meetings. They involve expert representatives from sectoral ministries of the Arctic states, government agencies, and researchers. Furthermore, observer states and observer organizations attend working group meetings and participate in specific projects.[26]

Questions surrounding observer status became contentious and politically sensitive in recent years. This status, set out in the Declaration on the Establishment of the Arctic Council and governed by the Arctic Council Rules of Procedure, is open to non-Arctic states, global and regional intergovernmental and inter-parliamentary organizations, and non-governmental organizations that the Council determines can contribute to its work. Twelve non-Arctic states, nine intergovernmental and inter-parliamentary organizations, and eleven non-government organizations are currently observers (popularly referred to as "permanent observers") to the Council – a status that allows these states and organizations to attend most Council meetings without obtaining permission on a meeting-by-meeting basis. In the initial years after its establishment, the Council seemed eager to accept states and organizations that showed an interest in its activities and applied as observers. With growing international interest in the Arctic, however, applicants attracted more critical scrutiny. For Canada, the most contentious application for observer status came from the European Union (EU), given its decision to ban the import of seal products in 2009. This sparked a major disagreement between the EU and Canada (with Canada being supported by other Arctic states and indigenous peoples), and led the Arctic Council to defer consideration of the EU request.[27] This in turn affected other applicants, including China.

Despite the admission of new observers, Prime Minister Harper stated in a January 2014 interview:

> There's been a lot of observer countries admitted. Our concern with that, and unfortunately, to be blunt about it, I think frankly this had already gone way too far before we became government. But given that that is the precedent that has been established, we're prepared to have a significant number of observers as long as they understand and respect the sovereignty of the permanent members. And as long as their presence doesn't override or impede upon the deliberations of the permanent members. So I think it's a matter of balance."[28]

Chinese scholars and government spokespersons stress that changes in the Arctic do not just bring challenges and opportunities to the Arctic states. "According to mainstream thinking among Chinese Arctic specialists," Jakobson and Peng observe, "China has a legitimate right to participate in Arctic governance because environmental changes in the Arctic have a major impact on China's ecological system and subsequently its agriculture and economic development." By extension, China envisages the Arctic Council as an important body for regional governance and cooperation. It has regularly attended Council sessions since 2007 as an ad hoc observer. Although the Council has never rejected China's request to attend a Council meeting, "permanent" observer status is perceived to be more than symbolic and "better positions non-Arctic states to participate in the governance of the Arctic region."[29] Jakobson and Peng indicate that "China's desire to become a permanent observer is linked both to an unspoken concern that at some point in the future it will not be a desired attendee and to China's aspiration that observers could over time attain more influence in the Arctic Council."[30]

China first requested "permanent" observer status in 2009, but its application was deferred – alongside applications from the European Union, Italy, and South Korea – when the Council member states could not reach consensus. The principle impediment to China's joining was Russia, which obstructed the process for years.[31] Nevertheless, foreign ministry representatives from Denmark, Finland, Iceland, Norway, and Sweden publicly supported China's application. In the case of Denmark, this position is consistent with its broader support for more observers, which recommends that "the Arctic Council should look for ways to further involve those that are ready to cooperate under the premise that the primary role of the Arctic Council is to promote sustainable development for the Peoples of the Arctic and the Arctic states."[32] Norway's Foreign Minister Jonas Gahr Støre officially endorsed China's application during a speech in Beijing in August 2010, and indicated his hope that the Council would reach a similar consensus.[33]

Canadian ambivalence to Chinese participation in the Arctic Council was evident right up until the final decision was made. Up to 2013, Canadian and American officials had neither opposed nor supported China's application, though American Secretary of State John Kerry ultimately helped to pave the way for the successful accession of China and other non-Arctic states to the Council that May.[34] This long deliberation reflects internal debates between the member states and permanent participants about the level of activity that observers should be able to play in various Arctic Council activities – as well as the absence of clear criteria to assess new applicants. Matthew Willis and Duncan Depledge have made a convincing case that the Arctic Council's consideration of China's application was always more of a question of the Council's growth and institutional direction more generally, and that China's application was never looked upon any differently than those of the other Asian and European applicants.[35]

At the Nuuk Ministerial in May 2011, the Council settled upon a formula, set explicit criteria for considering applications for observer status, and clarified the Council's expectations of observer states (see figure 5.1).[36] Later that year, China submitted a formal application for observer status in accordance with the new criteria and procedures. Although these applications were not public, official statements by Chinese officials indicate the basic elements of the country's case for admission. On November 6, 2012, Lan Lijun, China's ambassador to Sweden, explained on behalf of the vice foreign minister of China that he believed the participation of more non-Arctic states as observers would have a "positive significance to the work of the Council." Furthermore, he recognized that much of the region fell under national jurisdiction of the Arctic states. This recognition of the primacy of Arctic states' sovereignty, sovereign rights, and jurisdiction was also the principle factor in removing Russian objections.[37] His message was reassuring. "The participation of observers does not prejudice the dominant role of Arctic states in the Council," the ambassador suggested. "The participation of observers in the work of the Council is based on the recognition of Arctic states' sovereignty, sovereign rights and jurisdiction in the Arctic as well as their decision-making power in the Council."[38]

The process of China achieving accredited observer status elicited a great deal of comment and concern from the media - the rationale being, of course, that China was a powerful and even expansionist country (unlike Italy or South Korea for instance) whose presence on the Council might be destabilizing, or even a threat to Arctic state sovereignty. It is telling to note, however, that these views never held much authority within the halls of the Council itself. Through a series of interviews with Senior Arctic Officials (SAO), Willis and Depledge have shown that few, if any, diplomats had any real concerns about China's specific interests in the Arctic – in fact there had not been a single formal discussion specifically about China within the Council between 2006 and Kiruna (though there were, of course, informal conversations). During these interviews, the SAOs consistently emphasized that China's presence at the Council should not be feared. Some officials, particularly from the Nordic countries and the United States, said either that they welcomed and had always supported China's engagement or, at the very least, that they had no concerns whatsoever about its admission. Frequently, officials pointed out that the mass media's portrayal of China was heavily skewed and that Chinese diplomats had always behaved very well, both towards the Council states and the permanent participants.[39]

Transnational issues such as climate change and international shipping extend beyond the region. Arctic and non-Arctic states, therefore, have common interests in addressing these global issues, ambassador Lan suggested, and could do so through improved communication and cooperation. "By

5.1 Criteria and Role for Observers at the Arctic Council

Criteria for Admitting Observers:

As set out in the Declaration on the Establishment of the Arctic Council and governed by the Arctic Council Rules of Procedure, observer status in the Arctic Council is open to non-Arctic states; inter-governmental and inter-parliamentary organizations, global and regional; and non-governmental organizations that the Council determines can contribute to its work. In the determination by the Council of the general suitability of an applicant for observer status the Council will, inter alia, take into account the extent to which observers:

- Accept and support the objectives of the Arctic Council defined in the Ottawa declaration.
- Recognize Arctic states' sovereignty, sovereign rights, and jurisdiction in the Arctic.
- Recognize that an extensive legal framework applies to the Arctic Ocean including, notably, the Law of the Sea, and that this framework provides a solid foundation for responsible management of this ocean.
- Respect the values, interests, culture, and traditions of Arctic indigenous peoples and other Arctic inhabitants.
- Have demonstrated a political willingness as well as financial ability to contribute to the work of the permanent participants and other Arctic indigenous peoples.
- Have demonstrated their Arctic interests and expertise relevant to the work of the Arctic Council.
- Have demonstrated a concrete interest and ability to support the work of the Arctic Council, including through partnerships with member states and permanent participants bringing Arctic concerns to global decision making bodies.

Role of Observers:

Decisions at all levels in the Arctic Council are the exclusive right and responsibility of the eight Arctic states with the involvement of the permanent participants.

- Observers shall be invited to the meetings of the Arctic Council once observer status has been granted.
- While the primary role of observers is to observe the work of the Arctic Council, observers should continue to make relevant contributions through their engagement in the Arctic Council primarily at the level of working groups.
- Observers may propose projects through an Arctic State or a permanent participant but financial contributions from observers to any given project may not exceed the financing from Arctic states, unless otherwise decided by the SAOs.
- In meetings of the Council's subsidiary bodies to which observers have been invited to participate, observers may, at the discretion of the Chair, make statements after Arctic states and permanent participants, present written statements, submit relevant documents and provide views on the issues under discussion. Observers may also submit written statements at Ministerial meetings.

---

accepting observers, and therefore enhancing its openness and inclusiveness, the Council will help the international community to better appreciate its work, thus expanding its international influence," he argued. "Its exchanges and cooperation with the observers will help it review trans-regional issues from a broader perspective, which will facilitate effective settlement of relevant issues through international cooperation. This model of cooperation has been effective in addressing issues such as climate change and international shipping, and deserves further promotion. The Council should well respond to the desire expressed by relevant parties to participate in the work of the Council as observers."[40]

Casting China as a "near Arctic state," the ambassador also emphasized the significant impact that climate change and resource development in the Arctic had "on China's climate, ecological environment, agricultural production as well as social and economic development." Accordingly, China continues to invest in scientific research in the region – something best accomplished through cooperation with other states. The message sought to reassure the Member States that China's participation would not destabilize the Council or the region. In reaffirming the importance of "communication and dialogue with Arctic states on Arctic issues to enhance mutual understanding and trust," as well as China's willingness and ability "to contribute to the work of the Council and to strengthen cooperation with states in the Council for the peace, stability and sustainable development in the Arctic region,"[41] the ambassador's remarks also corroborate the findings of Jakobson and others that China fears being excluded from Arctic institutions.

Although Chinese officials have not publicly criticized the Nuuk criteria, Chinese scholars accused the Arctic Council member states of raising the political threshold for non-Arctic states to join at a time when "it is unimaginable that non-Arctic states will remain users of Arctic shipping lanes and consumers of Arctic energy without playing a role in the decision-making process."[42] On this subject, Guo Peiqing has mounted a sustained critique of the new criteria, alleging that "Observer status will bring more obligations but fewer rights" and thus is "not the best option for non-Arctic states to participate in Arctic governance." First, he considers the new criteria "as a rigorous and harsh requirement that is unprecedented in this history of international organizations." For example, one criterion stipulates that an applicant's suitability will be measured by the extent to which they "recognize Arctic states' sovereignty, sovereign rights and jurisdiction in the Arctic."[43] Rather than simply assuming that this is a blanket statement indicating that Arctic states have sovereignty, sovereign rights, and jurisdiction in the region, Peiqing reads it literally. He asserts that "the 'three recognitions' principle also calls on POs [permanent observers] to recognize sovereignty and jurisdiction that is not yet settled. The principle does not specify what aspects of disputed sovereignty or jurisdiction POs are recognizing or whether this implies recognition of settled boundaries in the future." In cases of conflicting member states' claims to Arctic lands or waters, applicants are placed in an irrational position where they must implicitly recognize "the legitimacy of both parties' claims to a contested area."[44] This unreasonable demand, as Guo sees it, imposed on non-Arctic states, obviously does not apply to Arctic states themselves.

In weighing the net benefit of observer status in light of the new admission criteria and practical aspects of actual involvement in the Council, Guo concludes that it "will bring non-Arctic states more obligations than rights and benefits." Observers are seldom allowed to speak at Ministerial or Senior Arctic Official meetings, and (citing Oran Young) the activities at the working-group level are not a conduit to "real dialogue regarding issues on the new Arctic policy agenda." In exchange, non-Arctic states "will likely lose the initiative and flexibility of diplomacy in the future because they have recognized Arctic states' 'sovereignty, sovereign rights and jurisdiction' in advance as a package deal," and thus will have given up any "potential residual rights in the Arctic Ocean by virtue of the new criteria." He also alleges specific discrimination by Arctic states against China in most international organizations, where they "work hard to control China's influence on rulemaking and implementation," insisting that China take on more responsibility but preventing China from rising to a level that can challenge Western dominance. "The new criteria place a high cost on China's entry into the Arctic club," Guo concludes. "China gains few practical benefits and gains little prestige by joining the Arctic Council." Instead, he urges China to exploit other multilateral institutions and bilateral diplomacy to influence Arctic governance.[16]

The logical extension of this argument could be that, rather than asking why the member states should let China in to the Council, they might consider asking "Why should China join us?"[46] Engaging China and other Asian countries as observers at the Arctic Council could prove useful for Canada in keeping its own agenda prominent in cooperative discussions.[47]

As Lackenbauer and Manicom have argued, the perception of China as a threat that may come to dominate the Arctic Council is flawed on three counts. First, such an assessment is inconsistent with China's track record of behaviour in international institutions – and with the nature of the Arctic Council and observer status itself. Second, and on the contrary, Chinese attitudes are characterized by a deep-seated mistrust of the Arctic Council as an effort by Arctic states to monopolize Arctic governance. Third, and on a related note, Chinese scholars point out that China does not *need* the Arctic Council to pursue its Arctic interests.

The literature on China and international institutions has also arrived at three general observations about Chinese behaviour.[48] First, Chinese interaction with institutions begins slowly and is characterized by merely observing the workings of the organization. Chinese participants say little and make few proposals. Second, China typically avoids taking on binding commitments in international institutions that would constrain its freedom of action. Third, China punches well below its weight in international affairs. Collectively, this

5.2 The Arctic Council, Changes at the Kiruna Meeting, May 2013.

Status	Party
Member States	Canada; Kingdom of Denmark (including Greenland and the Faroe Islands); Finland; Iceland; Norway; Russian Federation; Sweden; United States
Permanent Participants	Arctic Athabaskan Council; Aleut International Association; Gwich'in Council International; Inuit Circumpolar Council; Russian Association of Indigenous Peoples of the North (RAIPON); Saami Council
Observer States	Great Britain; Germany; The Netherlands; Poland; France; Spain
Non-state Observers	*Intergovernmental and Inter-Parliamentary Organizations (9):* International Union for the Conservation of Nature; Nordic Council of Ministers; Nordic Environment Finance Corporation; North Atlantic Marine Mammal Commission; International Federation of Red Cross and Red Crescent Societies; Standing Committee of the Parliamentarians of the Arctic Region; United Nations Development Program; United Nations Economic Commission for Europe; United Nations Environment Program *Non-government Organizations (11):* Advisory Committee on Protection of the Seas; Arctic Cultural Gateway; Association of World Reindeer Herders; Circumpolar Conservation Union; International Arctic Science Committee; International Arctic Social Sciences Association; International Union for Circumpolar Health; International Work Group for Indigenous Affairs; Northern Forum; University of the Arctic; World Wildlife Fund for Nature – Global Arctic Program
State Applicants for Observer status	China; India; Italy; Japan; Mongolia; Singapore; South Korea
Non-State Applicants for Observer status	Association of Oil and Gas Producers (OGP); Association of Polar Early Career Scientists (APECS); European Union*; Greenpeace; International Chamber of Shipping; International Hydrographic Organisation (IHO); Norwegian Scientific Academy for Polar Research; Oceana; OSPAR Commission; World Meteorological Organization (WMO) (*The Council website states that "The Arctic Council receives the application of the EU for Observer status affirmatively, but defers a final decision on implementation until the Council members are agreed by consensus that the concerns of the Council members, addressed by the President of the European Commission in his letter of 8 May are resolved, with the understanding that the EU may observe Council proceedings until such time as the Council acts on the letter's proposal.")

suggests that China does not wish to incur the costs of leadership for organizations in which it does not have a vital stake, or that are marginal to its primary national interests.[49] Chinese leadership and confidence in East Asian institutions, for example, emerged after China became well versed in regional protocols and as its confidence and power relative to the other members grew. These are not the characteristics of a country that seeks to dominate the Arctic Council – an organization controlled by the world's superpower, its NATO allies, and Russia.

Moreover, the role of observers in the Arctic Council does not allow for such dominance. In addition to outlining the criteria for observer status, the Nuuk Declaration placed constraints on the capacity of the observers to operate in the Council. Observers are there to observe. They are expected to contribute to the working groups and may, at the discretion of the chair, make statements and submit documents. Observers can only make written statements at Ministerial meetings, but they may propose projects through an Arctic state or permanent participant. In any event, the level of financial contribution from observers may not exceed that provided by the Arctic states, unless explicitly permitted by the Senior Arctic Officials. Furthermore, observer status is subject to review every four years, at which time observer states are expected to reiterate their interest in the status and share information about their activities in the Arctic Council. Although China could assert more influence at the working-group level than parties with more limited financial resources, the Nuuk criteria limits the amount an observer can commit to an initiative, reducing the odds that the working groups will become reliant on a single contributor. It could be argued that participation in Council meetings may afford China the informal opportunity to create mischief and exercise its influence, though where and how this could unfold is speculative. As argued throughout this book, inclusion and consultation are the ways to gain Chinese compliance. China will operate in the Arctic regardless of its status within Arctic Council. Though this does not obviate the need for vigilance and unity by Arctic Council member states, it is not sufficient grounds for keeping China out.

Second, Chinese attitudes to exclusion from Arctic Council are characterized by apathy (at best) and hostility (at worst). Zhang Xia, director of Strategic Studies at the Polar Research Institute of China, has asserted that "if many countries were to be excluded from the Arctic Council, the power of the council would be weakened and it would be difficult for it to remain the primary institution to negotiate Arctic affairs."[50] Rather than being concerned about Chinese domination, Arctic states should be concerned that China may seek to pursue its Arctic interests outside of the Arctic Council – thus diluting the Council's position as the premier forum for dialogue on Arctic issues – if Chinese officials do not believe that the forum is receptive to its involvement.

Third, given China's traditional wariness regarding both joining international institutions and assuming international obligations, some Chinese commentators have argued that it should stay out of the Arctic Council entirely and instead pursue its resource, shipping, and scientific interests by other means. Given that offshore resource development will likely take place in highly prospective areas closer to shore, China need only engage bilaterally with select Arctic states like Canada, Greenland, and Russia to pursue resource development. As a state with an abiding interest in deep-sea mining, Chinese activities in the Area in the central Arctic Ocean beyond coastal state jurisdiction need only involve the International Seabed Authority based in Kingston, Jamaica. Chinese fisheries interests can be pursued through the Fisheries and Agriculture Organization, and China, as a leading distant-water fishing state, can choose to remain outside efforts to construct a regional fisheries management organization (RFMO) in Arctic waters. China can pursue its shipping interests via the IMO and through coordinated efforts with other maritime states to resist Arctic state efforts to limit, police, or raise the costs of shipping in the Arctic.

Chinese scholars are quick to point out that other global and regional organizations have competencies not covered by the Arctic Council mandate (or which closely support the Council's work), including the International Maritime Organization, the International Arctic Science Committee, the International Association of Classification Societies, the Conference of Arctic Parliamentarians, the Barents Euro-Arctic Council, and the United Nations.[51] According to some Chinese scholars, this diverse array of institutions suggests that "a politically valid and legally binding Arctic governance system has yet to be established."[52] With China's accession to the Arctic Council as an accredited observer, China appears to have made a commitment to working within the Council for the time being and, according to Frédéric Lasserre and Linyan Huang, to have reached the immediate goal of making itself heard in the Arctic's premier regional governance forum.[53] Still, this neither gives China as much influence as some commentators suggest, nor does it preclude future forum-shopping.

Chinese officials and scholars have also begun to speak of Arctic governance as a question of "common destiny" or "a community of common destiny." This phrase was first officially adopted in Premier Hu Jintao's 17th National Party Congress report in 2007, in reference to the special relationship between China and Taiwan. Since then it has become a guiding principle of Chinese foreign policy, essentially implying the existence of common interests between China and its neighbours that will support peace and stability – with China playing a leading role.[54] This concept has since been applied in Chinese statements about the Arctic, always implying that China's presence will be constructive and helpful – but also central and indispensable.[55] Beijing has yet to clarify what exactly this may mean in practice, though it does succinctly encapsulate how China feels about its role in the Arctic. It is part of a community with common interests in an international region – and an important part at that.

The "Human Dimension" and Indigenous Governance

Geographer Sanjay Chaturvedi, in one of the most profound "think pieces" on Asia and the Arctic, concludes:

> On the note that as the rising Asian powers prepare and push their cases for observer status in the Arctic Council, it is vitally important that they give due space and attention to the "human dimension" of Arctic governance. In most reasoning advanced so far, what is missing by and large is the engagement with indigenous peoples of the circumpolar north; their knowledge systems, world-views and aspirations. It is useful to be reminded that "Arctic" (both on land and at sea) is not a "strategic void" and it is the *lived in* geographies of the Circumpolar North that are in the front line of adverse climate change consequences. What might appear as "opportunities" offered by climate change may in some cases pose serious "threats" to the livelihoods of Arctic communities; especially the indigenous peoples. It is vital in other words that the Asian efforts at confidence-building and alliance making go beyond the state actors in the Arctic Council.[56]

This message echoes that of the permanent indigenous participants to the Council, who identify "a pressing need for enhanced international exchange and cooperation in relation to the Arctic, particularly in relation to the dynamics and impacts of climate change and sustainable economic and social development."[57]

Canada is committed to "encourag[ing] a greater understanding of the human dimension of the Arctic to improve the lives of Northerners, particularly through the Arctic Council" and the Sustainable Development Working Group.[58] Senior officials, including the Hon. Leona Aglukkaq, Canada's minister for the Arctic Council during its 2013-15 chairmanship, insist that this is the government's foremost priority. Accordingly, some Canadian commentators have expressed concern that Asian decision-makers do not have a well-developed understanding of the Arctic as a homeland – as opposed to a resource, or a scientific frontier. Some cited this lack of knowledge as a justification to deny the applications of China and other Asian states for observer status to the Arctic Council.

In 2009, Arctic scholar Peter Kikkert noted concern among the permanent participants that "if more actors continue to gain access to the Council, the organization will begin to lose its specialized status and regional identity to the harm of the indigenous peoples and circumpolar states."[59] Although some Inuit representatives have downplayed the prevalence of this fear, Canada's 2010 Arctic foreign policy statement insisted that "as interest by non-Arctic players in the work of the Council grows, [it] will work to ensure that the central role of the permanent participants is not diminished or diluted."[60] Aglukkaq also emphasized a "people-first" approach, indicating that the criteria for evaluating new observers must incorporate "the respect and support of indigenous peoples in the Arctic region."[61]

Chinese officials insist that their countries have this respect, and wish to learn more about how to support indigenous peoples' development efforts. For example, Ambassador Zhao Jun insisted in January 2013 that China "respects the values, interests, culture and traditions of Arctic indigenous peoples and other Arctic inhabitants," and is open to exploring avenues for cooperation with northern peoples.[62] Some Canadian indigenous leaders, however, seem unconvinced that this is more than lip service. At an Ottawa conference later that month, Terry Audla, the president of Inuit Tapiriit Kanatami (ITK), warned that the Arctic Council should be cautious about opening up observer status to applicants (such as China) that did not have a strong track record of respecting indigenous rights. This posed a dilemma to Inuit, Audla explained. Although their culture embraced dialogue and negotiation, "the council runs the risk of seeing its agenda being diluted or sidetracked by special interests." He urged the Council to look "closely" at the applications of China and the European Union in particular.[63]

Inuit and other northern indigenous peoples insist that they have rights rooted in indigenous use and occupancy, international law, land claims, and self-government processes.[64] Accordingly, Inuit and other northerners place a high policy priority on "recognition that an effective Arctic strategy requires a high and sustained level of inter-governmental and government-aboriginal cooperation."[65] For example, the Inuit Circumpolar Council adopted *A Circumpolar Inuit Declaration on Sovereignty in the Arctic* in 2009, which emphasized that "the inextricable linkages between issues of sovereignty and sovereign rights in the Arctic and Inuit self-determination and other rights require states to accept the presence and role of Inuit as partners in the conduct of international relations in the Arctic." The declaration envisions Inuit playing an active role in all deliberations on environmental security, sustainable development, militarization, commercial fishing, shipping, health, and socio-economic development. In asserting that "the foundation, projection and enjoyment of Arctic sovereignty and sovereign rights all require healthy and sustainable communities in the Arctic," the declaration stipulates that: "In the pursuit of economic opportunities in a warming Arctic, states must act so as to: (1) put economic activity on a sustainable footing; (2) avoid harmful resource exploitation; (3) achieve standards of living for Inuit that meet national and international norms and minimums; and (4) deflect sudden and far-reaching demographic shifts that would overwhelm and marginalize indigenous peoples where we are rooted and have endured."[66]

How Chinese scholars or officials perceive this declaration is unknown. Nearly all Chinese social science commentary on Arctic is from a state-based perspective. Given recent indications that Canadian indigenous groups will use the legal rights recognized in land claims to disrupt resource exploration activities that they believe are prejudicial to their interests, and will sue the federal government for not implementing land claim provisions,[67] it is likely that they will hold the Canadian government responsible for protecting their interests.

Conclusions

In their 2012 report, Jakobson and Peng observed that the "vigorous public debate among Chinese scholars" since 2008 revealed an evolution in thinking about Arctic governance. Early "assertive and even hawkish stances" gave way to more subdued public proclamations after the Arctic Council's second deferral of China's observer application, when Chinese officials became "well aware of the suspicions that China's interest in the Arctic evokes and of the sensitivities of Arctic politics, especially in the realm of resources and sovereignty."[68] Although international legal scholar Donat Pharand suggests that "the limits of national sovereignties in the Arctic must be clarified before there can be any meaningful circumpolar stewardship,"[69] debates about appropriate forms of regional governance (and the role of non-Arctic states therein) will continue before all of the lines are drawn between Arctic states and "the area" in the central Arctic Ocean. Although a few Chinese commentators have articulated viewpoints demonstrating a lack of faith in the present system of Arctic governance,[70] or an abject disregard for international law, or a radically different interpretation of it, much of the debate among Chinese commentators on governance issues, documented by scholars like David Wright and Linda Jakobson, mirrors aspects of Western debates over the last decade.

Indeed, the complexities of transnational governance in the Arctic certainly invite debate. Oran Young has noted that the region

> features a mosaic of issue-specific arrangements rather than a single comprehensive and integrated regime covering an array of issues that constitute the region's policy agenda ... The continued success of region building in the Far North is by no means assured. The emerging mosaic of cooperative arrangements remains fragile ... What is more, the tides of global environmental change and globalization have triggered cascades of events that threaten to overwhelm efforts to carve out coherent agendas at the regional level and to pursue them without undue concern for the linkages between regional activities and planetary processes. Nowhere is this more apparent than in the Arctic, where externally driven environmental forces (for example, the impacts of climate change) together with the impacts of globalization (for

example, the consequences for Arctic communities of political pressures relating to marine mammals) threaten to swamp co-operative initiatives at the regional level.[71]

Nevertheless, the Arctic Council has enjoyed recent successes in developing guidelines for offshore oil and gas activity (2009), best practices in ecosystem-based oceans management (2009), and task forces that produced the Council's first legally binding multilateral instruments – a regional search and rescue agreement (2011), and an agreement on cooperation on marine oil pollution preparedness and response in the Arctic (2013).[72] Ongoing discussions about strengthening the Arctic Council, however, raise key questions about its structure and its future. Should the Council adopt more normative/prescriptive decisions in the future? What responsibilities should observers assume? What is the appropriate level of regional engagement for non-Arctic states? Should the Council address hard security issues?[73]

As Lackenbauer and Manicom have argued, rather than being concerned about China joining the Arctic Council as an accredited observer, member states should embrace this opportunity to enmesh China into their way of thinking about Arctic issues, if only to avoid the emergence of governance challenges that it (and other non-Arctic states) could design to undermine Arctic states' interests in the region. Although China seeks a more prominent role in Arctic affairs, there is no evidence that its observer status in the Arctic Council will allow it to pursue an agenda that is inconsistent with the spirit of the Nuuk Declaration. Rather, as a function of the global nature of many Arctic challenges, there is increasing scope for China to pursue its Arctic interests outside the Arctic Council through other multilateral bodies and assemblies.[74] These interests could certainly challenge Arctic state interests if China perceives itself as excluded from the key mechanisms of Arctic governance and chooses to sidestep the Council – and the Arctic states – in pursuit of its interests.[75] In many ways exclusion of China on the pretext that it is hostile to Arctic states' interests will become a self-fulfilling prophecy.[76]

6

The Way Ahead

*Through our Arctic foreign policy, we will deliver on the
international dimension of our Northern Strategy. We will
show leadership in demonstrating responsible stewardship while
we build a region responsive to Canadian interests and values,
secure in the knowledge that the North is our home and
our destiny.*

*Through our Arctic foreign policy, we are also sending a clear
message: Canada is in control of its Arctic lands and waters and
takes its stewardship role and responsibilities seriously. Canada
continues to stand up for its interests in the Arctic. When
positions or actions are taken by others that affect our national
interests, undermine the cooperative relationships we have built,
or demonstrate a lack of sensitivity to the interests or perspectives
of Arctic peoples or states, we respond.*

*Cooperation, diplomacy and respect for international law have
always been Canada's preferred approach in the Arctic. At the
same time, we will never waver in our commitment to protect
our North.*

Statement on Canada's Arctic Foreign Policy (2010)

The strongly worded conclusion from the *Statement on Canada's Arctic Foreign Policy*, quoted above, reflected the Harper government's desire to protect and project Canada's national interests and values. In defining these interests, the *Statement* explains, "the key foundation for any [international] collaboration will be acceptance of and respect for the perspectives and knowledge of northerners and Arctic states' sovereignty. As well, there must be recognition that the Arctic states remain best placed to exercise leadership in the management of the region."[1]

These guiding principles do not preclude an acknowledgement and recognition that non-Arctic states, including China, have legitimate interests in (and can make substantive contributions to) the Arctic region. Indian geographer Sanjay Chaturvedi notes that "the movers and shapers of Arctic governance discourse in general, and the Arctic Council in particular, can afford to dismiss or underplay the concerns of 'outside' stakeholders (as the 'Asian century' unfolds in all its complexities) only at the cost of undermining the legitimacy, authority and efficacy of their efforts."[2] This book has made clear that, although there is little evidence that China's intentions in the Arctic are malignant, it will not tolerate being excluded from the Arctic conversation. Furthermore, it is in no Arctic states' interests to attempt such an exclusion.

The following conclusions reflect upon China's polar behaviour and how it is likely to evolve over the next decade. We argue that, on balance, China is unlikely to pose a threat to Canadian Arctic interests, or those of any Arctic state. Rather, as a function of its interest in costly resource development, China's interest in the Arctic presents a tremendous opportunity. Throughout this volume we have noted areas of potential friction, but also areas of cooperation – and we believe that, on the whole, the opportunities presented by China's desire to be a "polar state" outweigh the dangers.

Indeed, given the maritime characteristics of the Arctic Ocean, excluding China entirely from the region would be impossible – from both a legal and a practical perspective. Attempting to do so would damage East-West relations to little purpose and ultimately end in failure. Rather, China's rise as an Arctic player can be managed, first, by robust international cooperation that includes Chinese input and, second, by strong domestic regulatory and investment institutions, many of which are already in place in Canada.

Justin Trudeau's Liberal Government: Shifting the Emphasis[3]

On October 19, 2015, Justin Trudeau's Liberal party won the Canadian federal election with a sweeping majority, replacing Stephen Harper's Conservatives. The new government has brought a change in political tone, affirming a renewed commitment to global climate change mitigation, a "return" to multilateralism and a foreign policy rooted in "responsible conviction," and a more constructive relationship with the United States.[4] Similar to previous Canadian governments, early indications suggest that Trudeau's Arctic agenda will prioritize domestic considerations (particularly those related to the health and resiliency of indigenous communities) but will continue to pursue positive international relationships that resonate with Canadian interests and values.

Respect for and reconciliation with indigenous peoples lies at the heart of the Liberal agenda. "No relationship is more important to me and to Canada than the one with indigenous Peoples," Trudeau highlighted in his mandate letter to each of his Cabinet ministers. "It is time for a renewed, nation-to-nation relationship with indigenous Peoples, based on recognition of rights, respect, co-operation, and partnership."[5] Accordingly, Canada will place the highest priority on ensuring that its activities in the Arctic (both domestic and international) acknowledge, protect, and promote indigenous peoples' rights – and, by extension, will insist that other Arctic stakeholders do the same. In May 2016, Canada officially lifted the qualifications to its endorsement of the United Nations Declaration on the Rights of Indigenous Peoples (UNDRIP) – qualifications that the Conservatives had registered over the requirement for "free, prior and informed consent" from indigenous peoples on issues that affected them. While disavowing that this new position gives indigenous groups a "veto" over development projects,[6] Canada's unqualified support of UNDRIP affirms a strong commitment to welcome "Indigenous peoples into the co-production of policy and joint priority-setting" within the Canadian political community.[7]

Prime Minister Trudeau has also declared that Canada "is back" when it comes to joining global efforts to mitigate climate change.[8] While the Harper government emphasized climate change adaptation measures in its Northern Strategy, the Liberals chastised their predecessors' alleged "refusal to take meaningful action on climate change," their lack of funding for science and "muzzling" of government scientists, and their prioritization of economic growth over environmental protection.[9] In signing the Paris Agreement on climate change, Canada has signalled its commitment to shift course, reduce greenhouse-gas emissions in concert with the international community, and promote a clean-energy future.[10] Along these lines, a major US-Canada Joint Statement of March 2016 articulated "a common vision of a prosperous and sustainable North American economy, and the opportunities afforded by advancing clean growth." Both Prime Minister Trudeau and President Obama cited the 2015 Paris Agreement as a pivotal moment, and committed to reduce methane emissions from the oil and gas sector as well as advance climate change action globally. They also reaffirmed "their commitment to working together to strengthen North American energy security, phase out fossil fuel subsidies, accelerate clean energy development to address climate change and to foster sustainable energy development and economic growth." Both countries also promised to "continue to respect and promote the rights of Indigenous peoples in all climate change decision making."[11]

Given Canada's longstanding position that its sovereignty in the Arctic is well established, there is unlikely to be any reversing of its basic stance on the rights and roles of Arctic states in regional governance. With Prime Minister Trudeau having criticized his predecessor for allegedly politicizing the scientifically informed legal process to delineate the outer limits of Canada's continental shelf in the Arctic, Canada is likely to emphasize openness, transparency, the rule of law, and science-based decision-making as it navigates the process established by article 76 of the LOSC for claims to extended continental shelves.[12] Similarly, the Liberal government is unlikely to succumb to alarmist narratives suggesting that military threats warrant a deviation from our established approach to managing outstanding sovereignty and status of water disputes.[13] While the new government is more likely to emphasize constructive diplomacy than adopt militant rhetoric on Arctic sovereignty issues, it is unlikely to adopt the de-militarization or nuclear-weapons free zone proposals promoted by a small number of left wing groups and commentators.[14] Instead, the Liberals have promised to maintain current National Defence spending levels, with "a renewed focus on surveillance and control of Canadian territory and approaches, particularly our Arctic regions, and will increase the size of the Canadian Rangers."[15] This continuity does not promote a "militarization" of the Arctic agenda, but simply represents a modest investment in appropriate defensive capabilities that help to deter would-be adversaries from attacking North America and, in a direct Arctic context, supports unconventional safety and security missions, such as law enforcement and disaster response.[16]

The Trudeau government is also emphasizing international cooperation in line with a more "nuanced" foreign policy. For example, newly appointed Minister of Global Affairs Stéphane Dion called for renewed "engagement" with Russia soon after taking office, despite Canada's ongoing displeasure with Russian expansionism and aggression in Ukraine.[17] This revised stance provoked debate among some Canadian commentators – who worried that it would send the wrong signals to an increasingly assertive Putin, who was already "pivoting" towards the Arctic as a "strategic frontier."[18] Others, however, applauded the desire to ensure that action on areas of common interest in the circumpolar world were not held hostage to geostrategic tensions in other parts of the world.[19]

While it is premature to determine whether the Trudeau government's policy priorities really "converge in Canada's North," thus investing the region with high political saliency in the country as a whole,[20] the prominent place of the Arctic in the Trudeau-Obama joint statement on environment, climate change, and Arctic leadership of March 2016 points in this direction. Emphasizing indigenous rights and knowledge, as well as "natural marine, land and air migrations that know no borders," the statement conceptualizes the Arctic as "the frontline of climate change" and articulates four main objectives relating to biodiversity, indigenous knowledge and decision-making, building a sustainable Arctic economy, and supporting Arctic communities.[21] These ideas are further developed in the joint statement of December 20, 2016, which identifies key actions to ensure "a strong, sustainable and viable Arctic economy and ecosystem, with low-impact shipping, science based management of marine resources, and free from the risks of offshore oil and gas activity."[22] Although articulated in a bilateral context, these statements provide the clearest indication of the international dimensions of the Trudeau government's "new" approach to Arctic leadership to date.

The first priority is conserving Arctic biodiversity through science-based decision-making by achieving national goals for land and marine protected areas. This entails working "directly with Indigenous partners, state, territorial and provincial governments" to set "a new, ambitious conservation goal for the Arctic based on the best available climate science and knowledge, Indigenous and non-Indigenous alike."[23] Realizing Arctic biodiversity goals will also require international partnerships. "Climate change is by far the most serious threat to Arctic biodiversity and exacerbates all other threats," the Arctic Council's Arctic Biodiversity Assessment (2013) concludes. Its findings also reinforce that many Arctic migratory bird species face threats from overharvesting and coastal and intertidal habitat changes while they are outside of the Arctic – particularly those that fly along the East Asian flyway. "Threatened migratory species require protection throughout the year, across their full migratory range and across multiple international boundaries," the assessment notes. "Arctic birds migrate far and wide, so Arctic migratory bird conservation is a truly global issue, of great importance to ecosystems and overall biodiversity in the Arctic and beyond."[24] Accordingly, Canada is likely to welcome the scientific involvement of China and other non-Arctic states in Arctic Council working groups on conservation issues, given that global partnerships are essential, in many cases, to achieve regional results.

The second objective – collaborating with "Indigenous and Arctic governments, leaders, and communities to more broadly and respectfully incorporate Indigenous science and traditional knowledge into decision-making"[25] – is a clear affirmation that the Trudeau Government intends to co-develop its Arctic domestic and foreign policies with northern indigenous interests at the forefront. In August 2016, the Government of Canada announced consultations to develop a "Shared Leadership Model" with northerners and other Canadian stakeholders to promote sustainability and "to ensure the many interests and uses of the Arctic are considered, particularly for those that make it their permanent home." It appointed Mary Simon, a prominent Inuit leader, as special representative on Arctic affairs to Minister of Indigenous and Northern Affairs Carolyn Bennett, to engage with Canadians to discern new goals for marine and terrestrial conservation, Arctic environmental health, and the well-being of northerners. Although the social, economic, and environmental considerations identified have a primarily domestic orientation, Simon's mandate also includes guidance to consider linkages to international efforts.[26] Given the fundamental principles promoted by Inuit Circumpolar Council Canada and the other permanent participants about the application of indigenous knowledge to the work of the Arctic Council and to scientific practice more generally, the Trudeau Government is likely to insist that foreign partnerships recognize, respect, and trust the importance of traditional knowledge holders in decision-making and policy development.[27]

The third goal is the Trudeau government's commitment to building a sustainable Arctic economy based on scientific evidence, with commercial activities occurring "only when the highest safety and environmental standards are met, including national and global climate and environmental goals, and Indigenous rights and agreements,"[28] The sub-priorities under this initiative are of obvious interest to other states, shipping companies, and resource developers. Canada and the US Coast Guard are pursuing the creation of low-impact shipping corridors and consistent policies for ship operations, taking into account sensitive ecological and cultural areas used by Indigenous communities, vessel traffic patterns, and the threat posed by hydrocarbons. Towards this end, Canada has committed to implement Northern Marine Transportation Corridors, beginning with a process of identifying necessary marine infrastructure and regional navigational and emergency response services, as well as initiating a new training program for northerners ("particularly indigenous peoples") who wish to join the marine field.[29] Furthermore, by engaging indigenous and Northern communities to develop a Canadian Arctic marine governance model "that is environmentally and socially responsible, including respecting modern northern treaties,"[30] the Canadian government is signalling a "for northerners, by northerners" approach that will more fully implement mechanisms such as the Nunavut Marine Council that empower northerners.[31] By identifying "sustainable shipping lanes" and providing more icebreaking, hydrographic, charting, and navigation services, this process will promote safe shipping activities and make Canadian Arctic waters more attractive to both domestic and international users, thus encouraging more maritime activity in the region.

Under the auspices of sustainable economic development, Canada and the United States also indicate a shared commitment to seek a binding international agreement to prevent the opening of unregulated fisheries in the Central Arctic Ocean, building "on a precautionary, science-based principle to commercial fishing that both countries have put in place in their Arctic waters."[32] This builds upon the July 2015 declaration by the five Arctic coastal states to prohibit unregulated commercial fishing on the Arctic high seas until a robust fisheries management regime is established to ensure sustainable management of stocks. Although fishing in the central Arctic Ocean is unlikely in the near future, and therefore the creation of an internationally recognized Regional Fishery Management Organization is not immediately necessary, the Arctic coastal states acknowledge that these interim measures do intersect with the international legal rights of other states. The "all interested States" that will need to be engaged "in a broader process to develop measures consistent with this Declaration"[33] include China.

The March bilateral statement also obliged Canada and the United States to ensure that oil and gas development and exploration activities "align with science-based standards between the two nations that ensure appropriate preparation for operating in Arctic conditions, including robust and effective well control and emergency response measures."[34] In light of low oil and gas prices, the low carbon climate agenda espoused by both Trudeau and Obama, and ongoing technical challenges associated with the extraction of hydrocarbons in the North American Arctic offshore,[35] one could argue that the political costs of signalling a pro-environmental political stand in this sector were slight. Accordingly, Canada announced in December 2016 that it "is designating all Arctic Canadian waters as indefinitely off limits to future offshore Arctic oil and gas licensing, to be reviewed every 5 years through a climate and marine science-based life-cycle assessment."[36] While dramatic symbolically, this action had little practical effect given the lack of exploration activity in these waters. Furthermore, Heather Exner-Pirot notes that the ban was announced without previous consultations with northern territorial and indigenous leaders (which seems to contradict the Liberals' overarching philosophy of northerner engagement in decision-making), indicating a "victory for global over local interests" that failed to address the "Arctic paradox" associated with non-renewable resource development that exacerbates global warming and the desire by northerners for sustainable development through a resource economy.[37] Although this particular announcement does not affect terrestrial energy exploration or the mining sector, it may also point to a Liberal government that is less supportive of promoting non-renewable resource development more generally both philosophically and as a way to differentiate itself from its Conservative predecessor.

Fourth, the Obama-Trudeau statement in March 2016 highlighted a joint commitment to support strong Arctic communities by "defining new approaches and exchanging best practices to strengthen the resilience of Arctic communities and continuing to support the well-being of Arctic residents, in particular respecting the rights and territory of Indigenous peoples."[38] Indigenous and environmental organizations in Canada applauded the statement, with national Inuit leader Natan Obed stating that "the final language in this document really spoke to Inuit" and heralding it "a tremendous breakthrough for Indigenous people who live in the Arctic."[39] By December, Canada committed:

> to co-develop a new Arctic Policy Framework, with Northerners, Territorial and Provincial governments, and First Nations, Inuit, and Métis People that will replace Canada's Northern Strategy. The Framework will focus on priority areas identified

by the Minister of Indigenous and Northern Affairs' Special Representative, including education, infrastructure, and economic development. The Framework will include an Inuit-specific component, created in partnership with Inuit, as Inuit Nunangat comprises over a third of Canada's land mass and over half of Canada's coast line, and as Inuit modern treaties govern the entirety of this jurisdictional space. In parallel, Canada is reducing the reliance of Northern communities on diesel, by deploying energy efficiency and renewable power. Canada will also, with Indigenous and Northern partners, explore how to support and protect the future of the Arctic Ocean's "last ice area" where summer ice remains each year.[40]

This domestically oriented agenda[41] indicates a return to the primacy of socio-cultural and environmental priorities over the more hard security, resource development focus of the Harper government.[42]

Despite the new Trudeau government's explicit efforts to create a "new Arctic Policy Framework" and its eschewing of conventional sovereignty-security rhetoric to frame its approach, the few political speeches that its representatives have given on Arctic issues resurrect the romantic, nationalistic terms extolling Canada's pride and unique responsibilities as a Northern nation that featured so prominently in the Harper government's speeches (and those of his political predecessors).[43] Parliamentary Secretary for Global Affairs Pamela Goldsmith-Jones, delivering a speech on behalf of Minister Dion to mark the twentieth anniversary of the Arctic Council in September 2016, proclaimed:

> Yes, we have a northern soul: 'The true north strong and free.' Few places on earth evoke more glorious images than the North. It is the land of the aurora, where the northern lights dance across the darkened sky at nightfall, and the land of the midnight sun and of polar days that go on forever under light that never fades.
>
> Our northern belonging fills us with pride – a pride that we owe first and foremost to the Canadians who actually live in the North … It is all the more important to remember that the

well-being of northern people is being challenged by great shifts in the North's physical and economic environments. The Arctic is attracting more and more economic activity. It will be the site of major, new economic projects. Its resources are increasingly coveted. Its navigation routes are opening. All the while, its ecosystem remains as fragile as ever.

The North is an essential part of our future and a place of extraordinary potential. More than ever, the world will count on Canada as a responsible steward of this great barometer of our planet. Northern resources, explored responsibly, offer huge potential for increased economic development. But if these resources are exploited irresponsibly, it will be a disaster not only for us but for all of humanity.[44]

A few weeks later, Goldsmith-Jones told the Arctic Circle in Reykjavik that, "for Canadians, the North captures our imagination like no other part of our country."[45] This idea of Canadian Arctic exceptionalism, which firmly embeds the North in identity politics, is evoked to inspire a sense of responsibility, serving as a call to action to protect northerners and the environment from emerging threats – an obligation that Canadians are asked to bear to all their country to realize its future potential and for the good of the planet as a whole. Where the interests of non-Arctic states, such as China, will fit in this agenda remains to be seen.

In his book *Engaging China*, Paul Evans argues that, under Harper's Conservatives "few if any ideas [were] in play" in terms of Canada's engagement strategy for China. "Nothing in Conservative foreign policy outlines an overarching strategy related to world order, China's place in it, and a comprehensive agenda of priorities," he observes. "There is little emphasis on the geopolitical dimensions of China's rise and a visible allergy to framing any Canadian role as a bridge or middle power in facilitating China's emergence as a responsible international actor. Instead, the emphasis is on managing and facilitating a transactional relationship focused on trade and investment."[46] Rather than pursuing "a narrowly mercantilist approach," Evans advocates for "an integrated commitment" involving "a combination of bilateral initiatives ... renewed support for regional institutions and cooperative security arrangements in addressing a range of conventional and non-traditional security issues; and a diplomatic commitment to playing a balancing role in encouraging a positive outcome in US-China relations."[47] In his plea for "China realism," former diplomat David Mulroney insists that Canadians need to wake up to China's increasing importance and influence – with all the opportunities and challenges this presents. "We should see China neither as the sum of all our fears nor as the answer to all our prayers," he suggests. "We need to see China steadily and see it whole, its dynamism and innovation, its aggressiveness and insecurity. And we need to craft an intelligently self-interested, thoughtful, and long-term approach to the relationship."[48]

The Trudeau government's approach to China, while still being defined, is clearly intended to increase engagement and trade and move away from the somewhat cold relationship that Prime Minster Harper had with the Communist government in Beijing. On the surface, that relationship has already been rejuvenated. Trudeau visited China in August 2016 where he was hailed for saying that "a stronger and deeper relationship with China is essential if we are to achieve our own objectives" and "any economic strategy that ignores China, or that treats that valuable relationship as anything less than critically important, is not just short-sighted, it's irresponsible."[49] The Chinese media approved of the message, with the Chinese newspaper *Global Times* noting that: "During Harper's time in office, China-Canada ties were constantly disturbed by issues such as human rights. The overall trend of bilateral relations was chilly." Quoting Wang Xuedong, Deputy Dean of Sun Yat-sun University, the paper contrasted this with Trudeau, who "is young and open-minded. He believes the world is developing and developed countries should not remain bound to an old mindset."[50] In a return visit the next month, Chinese Premier Li Keqiang effused: "this is the season for the fiery maple in Canada, symbolizing the prosperity of China-Canada all-round co-operation." His visit, he claimed, would bring together "true friends who feel close even when thousands of miles apart."[51] To make the point more dramatically, three Chinese warships paid a port visit to Victoria three months later, to much fanfare.[52]

In August 2016 Prime Minister Trudeau moved to establish more formal economic ties, with an application to join the Chinese-led Asian Infrastructure Investment Bank, an institution designed to provide low-cost development loans to Asian countries. Prime Minister Harper had made a point of opting out of this new organization when it was launched in 2015, and reversing that decision was seen as an early effort by the Liberals to build trust as well as political and economic ties with China.[53] On the trade file, Trudeau and Chinese Premier Li Keqiang also used the prime minister's September 2016 trip to China to announce the start of talks with the goal of doubling trade between the two countries by 2025 and, that December, International Trade Minister Chrystia Freeland announced that the two countries would begin exploring the possibility of a free trade agreement.[54] China is Canada's second largest trading partner after the United States and, with NAFTA jeopardized by the protectionist policies of President Donald Trump, Asian trade may prove more essential to Canadian prosperity.[55] Talking up its potential in a January 2016 interview with the *Globe and Mail*, Chinese Vice-Minister of Financial and Economic Affairs Han Jun stated that "if there is an FTA arrangement between China and Canada, you can see a flooding of potash, agricultural products and energy products from Canada to the market of China." However, Han said, China had its own demands, namely the removal of restrictions put in place by the Harper government on Chinese state-owned investments in Canada's oil and gas sector and a commitment to build an energy pipeline from the Alberta oil fields to the Pacific Coast.[56]

While the broad outlines of a Liberal China policy are clearly defined by a desire for improved diplomatic relations and increased trade, the government has been short on details about how Canada will proceed. Trudeau delivered no major policy speech on China in his first year in office, nor was that country mentioned in his mandate letters to any of his ministers.[57] Paul Evans notes that Canada lacks a "whole-country approach to China ... or even a whole-government approach," with different views prevailing in different ministries. Charles Burton, a former Canadian diplomat in China now based at Brock University, sees the Liberal policy as one of looking "to get the prosperity out of a rising China." Trudeau, he says, "sees [China] as inevitable to Canada's future, and therefore he's trying to satisfy Canadians' concerns over human rights and environment, but this seems to be mostly superficial and lacking in substance."[58] In short, Canada's new China policy remains a work in progress.

How the Trudeau government's strategic policy towards China will relate to the Arctic also remains uncertain. Chinese interest in Canadian Arctic resources would certainly be piqued by free (or freer) trade and by a relaxation of the government's restrictions on investments and acquisitions by Chinese SOEs. Likewise, a government warmer to the idea of Chinese investment in infrastructure might speed up projects like the stalled Izok Lake mines and open up the possibility of new partnerships. The security implications of this opening aside,[59] a more open and cordial Sino-Canadian trading relationship would only increase investment in the North and hasten development. Whether the Liberals can secure that investment without sacrificing too much in the way of security, and without suffering political damage for ignoring China's continuing human rights abuses, remains unanswered. This will be the tight-rope for the Liberals to walk, and the government's dexterity in this respect remains to be tested.

Debunking the Myths

China is a Threat to Arctic Regional Security

In 2008, PLA Senior Colonel Han Xudong warned that, because of sovereignty disputes, the possibility of the use of force cannot be ruled out in the Arctic.[60] A growing scholarly consensus suggests, however, a very low probability that Arctic coastal states will use military force to advance their sovereignty or jurisdictional claims. The Arctic Five have promoted a peaceful, diplomatic message since 2008 and, in spite of growing tensions with Russia, the Arctic remains a peaceful and well-governed region – a fact highlighted by recent boundary agreements and ongoing military cooperation between most circumpolar states.

China is unlikely to upset this framework. Its Arctic military capabilities are limited, in both quantity and quality, and it has no reason to enhance them. China possesses few aircraft with the range necessary to threaten the region and there would be little to threaten if it were to try. Its nuclear submarine fleet, while technically capable of under-ice travel, is small and ill-equipped for Arctic operations.[61] In short, China's ability to project military power into the region is minimal at best – a fact unlikely to change in the foreseeable future. Beijing is also publically committed to international norms on sovereignty, and it is probable that its core strategic focus will remain in its local Asian "neighbourhood." From a diplomatic standpoint, it is also unlikely that any particular Chinese military interest in the North will ever be worth upsetting Russia, Canada, or the United States – all major trading partners and/or suppliers of natural resources.

Chinese officials stress that "all Chinese activities in the Arctic are and will be solely for peaceful purposes." This is consistent with China's Information

Office of the State Council white paper on "China's Peaceful Development," released in September 2011.[62] In her influential 2010 article on the "Status and Prospects of China's Arctic Policy" (which has been translated into Chinese and is quoted widely), Russian Arctic commentator A.O. Baranikova argues that China will follow its traditional five principles of peaceful co-existence in foreign relations. China recognizes that Arctic states have the most important say in Arctic affairs and it will pursue its interests surrounding resources and shipping routes using diplomatic and economic strategies.[63]

Shipping

China will continue to express interest in the economic opportunities presented by a changing Arctic, and rather than working in opposition to coastal states it will likely engage more actively through existing regional and international instruments – such as the Arctic Council and the International Maritime Organization. Such multilateral institutions offer China a vehicle for influencing international law and shipping regulations (both in the Arctic and elsewhere) in a way that would not be possible through bilateral negotiations with Arctic states. This is not a uniquely Chinese approach; trading nations have long looked to international institutions and legal frameworks to guard their rights to transit and trade around the world, and the Arctic can be seen as an extension of that pattern.

Although the Chinese government does not have a clear policy regarding the Northern Sea Route, the "over the top" transpolar route, or the Northwest Passage, it may prepare for future Arctic shipping by enhancing its northeastern port infrastructure and building its experience in Arctic navigation by using the NSR to ship select commodities. Meanwhile, the risk of a Chinese ship transiting the Northwest Passage without seeking Canadian authorization is very low. There appears to be no benefit in doing so while the political fallout would surely impede the efforts of any Chinese company looking to win Canadian government approval for northern resource projects. The NSR will continue to be the better-serviced and more navigable route for the foreseeable future. Moreover, as argued in chapter three, Canada and China have a commonality of interest in their interpretations of the status of vital straits. Furthermore, unofficial comments by Chinese officials indicate that any Chinese shipping through Canada's internal waters will comply with Canadian regulations and controls. This position is supported by favourable assessments of Canada's sovereignty position by several Chinese scholars.

Arctic Resources

Although Western commentators debate the extent to which resources drive China's Arctic objectives, Beijing's strategic emphasis on secure resource imports will sustain its interest in the development of Arctic mineral and hydrocarbon projects. China perceives energy supply, in particular, through a security lens and has invested hundreds of billions of dollars to secure access to future and current oil and gas production from the Russian Arctic offshore and Siberian fields. Given China's desire to wean its energy sector off coal, and in light of Russia's increasing political and economic ostracization, the relationship between Chinese and Russian SOEs will likely expand even further.

This may be bad news for Canadian oil and gas producers, particularly if China feels its energy needs can be satisfied by Russian companies with infrastructure built by Chinese money. The recent moratorium on Arctic offshore energy development may dampen some of the boosterism around North American Arctic resources that has dominated media headlines over the past decade, but rich terrestrial energy and mineral deposits remain to be tapped. And China has demonstrated a strategic eye for resource development – preferring to vary its sources to ensure it is not beholden to any one power or group. As such, Chinese investment in Canadian Arctic oil and gas may be forthcoming once the Canadian regulatory regime is solidified and global oil prices begin to recover from their 2014–15 lows. In this Canada is already a leader: it has strong institutions, robust legal standards, stringent environmental regulations, and is increasingly cautious about the scale of state-owned investment in its economy. Although Chinese corporations are likely to place a higher priority on more easily accessible resources in other parts of the world, it is possible that well capitalized Chinese SOEs, with long investment timeframes, will continue to make strategic investments in the northern energy and mining sectors. Vigilance is required – not panic. If Canada aspires to feed Asian markets, and if Northern communities aspire to participate in the global economy, dealing with China is a must.

Globally, China's emphasis on resource acquisition often relegates environmental protection to a secondary consideration. Given Canada's explicit emphasis on sustainable development and environmental provisions in land claim agreements with indigenous groups, it should remain attentive to development projects in the North to ensure that they meet all of Canada's environmental regulations – and ensure that such regulations are sufficiently rigorous. Similarly, Canada should continue to pursue and implement instruments, both domestically and multilaterally, to ensure safe and secure Arctic shipping of resources.

Polar Research

Commentators who suggest that China's recent investments in Arctic science outclass Canada's might be considered key allies in China's implicit propaganda campaign to trumpet its polar status and achievements. While China's investments in icebreaking capabilities, polar research stations, and research personnel are impressive, media and scholarly depictions of Chinese capacity tends to inflate actual research outputs and their impact on decision-making bodies. Whereas Canada is a world leader in Arctic science, China aspires to be one.

Accordingly, there are opportunities for Canada to accede to China's request for more regular and formal scientific collaboration, particularly in the natural sciences. Welcoming Chinese specialists to come to Canada to undertake research, particularly in partnership with Canadian academic experts and indigenous knowledge holders, will provide opportunities to share best practices and to ensure that Chinese researchers develop a heightened respect for the place and value of indigenous knowledge and science in producing more holistic understandings of Arctic dynamics. Promoting Canada's new High Arctic Research Station (CHARS) in Cambridge Bay as a world-class hub for scientific and technological research will not only affirm Canadian leadership in polar science but also leverage growing Chinese expertise (and funding) on areas of common interest.[64] Using CHARS to facilitate joint projects also avoids the anxiety in some Canadian circles associated with China building its own research infrastructure on Arctic soil. Furthermore, encouraging more Sino-Canadian academic exchanges and conferences on Arctic themes, as the Nordic countries have done in recent years, will help to clarify our respective research interests and priorities in the natural and social sciences.

If China is serious about conducting substantive, high-level research and using this to influence regional and global decisions – with associated benefits for "political education" in China to boost government legitimacy and deflect attention from more contentious social issues – collaboration and cooperation with Arctic states will be essential. Conversely, Canada can take advantage of this fact by using such collaboration and cooperative opportunities to socialize China to the values and norms associated with Canada's Arctic priorities. If well orchestrated and based on mutual respect, polar research could serve as a conduit for positive relationship and awareness building, scientific burden-sharing, and the co-creation and dissemination of expert knowledge that can inform evidence-based policy-making in both countries – and throughout the circumpolar world.

Remaining Challenges

Arctic Governance

Broader international debates about Arctic governance (and the misperception that it is weak or lacking), coupled with a growing awareness that changes in the North will have global consequences, have opened the door for non-Arctic states such as China to stake a legitimate claim of interest in what is happening in the Arctic. The simple fact that some Chinese commentators have been aggressive in questioning the role and rights of the Arctic coastal states, the limitations of the Arctic Council, and the stability of the region should come as no surprise to Western scholars who have followed the debate among Arctic states over the past decade. According to some Chinese scholars, the diversity of institutions within which matters of relevance to the Arctic can be pursued suggests that "a politically valid and legally binding Arctic governance system has yet to be established."[65] While some of these Chinese viewpoints appear distorted from an expert perspective, it is important to remember that Canadian scholars have also based some bold assessments on ignorance of international law, selective use of evidence, misperceptions, and aspirations (rather than realities). Furthermore, it should come as no surprise that the conversation on China's appropriate roles and responsibilities in the Arctic is not monolithic. Diverse viewpoints should be encouraged, and, where these perspectives challenge the prevalent ideas offered by the Arctic states, those ideas should be countered through respectful debate.

While some Chinese commentators have questioned the current Arctic governance regime rooted in the primacy of Arctic states, China successfully applied for and received accredited observer status at the Arctic Council in 2013, indicating at least a basic acceptance of that system. Although its revised application to the Council remains classified, it was based upon the new Nuuk criteria for observers which requires an acknowledgement of the principles of state sovereignty and sovereign rights in the Arctic as well as indigenous rights. Accordingly, Chinese official statements, as well as most academic and media commentary in that country, have tended to emphasize the country's respect for or acquiescence to these principles since 2013.

Over the next decade, it is likely that China will continue to emphasize the importance of expanded international cooperation in the Arctic, particularly related to scientific research on climate change, rather than cooperation limited to the Arctic coastal states or Arctic Council member states. As part of its global search for resources, China will continue to express interest in energy and mineral deposits in Arctic regions. Given that the vast majority of these resources fall under the clear control of the Arctic states under international law, and resources in "the Area" (the central Arctic Basin beyond national jurisdiction) will not be viable for exploitation in the foreseeable future, Chinese interests can most efficiently and effectively secure access through investments and compliance with national regulations. The billions of dollars recently invested by Chinese SOEs in the Russian Arctic, and to a lesser extent in other circumpolar nations, is a clear sign that Beijing intends to take advantage of northern resources from within the framework of internationally recognized state sovereignty and jurisdiction.

China and the Area beyond National Jurisdiction

By far the most quoted line from Chinese officials by Western media and scholarly sources is Rear Admiral Yin Zhuo's quip that "The Arctic belongs to all the people around the world, as no nation has sovereignty over it ... China must play an indispensable role in Arctic exploration as we have one-fifth of the world's population."[66] This phrase is a convenient tool for Western writers to cast China as a revisionist actor that does not recognize Arctic state sovereignty or sovereign rights. Alarmist commentators, however, fail to acknowledge that Admiral Yin is correct, insofar as a large portion of the central Arctic Ocean does not fall under state sovereignty. Hence, Canada and other Arctic states had best prepare for China, and the rest of the world, to become more involved in Arctic affairs. This suggests the urgent need to put in place a regional fisheries management regime that polices Arctic fisheries so that they do not suffer the same fate as those off Canada's East Coast and in other areas where unsustainable practices persist around the world. The first step to this is to gather the essential data by studying the region's stocks and their movements, an inherently collaborative process that must include China. Convincing China to adhere to an Arctic fisheries management regime will be difficult; it has already rejected similar efforts in Antarctic waters. Nevertheless, it will certainly not adhere to a regime covering international waters that it has not had a role in developing.

Canada's Response: Engagement and Hedging

As in all other issues that surround China's rise, the best way forward is a combination of engagement and hedging.[67] Engagement begins with a circumspect and informed debate about the implications of China as an Arctic player. The Arctic states, including Canada, must clearly discern which issues are appropriately managed at the national, bilateral, regional, and global levels. To simply claim "rights," as some Chinese academics have done, without rigorously identifying what they are and why those rights exist at a given scale, is insufficient. Political scientist Timothy Wright notes that "catchy phrases, and notions of China having a right in the Arctic, amount to nothing more than *argument ad infinitum* or *argumentum ad nauseam*, varieties of the logical fallacy of proof by assertion. Commentators usually do not articulate justifications to back these phrases and seem to be based on the simple notion that China, as a major state, is entitled to pursue its self-interests in the Arctic. Reasoning such as this will not succeed against the Arctic Five's … more legitimate claims."[68] By extension, the sophisticated presentations from the Chinese Institute for Maritime Affairs and other Chinese scholars at the Sino-Canadian Exchanges on Arctic Issues from 2010–16 indicate a more nuanced appreciation of regional governance, where China fits, and how this respects the sovereignty and sovereign rights of the Arctic states.

Second, it is imperative to identify the limits of China's ambition. The polar regions are "convenient locations" for Beijing to demonstrate China's restored international status as a global power. Accordingly, it is important to discern what activities China would like to take or participate in to build "prestige," and what substantive contributions it believes are actually necessary. Both Jakobson and Wright note that the Chinese Communist Party recognizes that its rise to power and greater prominence evokes anxiety in the rest of the world.[69] The challenge for scholars, policy-makers, and security analysts is in distinguishing between which Chinese actions might be perceived as threatening from an Arctic-specific perspective and which developments should be assessed through a global strategic lens. In any event, with the world's eyes on China in the Arctic, its ability to behave in a fashion wildly inconsistent with the preferences of Arctic states should be limited provided those states engage China openly.

The third component of engagement is institutional enmeshing.[70] Countries the world over have had a modicum of success in enmeshing China into institutions as a way of modifying the excesses of Chinese behaviour. Allowing China to join the Arctic Council as an accredited observer is the first step in this process. Arctic states now have a venue to express their interests and preferences to China and to demonstrate an "Arctic" way of thinking. Simultaneously, the Arctic Council alone is insufficient to socialize China into Arctic norms. Engagement in every aspect of Arctic governance is necessary. Pursuant to its "shared Arctic leadership model" with the United States, Canada should pursue opportunities – within the Arctic Council, in other multilateral fora, and through bilateral channels – to work with China in pursuing Arctic conservation goals, ensuring that commercial activities conform to rigorous environmental and sustainable development standards, promoting the incorporation of indigenous science and traditional knowledge in Chinese research and decision-making, and sharing best practices through regular dialogue.

At the same time, it is important to guard against the potential for duplicity. Chinese policymakers believe they live in a Hobbesian world, where the powerful do what they can and the weak suffer what they must.[71] States around the world have hedged against the potential dark side of China's rise in various ways. First, it always helps to have a powerful ally and, in Canada's case, this means the United States.[72] While Canada's "special relationship" with its southern/northwestern neighbour has made the two "premier partners" in Arctic affairs since the early Cold War (a relationship reinforced by the recent joint statements between Trudeau and Obama), the transition to the new Trump Administration may challenge aspects of this relationship and heighten expectations about what Canada should contribute to Arctic defence.[73] Second, it is important to prevent China from gaining too much influence over smaller Arctic states (the kind of leverage demonstrated by China pressuring Cambodia to modify the agenda to its benefit at the 2011 meeting of ASEAN). Arctic states should thus support one another to develop strong investment and regulatory frameworks to avoid reliance on Chinese investment or labour to fulfill their national development aspirations.

The final component of hedging relates to national defence. It is appropriate for Arctic states to develop the capability to enforce their jurisdiction in their national waters, particularly as these waters become more accessible. This being said, investments in new defence capabilities should be clearly thought out and focused on realistic threats requiring a response. In the foreseeable future these threats will likely relate to environmental degradation, smuggling, search and rescue, criminal activity, and disaster relief.[74] Preparing to defend the Canadian Arctic from Chinese naval incursions (or those of any state for that matter) is simply not an immediate or realistic requirement. Preparing for Chinese-backed shipping or resource activities and attendant "soft" security challenges is a matter of more immediate concern. For example, Canadian Armed Forces assets may be useful in monitoring Chinese scientific research and resource development activities in the region as part of the government's broader public safety and security efforts – but they will have little value in defending either sovereignty or security. Accordingly, China's interests and activities in the Arctic should be considered as part of a more general consideration of the threats and hazards to which the Canadian Armed Forces, as part of a broader whole-of-government approach, should be prepared to respond in concert with the Government of Canada's broader Northern strategy over the next decade.[75]

China's interest in the Arctic does not exist in a vacuum. It is only one part of that country's broader push to secure resources and shipping routes around the world, while confirming its position as a power with global interests (if not necessarily global reach). Despite this, the Arctic is not a core Chinese interest. Its value to China is potential, not actual. As such, Beijing is unlikely to endanger any of its actual core interests or relationships while seeking greater influence in the Arctic region. The country's relationships with Russia and the United States are vital on both the economic and geopolitical level; any action that these states might perceive as either a challenge to their sovereignty or a threat to their northern security would have global ramifications, dramatically outweighing any benefit China may derive from an aggressive Arctic foreign policy. Likewise, China has worked hard to build economic relationships with Canada, Iceland, and Greenland – countries with bountiful resources that Beijing has an interest in developing. The popular backlash against the perception of growing Chinese influence in each of these countries demonstrates how carefully China and its SOEs must tread when doing business, and how damaging to its global interests a confrontation in the Arctic would be.

For these strategic and pragmatic reasons, China is playing out its Arctic ambitions through multilateral fora and bilateral channels in concert with the Arctic states and other interested parties. That has been Beijing's modus operandi thus far and looks to be the path China will continue to follow in the future. If this is the case, China's Arctic activities should not cause acute anxieties – and its involvement in the North may even lend greater legitimacy to Arctic state sovereignty, and to any international governance framework that emerges for Arctic areas outside of that state sovereignty. In his 2014 study of China's emerging Arctic strategies, Marc Lanteigne highlights an old Chinese proverb: "When the wind of change blows, some build walls, while others build windmills."[76] It is felicitous advice for Arctic powers struggling to adjust to China's expanding global interests. In matters of shipping, resource development, science, and even governance, Chinese interest in the region can be harnessed and turned to productive purposes and, with careful attention, may contribute constructively and substantively to positive circumpolar development.

Notes

Introduction

1 "The Arctic Council at 20 Years: More Necessary than Ever," Address by Parliamentary Secretary Pamela Goldsmith-Jones at Arctic Circle Assembly, October 8, 2016, Reykjavik, Iceland, http://news.gc.ca/web/article-en.do?nid=1139819.

2 Yang Jian, "China and Arctic Affairs," *2012 Arctic Yearbook*, ed. Lassi Heininen (Akureryi: Northern Research Forum, 2012), http://arcticyearbook.com/index.php/commentaries#commentary2.

3 *CBC News*, "Harper Promises to Defend Arctic Sovereignty," August 12, 2006. On Harper and Arctic sovereignty, see P. Whitney Lackenbauer, *From Polar Race to Polar Saga: An Integrated Strategy for Canada and the Circumpolar World* (Toronto: Canadian International Council, July 2009); P. Whitney Lackenbauer, "'Use it or Lose it,' History, and the Fourth Surge," in *Canada and Arctic Sovereignty and Security: Historical Perspectives*, ed. P. Whitney Lackenbauer (Calgary: Centre for Military and Strategic Studies/University of Calgary Press, 2011), 423–36; Klaus Dodds, "We are a Northern Country: Stephen Harper and the Canadian Arctic," *Polar Record* 47, no. 4 (2011): 371–4; Klaus Dodds, "Graduated and Paternal Sovereignty: Stephen Harper, Operation Nanook 10, and the Canadian Arctic," *Environment and Planning D: Society and Space* 30, no. 6 (2012): 989–1010; François Perreault, "The Arctic Linked to the Emerging Dominant Ideas in Canada's Foreign and Defence Policy," *Northern Review* 33 (2011): 47–67; Franklyn Griffiths, Rob Huebert, and P. Whitney Lackenbauer, *Canada and the Changing Arctic: Sovereignty, Security and Stewardship* (Waterloo: Wilfrid Laurier University Press, 2011); Petra Dolata, "A 'New' Canada in the Arctic? Arctic Policies under Harper," *Études canadiennes: Revue interdisciplinaire des études canadiennes en France* 78 (2015): 131–54; P. Whitney Lackenbauer and Ryan Dean, eds., *Canada's Northern Strategy under the Harper Conservatives: Key Speeches and Documents on Sovereignty, Security, and Governance, 2006–15* (Waterloo and Calgary: Centre on Foreign Policy and Federalism/Centre for Military, Security and Strategic Studies, 2016).

4 See P. Whitney Lackenbauer and Rob Huebert, "Premier Partners: Canada, the United States and Arctic Security," *Canadian Foreign Policy Journal* 20, no. 3 (2014): 320–33.

5 Rob Huebert, "Return of the Vikings," *Globe and Mail*, December 28, 2002.

6   For developments regarding Hans Island see Huebert, "Return of the 'Vikings': The
       Canadian-Danish Dispute over Hans Island – New Challenges for the Control of the
       Canadian North," in *Breaking Ice – Renewable Resource and Ocean Management in
       the Canadian North*, eds. Fikret Berkes et al. (Calgary: University of Calgary Press,
       2005), 319–36; Michael Byers, *International Law and the Arctic* (Cambridge: Cambridge
       University Press, 2013), 10–16.

7   See, for example, P. Whitney Lackenbauer, "Mirror Images? Canada, Russia, and the
       Circumpolar World," *International Journal* 65, no. 4 (Autumn 2010): 879–97; Kari
       Roberts, "Jets, Flags, and a New Cold War? Demystifying Russia's Arctic Intentions,"
       International Journal 65, no. 4 (2010): 957–76; Frédéric Lasserre, Jérôme Le Roy,
       and Richard Garon, "Is There an Arms Race in the Arctic?" *Journal of Military and
       Strategic Studies* 14, nos. 3–4 (2013); Aldo Chircop, Ivan Bunik, Moira L. McConnell,
       and Kristoffer Svendsen, "Course Convergence? Comparative Perspectives on the
       Governance of Navigation and Shipping in Canadian and Russian Arctic Waters,"
       Ocean Yearbook Online 28, no. 1 (2014): 291–327; Kari Roberts, "Why Russia Will Play
       by the Rules in the Arctic," *Canadian Foreign Policy Journal* 21, no. 2 (2015): 112–28;
       P. Whitney Lackenbauer, "Canada & Russia: Toward an Arctic Agenda," *Global Brief*
       (Summer/Fall 2016): 21–5.

8   On these themes in the Canadian context see, for example, Rob Huebert, "The Shipping
       News Part II: How Canada's Arctic Sovereignty Is on Thinning Ice," *International
       Journal* 58, no. 3 (Summer 2003), 295–308; Ken Coates, P. Whitney Lackenbauer, Bill
       Morrison, and Greg Poelzer, *Arctic Front: Defending Canada in the Far North* (Toronto:
       Thomas Allen and Son Ltd., 2008); Franklyn Griffiths, Rob Huebert, and P. Whitney
       Lackenbauer, *Canada and the Changing Arctic: Sovereignty, Security and Stewardship*
       (Waterloo: Wilfrid Laurier University Press, 2011); Michael Byers, *Who Owns the
       Arctic?* (Vancouver: Douglas and McIntyre, 2009). International overviews include:
       Scott G. Borgerson, "Arctic Meltdown: The Economic and Security Implications of
       Global Warming," *Foreign Affairs* (March/April 2008): 63–77; Barry Scott Zellen, *Arctic
       Doom, Arctic Boom: The Geopolitics of Climate Change in the Arctic* (Santa Barbara:
       Praeger, 2009); Charles Emmerson, *The Future History of the Arctic* (New York: Public
       Affairs, 2010).

9   See, for example, Rob Huebert, "How Russia's Move into Crimea Upended Canada's
       Arctic Strategy," *Globe and Mail*, April 2, 2014; Michael Byers, "Squeeze Putin, Yes,
       But the Arctic is Not Ukraine," *Globe and Mail*, May 1, 2014; Adam Lajeunesse and
       Whitney Lackenbauer, "Canadian Arctic Security: Russia's Not Coming," *Arctic Deeply*,
       April 19, 2016, https://www.opencanada.org/features/canadian-arctic-security-russias-
       not-coming/; Lackenbauer, "Canada & Russia: Toward an Arctic Agenda," *Global Brief*
       (Summer/Fall 2016): 21–5. In this volume, see "News Release: Baird Visits Norway,
       Reaffirms Canada's Position on Ukraine and the Arctic," August 22, 2014, doc. 237.

10   See, for example, P. Whitney Lackenbauer, "Mixed Messages from an 'Arctic
       Superpower'? Sovereignty, Security, and Canada's Northern Strategy," *Atlantisch
       Perspectief* 3 (2011): 4–8.

11   The Trudeau Government, elected in fall 2015, has indicated that it intends to "refresh"
       Canada's Northern Strategy and Arctic Foreign Policy in 2017. In August 2016, the
       Minister of Indigenous and Northern Affairs, Carolyn Bennett, appointed Mary

Simon as the Minister's Special Representative "responsible for leading engagements and providing advice to the Government of Canada on the development of a new Shared Arctic Leadership Model." The process remains ongoing as of January 2017. In his December 2016 joint statement with President Obama, Prime Minister Trudeau emphasized that "Canada is committing to co-develop a new Arctic Policy Framework, with Northerners, Territorial and Provincial governments, and First Nations, Inuit, and Métis People that will replace Canada's Northern Strategy." The statement indicated that this new framework "will include priority areas identified by the Minister of Indigenous and Northern Affairs' Special Representative, such as education, infrastructure, and economic development. The Framework will include an Inuit-specific component, created in partnership with Inuit, as Inuit Nunangat comprises over a third of Canada's land mass and over half of Canada's coast line, and as Inuit modern treaties govern this jurisdictional space." White House, "United States-Canada Joint Arctic Leaders' Statement" (December 20, 2016), https://www.whitehouse. gov/the-press-office/2016/12/20/united-states-canada-joint-arctic-leaders-statement. Anticipated developments are elaborated upon in our conclusion to this book.

12   Canada, Minister of Indian Affairs and Northern Development, *Canada's Northern Strategy: Our North, Our Heritage, Our Future* (July 2009).

13   Department of Finance, "Budget 2008: Responsible Leadership," Chapter 4 – Leadership at Home (2008).

14   Ibid., 13.

15   See P. Whitney Lackenbauer and Ryan Dean, eds., *Canada's Northern Strategy under the Harper Conservatives: Key Speeches and Documents on Sovereignty, Security, and Governance, 2006–15* (Waterloo and Calgary: Centre on Foreign Policy and Federalism/ Centre for Military, Security and Strategic Studies, 2016).

16   Department of Foreign Affairs and International Trade (DFAIT), *Statement on Canada's Arctic Foreign Policy: Exercising Sovereignty and Promoting Canada's Northern Strategy Abroad* (August, 2010). All quotations in this section are derived from this document unless otherwise specified.

17   Mary Simon, "The Arctic and Northern Dimensions of World Issues" Speech to *Canada-UK Colloquium*, Iqaluit (November 4, 2010).

18   We discuss this transition, with specific reference to offshore oil and gas development, in the conclusion.

19   DFAIT, *Statement on Canada's Arctic Foreign Policy*, 4, 11, 14.

20   Porismita Borah, "Conceptual Issues in Framing Theory: A Systematic Examination of a Decade's Literature," *Journal of Communication* 61, no. 2 (2011): 248, quoted in Rebecca Pincus and Saleem Ali, "Have You Been to 'The Arctic'? Frame Theory and the Role of Media Coverage in Shaping Arctic Discourse," *Polar Geography* 39, no. 2 (2016): 83–97.

21   For the most thorough analysis of Canadian Arctic discourse in Canada, see Mathieu Landriault, "La sécurité arctique 2000–2010: une décennie turbulente?" (unpublished Ph.D. dissertation, University of Ottawa, 2013).

22   Ilulissat Declaration, adopted at the Arctic Ocean Conference hosted by the
      Government of Denmark and attended by the representatives of the five costal states
      bordering on the Arctic Ocean (Canada, Denmark, Norway, the Russian Federation,
      and the US) held at Ilulissat, Greenland, May 27–29, 2008.

23   Chih Yuan Woon, "China, Canada and Framings of Arctic Geopolitics," in *Polar
      Geopolitics? Knowledges, Resources and Legal Regimes,* eds. Richard Powell and Klaus
      Dodds (London: Edward Elgar, 2014), 172–3. On framings of China in the *Globe and
      Mail* more generally, see Qinwen Yu, "A Canadian Press Perspective on China's Rise:
      An Analysis of *Globe and Mail* Editorials, 2001–2015" (unpublished M.A. thesis, Simon
      Fraser University, 2016).

24   Gang Chen, "China's Emerging Arctic Strategy," *Polar Journal* 2, no. 2 (2012): 1–2.

25   David Wright, *The Panda Readies to Meet the Polar Bear: China and Canada's Arctic
      Sovereignty Challenge* (Calgary: Canadian Defence and Foreign Affairs Institute, March
      2011), 1.

26   David Wright, "Canada Must Stand Up against China's Increasing Claim to Arctic,"
      Calgary Herald, March 7, 2011.

27   David Curtis Wright, *The Dragon Eyes the Top of the World: Arctic Policy Debate and
      Discussion in China* (Newport: Naval War College Press, China Maritime Studies
      Institute, 2011), 32.

28   Huebert, "The Shipping News Part II."

29   See, for example, "Harper Speaks up for Canada's Arctic," *Globe and Mail*, January 28,
      2006.

30   Rob Huebert, "Canada Must Prepare for the New Arctic Age," *Edmonton Journal*,
      August 4, 2008.

31   Rob Huebert quoted in Heather Yundt, "Canada's North Becomes a Battlefield in Arctic
      Video Game," *Nunatsiaq News*, February 9, 2012.

32   Victor Suthren, "Sinking the Navy In Afghanistan," *Ottawa Citizen*, November 2, 2006.

33   "China's Navy Making Waves," *Calgary Herald*, October 1, 2007. See also Shelagh
      Grant, "Troubled Arctic Waters," *Globe and Mail*, June 30, 2010. This assessment, while
      still far from proven, was given some support by the arrival of five PLAN warships
      in the Bering Sea in September 2015. The voyage, which coincided with the Glacier
      conference then being held in Alaska, was the closest the Chinese Navy had ever come
      to US territory without an invitation.

34   "China's Arctic Ambition," *Winnipeg Free Press*, October 25, 2014.

35   Diane Francis, "Is the Arctic Poised to Become the Next Suez?" *National Post*,
      December 14, 2013; the idea that China challenges Canada's sovereignty is found
      elsewhere as well – see, for example, Iain Hunter, "The North No Longer Cold War
      Bulwark," *Times Colonist*, August 25, 2013, and Robert Sibley, "Canada Ignores Arctic
      Sovereignty at Its Peril," *Ottawa Citizen*, October 2, 2015.

36   Sibley, "Canada Ignores Arctic Sovereignty"; Michel Byers and Scott Borgerson, "The
      Arctic Front in the Battle to Contain Russia," *Wall Street Journal*, March 8, 2016.

37 Nathan VanderKlippe, "Chinese Scientists Look to Canadian Arctic for Research Outpost," *Globe and Mail*, March 18, 2015.

38 Nathan VanderKlippe, "China Reveals Plans to Ship Cargo across Canada's Northwest Passage," *Globe and Mail*, April 20, 2016. This article was also reprinted in *Time* magazine as "China Could Be Preparing to Challenge Canada's Sovereignty over the Northwest Passage" (April 21, 2016)

39 Michael Byers, "Will China Become a Partner or Pariah after Court Decision?," *Globe and Mail*, July 12, 2016.

40 Frédéric Lasserre, *China and the Arctic: Threat or Cooperation Potential for Canada* (Toronto: International Council, June 2010). For another reassuring message that eschews "fear mongering" about Chinese Arctic interests, see Michael Byers in Randy Boswell, "China Moves to Become Major Arctic Player," *Nunatsiaq News*, March 3, 2010.

41 Frédéric Lasserre, "Case Studies of Shipping along Arctic Routes. Analysis and Profitability Perspectives for the Container Sector," *Transportation Research Part A: Policy and Practice* 66 (2014): 144–61; Lasserre, "Simulations of Shipping along Arctic Routes: Comparison, Analysis and Economic perspectives," *Polar Record* (2014): 1–21; Linyan Huang, Frédéric Lasserre, and Olga Alexeeva, "Is China's Interest for the Arctic Driven by Arctic Shipping Potential?," *Asian Geographer* 32, no. 1 (2015): 59–71; Pierre-Louis Têtu, Jean-François Pelletier, and Frédéric Lasserre, "The Mining Industry in Canada North of the 55th Parallel: A Maritime Traffic Generator?," *Polar Geography* 38, no. 2 (2015): 107–22; Olga Alexeeva, Frédéric Lasserre, and Pierre-Louis Têtu, "Vers l'affirmation d'une stratégie chinoise agressive en Arctique?," *Revue internationale et stratégique* 2 (2015): 38–47; Frédéric Lasserre, Linyan Huang, and Olga V. Alexeeva, "China's Strategy in the Arctic: Threatening or Opportunistic?," *Polar Record* (2015): 1–12; Frédéric Lasserre and Olga Alexeeva, "Analysis of Maritime Transit Trends in the Arctic Passages," in *International Law and Politics of the Arctic Ocean*, eds. Suzanne Lalonde and Ted McDorman (Leiden: Brill, 2015), 180–93; Leah Beveridge, Mélanie Fournier, Frédéric Lasserre, Linyan Huang, and Pierre-Louis Têtu, "Interest of Asian Shipping Companies in Navigating the Arctic," *Polar Science* (2016); Emmanuel Guy and Frédéric Lasserre, "Commercial Shipping in the Arctic: New Perspectives, Challenges and Regulations," *Polar Record* 52, no. 3 (2016): 294–304.

42 P. Whitney Lackenbauer, "Finding a Seat at the Top of the Globe," *Globe and Mail*, January 16, 2012; Lackenbauer, "Canada and the Asian Observers to the Arctic Council: Anxiety and Opportunity," *Asia Policy* 18, no. 1 (2014): 22–9.

43 P. Whitney Lackenbauer and James Manicom, "The Chinese Pole," *Policy Options* 34, no. 4 (April–May 2013): 12–15; P. Whitney Lackenbauer and James Manicom, "Canada's Northern Strategy and East Asian States' Interests in the Arctic," in *East Asia-Arctic Relations: Boundary, Security and International Politics*, eds. Ken Coates and Kimie Hara (Waterloo: Centre for International Governance Innovation, 2014), 78–117; James Manicom and P. Whitney Lackenbauer, "East Asian States and the Pursuit of Arctic Council Membership," in ibid., 199–216; James Manicom and P. Whitney Lackenbauer, "Asian States and the Arctic: National Perspectives on Regional Governance," in *The Handbook of the Politics of the Arctic*, eds. Leif Christian Jensen and Geir Hønnelan (Cheltenham, UK: Edward Elgar, 2015), 517–32.

44   See, for example, Aldo Chircop, "The Emergence of China as a Polar-Capable State," *Canadian Naval Review* 7, no. 1 (2011): 9–14; Whitney Lackenbauer and Adam Lajeunesse, "China's Mining Interests in the North American Arctic" in *Governing the North American Arctic: Lessons from the Past, Prospects for the Future*, eds. Dawn Berry, Nigel Bowles, and Halbert Jones III (London: Palgrave MacMillan, 2016), 74–99; Matthew Willis and Duncan Depledge, "How We Learned to Stop Worrying about China's Arctic Ambitions: Understanding China's Admission to the Arctic Council, 2004–2013," *Handbook of the Politics of the Arctic*, eds. Leif Christian Jensen and Geir Hønneland (Cheltenham: Edward Elgar, 2015), 388–407; Hugh Stephen, *The Opening of the Northern Sea Routes: The Implications for Global Shipping and for Canada's Relations with Asia*, University of Calgary School of Public Policy *Research Papers* 9, no. 19 (May 2016), http://arcticjournal.com/sites/default/files/northern-sea-routes-stephens.pdf; Adam Lajeunesse, "China Prepares to Use the Northwest Passage," *Arctic Deeply* (September 19, 2016); Pierre-Louis Têtu, "Stratégies des entreprises chinoises dans le secteur extractif dans l'Arctique" (unpublished Ph.D. dissertation, Laval University, 2016).

45   Linda Jakobson and Jingchao Peng, *China's Arctic Aspirations*, SIPRI Policy Paper 34 (Stockholm: Stockholm International Peace Research Institute, 2012), 1–2.

46   See, for example, Per Erik Solli, Elana Wilson Rowe, and Wrenn Yennie Lindgren, "Coming into the Cold: Asia's Arctic Interests," *Polar Geography* 36, no. 4 (2013): 253–70; Sanna Kopra, "China's Arctic Interests," *Arctic Yearbook 2013: The Arctic of Regions versus the Globalized Arctic*, ed. Lassi Heilinen (Akureyri: Northern Research Forum, 2013); Li Xing and Rasmus Gjedssø Bertelsen, "The Drivers of Chinese Arctic Interests: Political Stability and Energy Transportation Security," in ibid., 53–68; Olav Schram Stokke, "The Promise of Involvement: Asia in the Arctic," *Strategic Analysis* 37, no. 4 (2013): 474–9; Linda Jakobson, "China Wants to be Heard on Arctic Issues," *Global Asia* 8, no. 4 (2013): 98–101; Oran Young, Jong Deog Kim, and Yoon Hyung Kim, eds., *The Arctic in World Affairs: A North Pacific Dialogue on International Cooperation in a Changing Arctic* (Honolulu: East-West Center, 2014); Kai Sun, "Beyond the Dragon and the Panda: Understanding China's Engagement in the Arctic," *Asia Policy* 18, no. 1 (2014): 46–51; Aki Tonami, "The Arctic Policy of China and Japan: Multi-Layered Economic and Strategic Motivations," *Polar Journal* 4, no. 1 (2014): 105–26; Njord Wegge, "China in the Arctic: Interests, Actions and Challenges," *Nordlit* 32 (2014): 83–98; Nong Hong, "Emerging Interests of Non-Arctic Countries in the Arctic: A Chinese Perspective," *Polar Journal* 4, no. 2 (2014): 271–86; Su Ping and Marc Lanteigne, "China's Developing Arctic Policies: Myths and Misconceptions," *Journal of China and International Relations* 3, no. 1 (2015): 1–25; Chunjuan Wang, Dahai Liu, Meng Xu, Ying Yu, Xiaoxuan Li, Junguo Gao, and Wenxiu Xing, "The Sustainable Relationship between Navigation of Arctic Passages, Arctic Resources, and the Environment," *Journal of Sustainable Development* 9, no. 2 (2016): 127–36.

47   See, for example, the recent volume Leiv Lunde, Yang Jian, and Iselin Stensdal, *Asian Countries and the Arctic Future* (Singapore: World Scientific, 2016).

48   See, for example, Olya Gayazova, "China's Rights in the Marine Arctic," *International Journal of Marine and Coastal Law* 28, no. 1 (2013): 61–95; John K.T. Chao, "China's Emerging Role in the Arctic," in *Regions, Institutions, and Law of the Sea: Studies in*

Ocean Governance, eds. Harry Scheiber and Jin-Hyun Park (Leiden: Brill, 2013), 467–89; Andrea Beck, "China's Strategy in the Arctic: A Case of Lawfare?," *Polar Journal* 4, no. 2 (2014): 306–18; Jingchao Peng and Njord Wegge, "China and the Law of the Sea: Implications for Arctic Governance," *Polar Journal* 4, no. 2 (2014): 287–305; Anne-Marie Brady, "Polar Politics and History," *Polar Journal* 4, no. 2 (2014): 247–52; Valur Ingimundarson, "Managing a Contested Region: The Arctic Council and the Politics of Arctic Governance," *Polar Journal* 4, no. 1 (2014): 183–98; Jun Zhao, "China's Emerging Arctic Strategy and the Framework of Arctic Governance," in *Science, Technology, and New Challenges to Ocean Law*, eds. Harry Scheiber, James Kraska, and Moon-Sang Kwon (Leiden: Brill, 2015), 367–94; Sandra Cassotta, Kamrul Hossain, Jingzhemg Ren, and Michael Evan Goodsite, "Climate Change and China as a Global Emerging Regulatory Sea Power in the Arctic Ocean: Is China a Threat for Arctic Ocean Security," *Beijing Law Review* 6 (2015): 199–207; Mia Bennett, "How China Sees the Arctic: Reading Between Extraregional and Intraregional Narratives," *Geopolitics* 20, no. 3 (2015): 645–68; Jiayu Bai and Huijun Hu, "Transcending Divisions and Harmonizing Interests: How the Arctic Council Experience Can Inform Regional Cooperation on Environmental Protection in the South China Sea," *Chinese Journal of International Law* 15, no. 4 (2016): 935–45.

49 People's Republic of China (PRC), Ministry of Foreign Affairs, "China's View on Arctic Cooperation" (July 30, 2010).

50 Ekos Research Associates, *Rethinking the Top of the World: Arctic Security Public Opinion Survey* (January, 2011). A revised survey was also published in 2015.

51 Munk-Gordon Arctic Security Program, *Rethinking the Top of the World: Arctic Public Opinion Survey* 2 (April 22, 2015).

52 Asia Pacific Foundation of Canada (APFC), *2012 National Opinion Poll: Canadian Views on Asia* (2012), 12, 16.

53 Ibid., 4, 9, 26.

54 Ibid., 3–5, 14, 17, 29–30.

55 Ibid., 3.

56 Asia Pacific Foundation of Canada (APFC), *2012 National Opinion Poll: Canadian Views on Asia* (2012), 6–7, 9–11, 21, 23–4, 37, 44–5.

57 Ibid., 7–8, 11, 31–2, 41–3, 48.

58 Paul Evans, *Engaging China: Myth, Aspiration, and Strategy in Canadian Policy from Trudeau to Harper* (Toronto: University of Toronto Press, 2014), xi–xii.

59 Ibid., 3, 9.

60 David Mulroney, *Middle Power, Middle Kingdom: What Canadians Need to Know about China in the 21st Century* (Toronto: Allen Lane, 2015), 61–2. On Sino-Canadian relations under Harper, see also Kim Richard Nossal and Leah Sarson, "About Face: Explaining Changes in Canada's China Policy, 2006–2012," *Canadian Foreign Policy Journal* 20, no. 2 (2014): 146–62.

61 Paul Evans, *Engaging China: Myth, Aspiration, and Strategy in Canadian Policy from Trudeau to Harper* (Toronto: University of Toronto Press, 2014), 75.

62   Mulroney, *Middle Power, Middle Kingdom*, 16.

63   On this fear see, for instance, the Huang Nubo controversy in Iceland and Norway outlined in more detail in chapter 4.

64   Workshop Report, "Sino-Canadian Workshop on the Arctic," Beijing and Shanghai (February 25–27, 2010).

65   Njord Wegge, "China in the Arctic: Interests, Actions and Challenges," *Nordlit* 32 (2014): 88.

66   Anne-Marie Brady, "Polar Stakes: China's Polar Activities as a Benchmark for Intentions," *China Brief* 12, no. 14 (2012): 11.

67   MELAW, Final Workshop Report, "Second Sino-Canadian Exchange on the Arctic," Halifax (June 25–26, 2012)

68   See, for example, Oran R. Young, "Whither the Arctic? Conflict or Cooperation in the Circumpolar North," *Polar Record* 45, no. 232 (2009); P. Whitney Lackenbauer, "Polar Race or Polar Saga? Canada and the Circumpolar World," in *Arctic Security in an Age of Climate Change*, ed. James Kraska (Cambridge: Cambridge University Press, 2011), 218–43; Ian G. Brosnan, Thomas M. Leschine, and Edward L. Miles, "Cooperation or Conflict in a Changing Arctic?" *Ocean Development & International Law* 42, nos. 1–2 (2011): 173–210; Frédéric Lasserre, Jérôme Le Roy, and Richard Garon, "Is There an Arms Race in the Arctic?" *Journal of Military and Strategic Studies* 14, nos. 3–4 (2012): 1–56; Christian Le Mière and Jeffrey Mazo, *Arctic Opening: Insecurity and Opportunity* (Abingdon: Routledge for the IISS, 2013); Rolf Tamnes and Kristine Offerdal, *Geopolitics and Security in the Arctic: Regional Dynamics in a Global World* (London: Routledge, 2014); Lackenbauer and Adam Lajeunesse, "The Canadian Armed Forces in the Arctic: Building Appropriate Capabilities." *Journal of Military and Strategic Studies* 16, no. 4 (2016): 7–66.

69   See, for example, Rob Huebert, Heather Exner-Pirot, Adam Lajeunesse, and Jay Gulledge, *Climate Change & International Security: The Arctic as a Bellwether* (Arlington: Centre for Climate and Energy Solutions, 2012); Rob Huebert, *The Newly Emerging Arctic Security Environment* (Calgary: Canadian Defence and Foreign Affairs Institute, 2010); Roger Howard, *Arctic Gold Rush: The New Race for Tomorrow's Natural Resources* (London: Continuum, 2010); Michael Byers, *Who Owns the Arctic? Understanding Sovereignty Disputes in the North* (Vancouver: Douglas & McIntyre, 2010); Kristian Åtland, "Interstate Relations in the Arctic: An Emerging Security Dilemma?" *Comparative Strategy* 33, no. 2 (2014): 145–66; Richard Sale and Evgenii Potapov, *The Scramble for the Arctic: Ownership, Exploitation and Conflict in the Far North* (London: Frances Lincoln, 2010); Scott Borgerson, "Arctic Meltdown: The Economic and Security Implications of Global Warming," *Foreign Affairs* (March–April 2008): 63–77; Borgerson, "Coming Arctic Boom: As the Ice Melts, the Region Heats Up," *Foreign Affairs* (2013): 76–89. On their use in a Chinese context, see Kai Sun, "Comments on Chapter 4: Chinese Perspective," in *The Arctic in World Affairs: A North Pacific Dialogue on the Future of the Arctic*, eds. Oran Young, Jong Deog Kim, and Yoon Hyung Kim (Seoul: Korea Maritime Institute and East-West Center, 2013), 323.

70　See, for example, "Admiral Urges Government to Stake Claim In the Arctic," *South China Morning Post*, March 6, 2010; Linda Jakobson, *China Prepares for an Ice-Free Arctic*, 7.

71　For a Russian example, a 2009 article in *Dongbei zhi chuang (Window on the Northeast)* quotes a recent prediction in the Russian tabloid *Komsomolskaya Pravda* (the Communist Youth League version of *Pravda*, still in publication today and in fact the top-selling newspaper in Russia) about the likelihood of a Third World War breaking out in the Arctic: "With the continual discoveries of new resources beneath the Arctic Ocean, this previously neglected land of snow and ice has become a treasure house at which each country gazes with the cruel greed of a tiger. Although the land areas of the Arctic are owned by the eight countries Canada, Denmark, Finland, Iceland, Norway, Sweden, the United States, and Russia, the strife over Arctic sovereignty has not only not subsided, but has become more vehement over time. Russia's *Komsomolskaya Pravda* even predicts that "because there are serious discrepancies over the division and delimitation of Arctic interests, the World War III of the future may well break out in the Arctic." Translated by David Curtis Wright in *The Dragon Eyes the Top of the World*, 5.

72　MELAW, Second Sino-Canadian Exchange on the Arctic, Halifax (June 25–26, 2012), Final Workshop Report, December 2012. Identity of the speaker withheld due to Chatham House rules. The presenter stressed that China is the only nuclear-weapon country that has publicly stated it will not be the first to use nuclear weapons, or use or threaten to use nuclear weapons against non-nuclear-weapon states. He also noted that China calls for settlement of disputes over territory and maritime rights and interests with neighbouring countries through dialogue and negotiation (and has settled historical boundary issues peacefully with twelve land neighbours).

73　For a more extensive discussion of defence and security considerations related to China's Arctic interests, see Timothy Wright, "China's Race towards the Arctic: Interests, Legitimacy, and Canadian Security Implications" (unpublished M.A. thesis, University of Calgary, 2014).

74　Linda Jakobson and Jingchao Peng, *China's Arctic Aspirations*, 23.

75　On these themes see Chih Yuan Woon, "China, Canada and Framings of Arctic Geopolitics," 175.

Chapter 1 - Situating the Arctic in China's Strategy

1　Gang Chen, "China's Emerging Arctic Strategy," *Polar Journal* 2, no. 2 (2012): 10.

2　OECD, *OECD Economic Surveys: China 2013* (OECD Publishing, 2013).

3　United States, Central Intelligence Agency (CIA), "World Factbook: China," https://www.cia.gov/library/publications/the-world-factbook/.

4　National Intelligence Council, *Global Trends 2030: Alternative Worlds*, December 2012. http://www.dni.gov/files/documents/GlobalTrends_2030.pdf.

5　World Bank, "Multipolarity: The New Global Economy," 2011, 46.

6   Andrew S. Erickson and Adam P. Liff, "A Player But No Superpower," *Foreign Policy*, March 7, 2013. These authors note that the US National Intelligence Council predicts that China's GDP will surpass that of the United States in purchasing-power-parity terms in 2022, and near 2030 at market exchange rates. For a Canadian perspective on these trends, see Elinor Sloan, "Responding to China's Military Build-Up," *OpenCanada.org*, Canadian International Council, March 20, 2013.

7   Wang Jisi, "China's Search for a Grand Strategy," *Foreign Affairs* (March/April 2011).

8   William A. Callahan, *Contingent States: Greater China and Transnational Relations* (Minneapolis: University of Minnesota Press, 2004), 82.

9   See, for example, John J. Mearsheimer, *The Tragedy of Great Power Politics* (New York: W.W. Norton and Co., 2001).

10   For a useful overview and critique of both revisionist and integrationist perspectives see Jeffrey W. Legro, "What Will China Want: The Future Intentions of a Rising Power," *Perspectives on Politics* 5, no. 3 (2007).

11   There is some debate as to how this changed after the end of the Cold War. See Ian Clark, *The Post-Cold War Order: The Spoils of Peace* (Oxford: Oxford University Press, 2001); John Ikenberry, "Power and Liberal Order: America's Postwar World Order in Transition," *International Relations of the Asia-Pacific* 5, no. 2 (2005): 133–52.

12   See, for example, Jacek Kugler, "The Asian Ascent: Opportunity for Peace or Precondition for War?" *International Studies Perspectives* 7 (2006): 36–42.

13   John Ikenberry, "The Rise of China and the Future of the West," *Foreign Affairs* (January–February 2008).

14   Barry Buzan, "China in International Society: Is Peaceful Rise Possible?" *Chinese Journal of International Politics* 3 (2010): 5–36.

15   Rosemary Foot, "Chinese Strategies in a US-Hegemonic Global Order: Accommodating and Hedging," *International Affairs* 82, no. 1 (2006): 77–97; Avery Goldstein, "Power Transitions, Institutions, and China's Rise in East Asia: Theoretical Expectations and Evidence," *Journal of Strategic Studies* 30, nos. 4–5 (2007): 639–82.

16   Nina Hachigian, China's Engagement in the International System: In the Ring, But Punching below Its Weight (Washington: Center for American Progress, 2009).

17   Mingjiang Li, "Rising from Within: China's Search for a Multilateral World," *Global Governance* 17 (2011): 347.

18   Gregory Chin and Ramesh Thakur, "Will China Change the Rules of Global Order?" *Washington Quarterly* 33, no. 4 (2010): 119–38.

19   Alistair Iain Johnston, *Social States: China in International Institutions 1980–2000* (Princeton: Princeton University Press, 2008)

20   Ann Kent, China, The United Nations and Human Rights: The Limits of Compliance (Philadelphia: University of Philadelphia Press, 1999).

21   Michael D. Swaine and Ashley J. Tellis, *Interpreting China's Grand Strategy: Past, Present and Future* (Santa Monica: RAND, 2000), 113–14.

22 For a discussion on PRC calculations on international regimes, see Michael D. Swaine and Ashley J. Tellis, *Interpreting China's Grand Strategy: Past, Present and Future*, 133–40; Alastair Iain Johnston and Paul Evans, "China's Engagement with Multilateral Security Institutions," *Engaging China: The Management of an Emerging Power*, eds. Alastair Iain Johnston and Robert S. Ross (Routledge, London, 1999), 235–72.

23 J. Mohan Malik, "China and the Nuclear Non-proliferation Regime," *Contemporary Southeast Asia* 22, no. 3 (2000): 447.

24 Bates Gill, "Two Steps Forward, One Step Back: The Dynamics of Chinese Non-proliferation and Arms Control Policy Making in the Era of Reform," in *The Making of Chinese Foreign and Security Policy in the Era of Reform*, ed. David M. Lampton (Stanford: Stanford University Press, 2001), 281.

25 See, for example, Alistair Iain Johnston, "Treating International Institutions as Social Environments," *International Studies Quarterly* 45, no. 4 (2001): 490; Xiaoyu Pu, "Socialization as a Two-Way Process: Emerging Powers and the Diffusion of International Norms," *Chinese Journal of International Politics* (2012): 18–19.

26 Mark Burles and Abram Shulsky, *Patterns in China's Use of Force: Evidence from History and Doctrinal Writings* (Santa Monica: RAND, 2000), 31. The PLA has identified five likely types of conflict: small scale border conflicts; conflicts over territory, seas, or islands; surprise air attacks; resistance against hostile intrusions; and punitive counter-attacks.

27 You Ji has argued that the doctrine was contradictory. See You Ji, "The Revolution in Military Affairs and China's Strategic Thinking," *Contemporary Southeast Asia* 21, no. 3 (1999): 352–5.

28 Viacheslav A. Frolov, "China's Armed Forces Prepare for High-Tech Warfare," *Defense and Foreign Affairs Strategic Policy* 26, no. 1 (1998): 7.

29 James Mulvenon, "Chinese Nuclear and Conventional Weapons," *China Joins the World: Progress and Prospects*, eds. Elizabeth Economy and Michel Oksenberg (New York: Council on Foreign Relations, 1999), 331–3.

30 Zachary Keck, "China's Building Second Aircraft Carrier," *Diplomat*, January 20, 2014.

31 David Shambaugh, "China Engages Asia: Reshaping the Regional Order," *International Security* 29, no. 3 (2004/2005): 64–99; Nicholas Khoo, Michael L.R. Smith, and David Shambaugh, "Correspondence: China Engages Asia? Caveat Lector," *International Security* 30, no. 1 (2005): 196–213.

32 Leszek Buszynski, "ASEAN, the Declaration on Conduct and the South China Sea," *Contemporary Southeast Asia* 25, no. 3 (2003): 343–62.

33 People's Republic of China and the governments of the ASEAN States, "Declaration on the Conduct of Parties in the South China Sea" (2002).

34 James Manicom, "Beyond Boundary Disputes: Understanding the Nature of China's Challenge to Maritime East Asia," *Harvard Asia Quarterly* 12, nos. 3–4 (2010): 46–53.

35 See, for example, Michael T. Klare, *Resource Wars* (New York: Henry Holt and Co., 2002), 109–37; Mamdouh G. Salameh, "China, Oil and the Risk of Regional Conflict,"

Survival 37, no. 4 (1995–96): 133–46; Felix K. Chang, "Beyond the Unipolar Moment: Beijing's Reach in the South China Sea," *Orbis* 40, no. 3 (1996): 353–74.

36   For details, see Carlyle A. Thayer, "Chinese Assertiveness in the South China Sea and Southeast Asian Responses," *Journal of Current Southeast Asian Affairs* 30, no. 2 (2011): 77–104; Leszek Buszynski, "The South China Sea: Oil, Maritime Claims and US-China Strategic Rivalry," *Washington Quarterly* 35, no. 2 (2012): 139–56.

37   Carl Thayer, "China's New Fishing Regulations: An Act of State Piracy?" *Diplomat*, January 13, 2014 and Taylor Fravel "Hainan's New Fishing Rules: A Preliminary Analysis," *Diplomat*, January 10, 2014.

38   On US reactions to the possibility to a SCS ADIZ, see Zachary Keck, "US Warns China against a South China Sea ADIZ," *Diplomat*, December 18, 2013. On the East China Sea ADIZ, see David A. Welch, "What's an ADIZ: Why the United States, Japan, and China Get it Wrong," *Foreign Affairs*, December 9, 2013.

39   United States, Office of the Press Secretary, "Remarks By President Obama to the Australian Parliament," November 17, 2011. For a recent update on Obama's "strategic pivot" toward the Asia-Pacific region, see Brian Spegele and Jeremy Page, "Beijing to Shake Up Foreign-Policy Team," *Wall Street Journal*, March 10, 2013.

40   The White House, Sustaining US Global Leadership: Priorities for 21ˢᵗ Century Defence (Washington, DC: 2012).

41   Teddy Ng, "Xi Sets Out Priorities for Foreign Policy," *South China Morning Post*, October 26, 2013.

42   Malte Humpert an Andreas Raspotnik, "From 'Great Wall to 'Great White North': Explaining China's Politics in the Arctic," *Longpost*, August 17, 2012.

43   David Curtis Wright, *The Dragon Eyes the Top of the World: Arctic Policy Debate and Discussion in China* (Newport: Naval War College Press, China Maritime Studies Institute, 2011), 38.

44   Roger W. Robinson, "China's 'Long Con' in the Arctic Must Be Countered," *Ottawa Citizen*, September 14, 2013.

45   Quoted in J. Dana Stuster, "The Case for Canamerica: The Far-Out, Incredibly Earnest Argument for Why the US Should Merge with Its Northern Neighbor," *Foreign Policy*, October 3, 2013.

46   Gang Chen, "China's Emerging Arctic Strategy," *Polar Journal* 2, no. 2 (2012): 361.

47   Vlado Vivoda and James Manicom, "Oil Import Diversification in Northeast Asia: A Comparison between China and Japan," *Journal of East Asian Studies* 11, no. 2 (2011): 223–54.

48   International Energy Agency, *China's Worldwide Quest for Energy Security* (2000), 8; Roland Dannreuther, "Asian Security and China's Energy Needs," *International Relations of the Asia-Pacific* 3, no. 2 (2003): 201.

49   Nick Owen, "Disputed South China Sea Oil in Context," in *Maritime Energy Resources in Asia: Energy and Geopolitics*, ed. Clive Schofield (Washington, DC: The National Bureau of Asia Research, 2011), 11–38.

50 Wang has advocated rephrasing the principle of "keeping a low profile" to a strategy of "modesty and prudence." Wang Jisi, "China's Search for a Grand Strategy," *China 3.0*, ed. Mark Leonard (European Council on Foreign Relations, November 2012), 118.

51 Wang, "China's Search."

52 See, for example, PRC, Ministry of Foreign Affairs, "China's View on Arctic Cooperation," July 30, 2010; Workshop Report, "Sino-Canadian Workshop on the Arctic," Beijing/Shanghai, February 25–27, 2010.

53 Wang, "China's Search."

54 Ibid.

55 Ibid.

56 Canada and Russia are both G20 members and Canada is influential at the International Monetary Fund and other financial institutions.

57 Wang, "China's Search."

58 International Crisis Group, "Stirring Up the South China Sea," *Asia Report* 223 (2012).

59 This section is based upon Gang Chen, "China's Emerging Arctic Strategy," *Polar Journal* 2, no. 2 (2012): 1–11; Linda Jakobsen and Jingchao Peng, *China's Arctic Aspirations*, SIPRI Policy Paper 34 (Stockholm: Stockholm International Peace Research Institute, November 2012), 3–4; Anne-Marie Brady, "China's Antarctic Interests," *The Emerging Politics of Antarctica*, ed. Anne Marie Brady (Abingdon: Routledge, 2012), 32–3. For fuller discussions see T. Qu et al., eds., "Research on Arctic Issues" [北极问题研究], (Ocean Press: Beijing, June, 2011). Although it is beyond the scope of this paper to elaborate on the Chinese foreign policy-making process, Chen provides a succinct overview in his article.

60 Chen, "China's Emerging Arctic Strategy," 367–8.

61 Ibid., 368.

62 Jakobsen and Peng, *China's Arctic Aspirations*, 4.

63 Chen, "China's Emerging Arctic Strategy," 369.

64 Susan V. Lawrence, "China's Political Institutions and Leaders in Charts," *CRS Report to Congress,* R43303, November 12, 2013, 44.

65 Chen, "China's Emerging Arctic Strategy," 368–9.

66 State Oceanic Administration People's Republic of China, "The Main Duties of the State Oceanic Administration" [国家海洋局主要职责], April 9, 2010.

67 "Final Workshop Report – Second Sino-Canadian Exchange on the Arctic," Halifax, December, 2012, 10.

68 The CACPR comprises experts from thirteen Chinese ministries or bureaus under the State Council and the General Staff Department of the PLA.

69 Chen, "China's Emerging Arctic Strategy," 369.

70   Gordon Chang, "China's Arctic Play," *Foreign Policy*, March 9, 2010; Luo Jianwen, "Navy Major General: China Cannot Afford to Lose Out on Developing the Arctic Ocean," *Zhongguo Xinwen She*, August 28, 2010.

71   United Nations, *Convention on the Law of the Sea*, [hereafter LOSC], signed December 10, 1982 at Montego Bay, Jamaica, came into effect November 16, 1994, Preamble and Article 136.

72   "CPC Central Committee's Proposal on Formulating the 12th Five-Year Program on National Economic and Social Development," *Xinhua*, October 30, 2010; "China: Measures Aim to Bolster Control of Maritime Interests," *OSC Analysis*, May 31, 2007.

73   State Oceanic Administration, *China National Offshore Development Report 2011*.

74   Katrin Hille, "Hu Calls for China to be Maritime Power," *Financial Times*, November 8, 2012.

75   Olga Alexeeva and Frédéric Lasserre, "China and the Arctic," *Arctic Yearbook* (2012): 80–90; James Manicom and P. Whitney Lackenbauer, "The Chinese Pole," *Policy Options* (April–May 2013): 16–18.

76   Translated and quoted in David Curtis Wright, *The Dragon Eyes the Top of the World: Arctic Policy Debate and Discussion in China*, 18–20.

77   For Chinese commentaries on this, see Gao Lanjun, "Arctic Security Governance: Nature, Challenge and Solution" [北极地区的安全治理问题:内涵、困境与应对], *Seeker* [求索] 11 (2015); Kai Sun, "China's Contribution to Arctic Governance [为北极治理作出中国贡献], *Journal of China Social Sciences* [中国社会科学报], December 30, 2015.

78   Linda Jakobson, *China Prepares for an Ice-Free Arctic* (Stockholm: Stockholm International Peace Research Institute, March 2010).

79   Workshop Report, "Sino-Canadian Workshop on the Arctic," Beijing/Shanghai (February 25–27, 2010).

80   Presentation at "The Second Sino-Canadian Workshop on the Arctic," Halifax, June 25–26, 2012. Name withheld pursuant to Chatham House Rules.

81   Quoted in Sanjay Chaturvedi, "Geopolitical Transformations: 'Rising' Asia and the Future of the Arctic Council" (2012), 230.

82   Chen, "China's Emerging Arctic Strategy," 360.

83   Aaron Friedberg, *A Contest for Supremacy: China, America, and the Struggle for Mastery in Asia* (New York: W.W. Norton, 2011), 144.

Chapter 2 - *The Snow Dragon: China, Polar Science, and the Environment*

1   Ministry of Foreign Affairs of the PRC, "Keynote Speech by Vice Foreign Minister Zhang Ming at the China Country Session of the Third Arctic Circle Assembly," Speech to the Third Arctic Circle Assembly, Iceland, October 17, 2015.

2   Ed Struzik, "Canada Urged to Take Lead in Polar Research," *Edmonton Journal*, February 25, 2009; Ed Struzik, "The True North Strong and Free but Not Cheap,"

Toronto Star, December 1, 2007; Canadian Polar Commission, *International Polar Year Canadian Science Report: Highlights* (Ottawa: Canadian Polar Commission, 2012).

3   Council of Canadian Academies, *Vision for the Canadian Arctic Research Initiative: Assessing the Opportunities* (2008), 4.

4   Canadian Polar Commission, *The State of Northern Knowledge in Canada* (Ottawa: Canadian Polar Commission, 2014), as well as the new Polar Knowledge Canada (POLAR) established in June 2015 to sit "on the cutting edge of Arctic issues and [strengthen] Canada's position internationally as a leader in polar science and technology." Government of Canada, "Polar Knowledge Canada," June 11, 2015, http://www.canada.ca/en/polar-knowledge/.

5   Jingchao Pen and Njord Wegge, "China's Bilateral Diplomacy in the Arctic," *Polar Geography* 38, no. 3 (2015): 238. See also Zhang Jiansong, "China's Scientists Will Play a More Active Role in the Arctic Scientific Research" [中国科学家将在北极科学研究舞台扮演更积极角色] *Xinhua News* [新华网] (January 24, 2015).

6   Huigen Yang, "Development of China's Polar Linkages," *Canadian Naval Review* 8, no. 3 (Fall 2012): 30.

7   Final Workshop Report, "Second Sino-Canadian Exchange on the Arctic," Halifax, June 25–26, 2012.

8   The First Sino-Canadian Exchange on the Arctic brought together senior Canadian and Chinese academics and experts to exchange views with respect to the international legal and political ramifications of current activities in the Arctic Ocean. It was convened in Beijing and Shanghai from February 25–27, 2010 by the China Institute of Marine Affairs in cooperation with the Polar Research Institute of China (PRIC), Marine and Environmental Law Institute of the Schulich School of Law at Dalhousie University, the Ocean Management Research Network, and the Faculty of Law of the University of Victoria. MELAW convened the Second Exchange from 25–26 June 2012 at Dalhousie University in cooperation with the Faculty of Law of the University of Victoria and the Centre for Foreign Policy Studies at Dalhousie in Canada, and the CIMA in Beijing. The report of the second workshop noted: "The First Sino-Canadian Exchange was the first bilateral meeting between academic and experts from the two countries. The purpose of the exchange was to enable a better understanding among Canadian and Chinese participants of each country's respective interests and activities as they relate to Arctic waters. The meeting occurred against the backdrop of growing international interest in the region as a result of greater accessibility resulting from impacts of climate change and in particular a decrease in sea ice cover, especially during the critical summer season. These changes are resulting in increased international activities in the region, notably for resource exploration and development, international shipping and navigation, fishing and marine scientific research."

9   Workshop Report, "Sino-Canadian Workshop on the Arctic," Beijing/Shanghai, February 25–27, 2010.

10   Chinese Arctic and Antarctic Administration, "Home," http://www.chinare.gov.cn/en/index.html.

11   Brady, "Polar Stakes," 11, 15.

12   Anne-Marie Brady, "China's Antarctic Interests," 31.

13   Rob Huebert, "Canada and China in the Arctic: A Work in Progress," *Meridian Newsletter* (2012).

14   Todd Sharp, "The Implications of Ice Melt on Arctic Security," *Defence Studies* 11, no. 2 (June 2011): 298; Joshua Ho, "The Opening of the Northern Sea Route," *Maritime Affairs* 7, no. 1 (Summer 2011): 106; Ho, "The Implications of Arctic Sea Ice Decline on Shipping," *Marine Policy* 34 (2010): 713. Many other multidisciplinary studies confirm the rate of climate change is increasing at an unprecedented rate.

15   Ho, "The Opening of the Northern Sea Route," 106; James Astill, "The Melting North," *Economist*, June 16, 2012.

16   United Nations Environment Programme, "Revised Draft Decision on Sustainable Development of the Arctic Region," February 1, 2008.

17   See, for example, Arctic Climate Impact Assessment (hereafter ACIA), *Impacts of a Warming Arctic: ACIA Overview Report* (Cambridge: Cambridge University Press, 2004).

18   ACIA; Hua Xu et al., "The Potential Seasonal Alternative of Asia-Europe Container Service via Northern Sea Route under the Arctic Sea Ice Retreat," *Maritime Policy and Management* 28, no. 5 (September 2011): 541.

19   Josefino C. Comiso, "Accelerated Decline in the Arctic Sea Ice Cover," *Geophysical Research Letters* 35 (2008): 6.

20   Sharp, "Implications of Ice Melt on Arctic Security," 298.

21   See, for example, Borgerson, 66.

22   Marika Holland, Cecilia M. Bitz, and Bruno Tremblay, "Future Abrupt Reductions in the Summer Arctic Sea Ice," *Geophysical Research Letters* 33 (2006); M. Winton, "Does the Arctic Sea Ice Have a Tipping Point," *Geophysical Research Letters* 33 (2006); Muyin Wang and James Overland, "A Sea Ice Free Summer Arctic within 30 Years?" *Geophysical Research Letters* 36, no. 7 (2009); Review Commission Staff Research Report, "China and the Arctic: Objectives and Obstacles," *US-China Economic and Security* 13 (April 2012), 3.

23   Estimates vary among scientists and projection models. In terms of commentaries on China and the Arctic, examples include the study by Joseph Spears, "A Snow Dragon in the Arctic," *Asia Times Online* (February 8, 2011), who had estimated that the Arctic would be ice-free during the summer months as early as 2013. Other estimates include Brady, "Polar Stakes," whose projected date is 2020; Ho, "The Opening of the Northern Sea Route," who estimates between 2026 and 2046; and in "Semantic-Based Web Service Discovery and Chaining for Building an Arctic Spatial Data Infrastructure," W. Li. et al. estimate 2050.

24   EU, *Climate Change and International Security*, 2.

25   Thomas Homer-Dixon, "Climate Change, the Arctic, and Canada: Avoiding Yesterday's Analysis of Tomorrow's Crisis," *Securing Canada's Future in a Climate-Changing World*, National Round Table on the Environment and the Economy, October 30, 2008, 89.

26 AAC, "Europe and the Arctic"; ITK and ICC (Canada), *Building Inuit Nunaat*; Sheila Watt-Cloutier. "Connectivity: The Arctic – The Planet," Speech at Oslo Sophie Prize Ceremony, June 15, 2005.

27 Ma Jianmin et al., "Revolatilization of Persistent Organic Pollutants in the Arctic Induced by Climate Change," *Nature Climate Change* 1, no. 5 (2011): 255–60.

28 Ho, "The Opening of the Northern Sea Route," 108.

29 See, for example, A. Stohl et al., "Black Carbon in the Arctic: The Underestimated Role of Gas Flaring and Residential Combustion Emissions," *Atmospheric Chemistry and Physics* 13 (2013): 8833–55.

30 See, for example, DKB Perovich et al., "Increasing Solar Heating of the Arctic Ocean and Adjacent Seas, 1979–2005: Attribution and Role in the Ice-Albedo Feedback," *Geophysical Research Letters* 34, no. 19 (2007).

31 See, for example, National Research Council, *Abrupt Impacts of Climate Change: Anticipating Surprises* (Washington, DC: The National Academies Press, 2013). For a paper with an Arctic focus, see Timothy M. Lenton, "Arctic Climate Tipping Points," *AMBIO* 41, no. 1 (2012): 10–22.

32 ACIA.

33 Oran Young, "Review Article, The Future of the Arctic: Cauldron of Conflict or Zone of Peace?" *International Affairs* 87, no. 1 (2011): 187.

34 Ho, "The Opening of the Northern Sea Route," 109–10. For more on the impacts of climate change in China, see also Wai-Shin Chan and Zoe Knight, "China's Rising Climate Risk: The 20 Questions Investors Need to Ask," *HSBC Global Research* (2011); Brad Plumer, "These 20 Cities Have the Most to Lose from Rising Sea Levels," *Washington Post Wonkblog*, August 20, 2013.

35 Frédéric Lasserre and Olga Alexeeva, "China and the Arctic," *Arctic Yearbook 2012* (2012), 83.

36 IPCC, *Climate Change 2014: Impacts, Adaptation and Vulnerability*, http://www.ipcc.ch/.

37 Dr. Huigen Yang, "Development of China's Polar Linkages," *Canadian Naval Review* 8, no. 3 (Fall 2012): 30. See also Chris Buckley, "China Report Spells out 'Grim' Climate Change Risks," *Reuters*, January 17, 2012.

38 Olga Alexeeva and Frédéric Lasserre (2012), "Le Dragon des Neiges: les stratégies de la Chine en Arctique," *Perspectives Chinoises* 3, 63; Caitlin Campbell, "China and the Arctic: Objectives and Obstacles," *US-China Economic and Security Review Commission Staff Research Report* 13 (April, 2012): 3.

39 Lasserre and Alexeeva, "China and the Arctic," 82.

40 Aldo Chircop, "The Emergence of China as a Polar-Capable State," *Canadian Naval Review* 7, no. 1 (Spring 2011): 9.

41 Brady, "China's Arctic Interests," 31–49.

42   For summaries see Lasserre and Alexeeva, "China and the Arctic," 81; Frédéric Lasserre and Olga Alexeeva, "The Snow Dragon: China's Strategies in the Arctic," *China Perspectives* 3 (2012): 62; Linda Jakobson, *China Prepares for an Ice-Free Arctic* (Stockholm: Stockholm International Peace Research Institute, March 2010): 3–4.

43   Lasserre and Alexeeva, "China and the Arctic," 81.

44   Linda Jakobsen and Jingchao Peng, *China's Arctic Aspirations*, Stockholm International Peace Research Institute (SIPRI) Policy Paper 34 (November 2012): 3.

45   Chinese Arctic and Antarctic Administration, "About Us," http://www.chinare.gov.cn/en/index.html?pid=about.

46   Jakobson, *China Prepares for an Ice-Free Arctic*, 4.

47   Workshop Report, "Sino-Canadian Workshop on the Arctic," Beijing/Shanghai, February 25–27, 2010.

48   Jakobsen and Peng, *China's Arctic Aspirations*, 5.

49   PRIC, "Polar Information Centre," http://www.pric.gov.cn/enindex.asp?sortid=14 (last accessed 2014, no longer available online in English). The new website for the PIC is http://www.coi.gov.cn/english/eoverview/ejd/jd9.htm, which includes updated statistics in a revised format.

50   W. Li et al, "Semantic-Based Web Service Discovery and Chaining for Building an Arctic Spatial Data Infrastructure," *Computers and Geosciences* 37 (2011); Chaowei Yang et al., "Establishing a Sustainable and Cross-Boundary Geospatial Cyber Infrastructure to Enable Polar Research," *Computers and Geosciences* 37 (2011). There is a proof-of-concept prototype available at http://eie.cos.gmu. edu/VASDI.

51   Jakobson, *China Prepares for an Ice-Free Arctic*, 4.

52   Yizhi Li and Xuan Zhang, "International Observation: China's Cooperation with Northern Europe in the Arctic Has Had Steady Progress" [国际观察: 中国与北欧国家北极合作稳步推进], *Xinhua Web* [新华网], June 4, 2016.

53   Xiaoyi Wang, "American Media: Russia Has Changed its Mind and Has Started to Attract China to Arctic Exploitation" [美媒: 俄转变立场, 吸引中国开发北极], *Wangyi Finance* [网易财经], October 3, 2016.

54   Kai Sun, "China and the Arctic: China's Interests and Participation in the Arctic," paper for the Workshop on East Asian-Arctic Relations, Whitehorse, Yukon, March 2–3, 2013. Cited with permission of the author.

55   Lasserre and Alexeeva, "China and the Arctic," 82.

56   Jakobson, *China Prepares for an Ice-Free Arctic*, 3. According to plans currently being developed, the new icebreaker could conduct up to two research cruises to the Arctic during the summer months. This would allow for long-term monitoring of changing Arctic marine environments and allow Chinese researchers to make observations that would provide insight into how a changing Arctic might influence weather and climate in China. Jean de Pomereu, "China Spreads its Polar Wings: Investing in Infrastructure," *Science Poles*, December 5, 2012.

57 Franz-Stefan Gady, "China Begins Construction of Polar Icebreaker," *Diplomat*, December 22, 2016.

58 Brady, "Polar Stakes," 11–12. Brady notes that the Dome A project for deep space research is a collaborative effort by Australian, Chinese, and US scientists, but Chinese-language reports only highlight China's involvement.

59 Brady, "Polar Stakes," 12. China's future Antarctic expeditions will include a Bastler 67 type airframe to support operations (particularly at Dome A) and facilitate airborne remote sensing and atmospheric observation. Yang, "Development of China's Polar Linkages," 32.

60 See, for example, Muhammad Makki, China's Quest for Arctic Access and Resources, April 19, 2012; Huebert, "Canada and China in the Arctic."

61 Brady, "China's Antarctic Interests," 33.

62 Brady, "Conflict or Cooperation? The Emerging Politics of Antarctica," 6.

63 Workshop Report, "Sino-Canadian Workshop on the Arctic," Beijing/Shanghai, February 25–27, 2010.

64 PRIC, "Polar Information Centre," http://www.pric.gov.cn/enindex.asp?sortid=14. In 1988, the Chinese Academy of Sciences released the first issue of the *Chinese Journal of Polar Science* to communicate the findings of Chinese polar researchers, which included a semi-annual English edition beginning in 1990. As Olga Alexeeva and Frédéric Lasserre document, most of the articles that Chinese scientists published in Chinese journals from 1988–2008 focused on Arctic glaciology, climatology, oceanographic science, upper atmospheric physics, and biological and environmental studies. Frédéric Lasserre and Olga Alexeeva, "China and the Arctic," 81.

65 Chinese Arctic and Antarctic Administration, "Science and Data."

66 Nancy Teeple, "A Brief History of Intrusions into the Canadian Arctic," *Canadian Army Journal* 12, no. 3 (Winter 2010): 52.

67 Teeple, "Brief History," 53; Huebert, "Canada and China in the Arctic."

68 See, for example, Jane George, "Arctic Borders Need Tighter Control, Former Commander Says," *Nunatsiaq News*, February 2, 2001; "Arctic Terror Threats Real: Security Agencies," *CBC News North*, November 10, 2010.

69 Sébastien Pelletier and Frédéric Lasserre, "Les Chinois dans l'Arctique: une présence qui ne date pas d'Hier – Analyse de l'incident de Tuktoyaktuk, TNO," *Monde Chinois* 41 (2015/1): 109–29.

70 Chinese Arctic and Antarctic Administration, "Science and Data," http://www.chinare.gov.cn/en/index.html?pid=science.

71 At the Arctic Science Summit held at Kunming, Yunnan Province in 2005, China was invited to join the Ny-Ålesund Science Managers Committee – a committee established in 1994 to enhance cooperation among the research centres at Ny-Ålesund. Jakobson, *China Prepares for an Ice-Free Arctic*, 4.

72 Chaowei Yang et al., "Establishing a Sustainable and Cross-Boundary Geospatial Cyber Infrastructure," 1721.

73   Yang, "Development of China's Polar Linkages."

74   Aldo Chircop, "The Emergence of China as a Polar-Capable State," 12–13; Anne-Marie Brady, "Polar Stakes: China's Polar Activities as a Benchmark for Intentions," *China Brief* 12, no. 14 (2012).

75   Brady, "Polar Stakes," and Bhavna Singh, "China and The Arctic: The Next 'Strategic' Frontline," *Institute of Peace and Conflict Studies*, November 9, 2012.

76   Jakobson and Peng, *China's Arctic Aspirations*, 1.

77   "Icebreaker *Xuelong* Concludes Arctic Expedition," *China Daily*, September 27, 2012.

78   "Chinese Arctic Expedition Team Returns Home," *Xinhuanet*, September 26, 2016.

79   Zhang Rui. 张锐 Exploitation in the Arctic: China cannot be left behind. [北极开发：中国不能落下[N]. China Economic Times [中国经济时报], November 3, 2011.

80   Chinese representative's presentation to the Second Sino-Canadian Arctic Exchange (2012). Meeting held under Chatham House rules.

81   Matthew Willis and Duncan Depledge, "How We Learned to Stop Worrying about China's Arctic Ambitions: Understanding China's Admission to the Arctic Council, 2004," in *Handbook of the Politics of the Arctic*, eds. Leif Christian Jensen and Geir Hønneland (Northampton: Edward Elgar Publishing Limited, 2015), 766.

82   Workshop Report, "Sino-Canadian Workshop on the Arctic," Beijing/Shanghai, February 25–27, 2010.

83   Li Zhenfu, "Obstacles and Countermeasures: China's Participation in International Mechanisms of the Arctic Route" [中国参与北极航线国际机制的障碍及对策], *China Navigation* [中国航海] 32, no. 2 (2009).

84   Quoted in Jakobson, *China Prepares for an Ice-Free Arctic*, 7.

85   Yang, "Development of China's Polar Linkages," 32.

86   Kai Sun, "China and the Arctic: China's Interests and Participation in the Region," in *East Asia-Arctic Relations: Boundary, Security and International Politics*, eds. Kimie Hara and Ken Coates (Waterloo: Centre for International Governance Innovation, 2014), 34–5.

87   Workshop Report, "Sino-Canadian Workshop on the Arctic," Beijing/Shanghai, February 25–27, 2010.

88   Final Workshop Report, "Second Sino-Canadian Exchange on the Arctic," December 2012, 3.

89   Presentation to the Second Sino-Canadian Exchange (Chatham House rules).

90   LOSC, Articles 238 and 239.

91   LOSC, Article 240. MSR in the Canadian Arctic must also comply with territorial scientific licensing processes.

92   LOSC, Article 232.

93   Lasserre, *China and the Arctic: Threat or Cooperation*, 4

94 See, for example, Guo Zhen, "China's Ocean Rights on the Arctic – Based on the Analysis of UNCLOS [中国在北极的海洋权益及其维护——基于《联合国海洋法公约》的分析], *Theoretical Studies on PLA Political Work* [军队政工理论研究] 15, no. 1 (2014) and Huang Deming and Zhang Cheng, "The Legal Issues of the Arctic Outer Continental Shelf Boundary from the Perspective of China's Overseas Security" [中国海外安全利益视角下的北极外大陆架划界法律问题], *Nanjing Journal of Social Sciences* [南京社会科学] 7 (2014).

95 See, for example, final Workshop Report, "Second Sino-Canadian Exchange on the Arctic" (December 2012), 3.

96 NSERC/SSHRC, "From Crisis to Opportunity: Rebuilding Canada's Role in Northern Research" (Ottawa: 2000), 2, 8.

97 Liu quoted in Jakobson and Jingchao, *China's Arctic Aspirations*, 16.

98 Karen T. Litfin quoted in Chaturvedi, "Geopolitical Transformations," 245.

99 Jakobson and Jingchao, *China's Arctic Aspirations*, 16.

100 John Ibbitson, "Stephen Harper's Frisky Northern Renaissance," *Globe and Mail*, August 27, 2010.

101 Grégoire Coté and Michelle Picard-Aitken, *Arctic Research in Canada: A Bibliometric Analysis* (Montreal: Science-Metrix), report to Indian and Northern Affairs Canada, March 31, 2009.

Chapter 3 - Sovereignty and Shipping

1 Bloomberg News, "China Eclipses US and Biggest Trading Nation," February 10, 2013.

2 Nong Hong, "The Melting Arctic and Its Impact on China's Maritime Transport," *Research in Transportation Economics* 35, no. 1 (2012): 50–7.

3 Ibid., 50.

4 Michael Byers, "Asian Juggernaut Eyes Our 'Golden' Waterways," *Globe and Mail*, August 29, 2011.

5 Shou Jianmin Feng Yuan, "A Study on Container Transport Potential of the Northeast Passage Based on Shipping Cost" [基于航运成本的北极东北航道集装箱运输潜力研究], *Journal of Polar Research* [极地研究] 27, no. 1 (2015).

6 Linyan Huang, Frédéric Lasserre, and Olga Alexeeva, "Is China's Interest for the Arctic Driven by Arctic Shipping Potential?," *Asian Geographer* 32, no. 1 (2015).

7 Linda Jakobson, "China: Potential Benefits of Arctic Melting," *University World News*, May 28, 2010; Jakobson, *China Prepares for an Ice-Free Arctic* (Stockholm: Stockholm International Peace Research Institute, March 2010).

8 "Short and Sharp," *Economist*, June 16, 2012.

9 International Chamber of Commerce, "IMB Piracy and Armed Robbery Map 2012," http://www.icc-ccs.org.

10   Marc Lanteigne, "China's Maritime Security and the 'Malacca Dilemma,'" *Asian Security* 4, no. 2 (2008): 143–61.

11   Ian Storey, "China's Malacca Dilemma," *China Brief* 6, no. 8 (2006).

12   Commander (Retd.) Neil Gadihoke, "Arctic Melt: The Outlook for India," *Maritime Affairs* 8, no. 1 (Summer 2012): 4–5; Lei Shan and Yin Jinyin, "An Analysis of Arctic Oil and Gas Exploitation and Strategic Thinking [北极油气开发现状分析与战略思考], *China Mining* [中国矿业] 23, no. 2 (2014).

13   Stephen Blank, "The Arctic: A Future Source of Russo-Chinese Discord?," *China Brief* 10, no. 24 (December 3, 2010): 7–9.

14   Linda Jakobson, "Preparing for an Ice-Free Arctic: Part 2 – The Commercial Lure of Melting Ice," and "China Prepares for an Ice-Free Arctic," *SIPRI Insights on Peace and Security* 2 (March 2010).

15   Joseph Spears, "The Snow Dragon Moves into the Arctic Ocean Basin," *China Brief* 11, no. 2 (January 28, 2011): 12–15.

16   Timothy Curtis Wright, "China's Race towards the Arctic: Interests, Legitimacy, and Canadian Security Implications," (M.A. thesis, University of Calgary, 2014), 55.

17   On the Northwest Passage see Donat Pharand, "The Arctic Waters and the Northwest Passage: A Final Revisit," *Ocean Development & International Law* 38, nos. 1–2 (2007): 3–69; Suzanne Lalonde and Michael Byers, "Who Controls the Northwest Passage?" *Vanderbilt Journal of Transnational Law* 42 (2009): 1133–1210; James Kraska, "International Security and International Law in the Northwest Passage," *Vanderbilt Journal of Transnational Law* 42 (2009): 1109–32; Suzanne Lalonde and Frédéric Lasserre, "The Position of the United States on the Northwest Passage: Is the Fear of a Precedent Warranted?" *Ocean Development and International Law* 44, no. 1 (2013): 28–72.

18   On the Manhattan voyages see John Kirton and Don Munton, "The *Manhattan* Voyages and their Aftermath," in *Politics of the Northwest Passage*, ed. Franklyn Griffiths (Kingston: McGill-Queen's University Press, 1987), 67–97; Matthew Willis, "The *Manhattan* Incident Forty Years On: Re-assessing the Canadian Response," in *Canada and Arctic Sovereignty and Security: Historical Perspectives*, ed. P. Whitney Lackenbauer (Calgary: Centre for Military and Strategic Studies, 2011), 259–82; and the detailed recent study by Ross Coen, *Breaking Ice for Arctic Oil: The Epic Voyage of the SS Manhattan through the Northwest Passage* (Anchorage: University of Alaska Press, 2012).

19   Arctic Council, *Arctic Marine Shipping Assessment 2009 Report* (Protection of the Arctic Marine Environment, 2009); Frédéric Lasserre and Sébastien Pelletier, "Polar Super Seaways? Maritime Transport in the Arctic: An Analysis of Shipowners' Intentions," *Journal of Transport Geography* 19, no. 6 (2011): 1465–73; Adam Lajeunesse, "A New Mediterranean? Arctic Shipping Prospects for the Twenty-First Century," *Journal of Maritime Law and Commerce* 43, no. 44 (October 2012); P. Whitney Lackenbauer and Adam Lajeunesse, *On Uncertain Ice: The Future of Arctic Shipping and the Northwest Passage* (Calgary: Canadian Defence & Foreign Affairs Institute, 2014).

20   See, for example, Guo Zhen, "China's Ocean Rights in the Arctic – Based on an
     Analysis of UNCLOS [中国在北极的海洋权益及其维护——基于《联合国海洋法公
     约》的分析], *Theoretical Studies on PLA Political Work* [军队政工理论研究] 1 (2014);
     Wu Jun and Wu Leizhao, "An Analysis of China's Ocean Rights in the Arctic – Based
     on the Perspective of International Maritime Law [中国北极海域权益分析——以国际
     海洋法为基点的考量], *Wuhan University Journal* (Philosophy & Social Sciences) [武汉
     大学学报(哲学社会科学版] 67, no. 3 (2014).

21   See, for example, Dong Aibo et al. "China and Russia to Build a Large-Scale Upgrade
     of the Arctic Ocean "Golden Waterway" Freight Hub" [中俄共建港口 提升北极"黄金
     水道"成色], *Pearl River Water Transport* [珠江水运] 20 (2014); Jiayu Bai, "The Study of
     the Arctic States Shipping Regulation Evolution – Starting from the Dispute over Water
     [北极航道沿岸国航道管理法律规制变迁研究——北极航道及所在水域法律地位之争
     谈起], *Journal of Social Sciences* [社会科学] 8 (2014); and Hongyan Guo, "Inquiries on
     the Northwest Passage" [论西北航道的通行制度], *Journal of CUPL* [中国政法大学学
     报] 6 (2015).

22   Ben Blanchard, "China Wants Ships to Use Faster Arctic Route Opened by Global
     Warming," *Reuters*, April 20, 2016.

23   See, for example, Nash Jenkins, "China Could Be Preparing to Challenge Canada's
     Sovereignty Over the Northwest Passage," *Time*, April 21, 2016.

24   The Maritime Safety Administration of the People's Republic of China, *Guidances on
     Arctic Navigation in the Northwest Route/2015* (Beijing: China Communications Press,
     2015).

25   Ibid., 34–5.

26   Ibid., 125.

27   See, for example, Paul Waldie, "A Reality Check on the Northwest Passage Boom,"
     Globe and Mail, January 7, 2014.

28   See, for example, Miaojia Liu and Jacob Kronbak, "The Potential Economic Viability
     of using the Northern Sea Route (NSR) as an Alternative Route between Asia and
     Europe," *Journal of Transport Geography* 18, no. 3 (2010): 434–44; Xu Hua, "Comments
     on Chapter 2: Chinese Perspective," in *The Arctic in World Affairs: A North Pacific
     Dialogue on the Future of the Arctic – 2012 North Pacific Arctic Conference Proceedings*,
     Oran Young, Jong Deog Kim, and Yoon Hyung Kim eds. (Seoul: Korea Maritime
     Institute and East-West Center, 2012), 84–9, 94–102; Masahiko Furuichi and Natuhiko
     Otsuka, "Proposing a Common Platform of Shipping Cost Analysis of the Northern Sea
     Route and the Suez Canal Route," *Maritime Economics & Logistics* 17, no. 1 (2014): 1–23.

29   Although the Danish bulk carrier *Nordic Orion* completed the first commercial transit
     of the Northwest Passage in October 2013, it did not complete its planned voyages in
     2014 owing to heavy ice conditions that effectively cancelled the shipping season. P.
     Whitney Lackenbauer and Adam Lajeunesse, "More Ships in the Northwest Passage
     Will Boost Our Arctic Claim," *Globe and Mail*, January 5, 2015.

30   "Commercial Operation Outlook of North Pole Navigation Routes" [北极航道商业
     化运营的前景], Ministry of Commerce, Beijing, via the Chinese Embassy in Norway,
     September 11, 2013.

31   Martine Erika Beiermann Wahl and Erik Kristoffersen, "Speed Optimization for Very Large Crude Carriers: Potential Savings and Effects of Slow Steaming," *Norwegian School of Economics* (Spring 2012): 60.

32   Lajeunesse, "A New Mediterranean?" 522–6; John Higginbotham, Andrea Charron, James Manicom, and Zhou Leilei et al. "A Comparative Study of the Northwest Passage and the Northeast Passage [加拿大西北航道与俄罗斯北方海航道管理的对比研究]. *Chinese Journal of Polar Research* [极地研究] 26, no. 4 (2014): 515–21; Canada-US Arctic Marine Corridors and Resource Development," *CIGI Policy Brief* 24 (November 2012); Frédéric Lasserre, "Case Studies of Shipping along Arctic Routes: Analysis and Profitability Perspectives for the Container Sector," *Transportation Research Part A* 66 (2014): 144–61.

33   Zhou Leilei et al.

34   Luo Qiaoyun, "An Analysis of Arctic LNG Shipping Profitability and its Future [北极东北航道运输经济性与前景分析], *Journal of Dalian Maritime University* [大连海事大学学报] 3 (2016).

35   Stewart et al., "Sea Ice in Canada's Arctic: Implications for Cruise Tourism," *Arctic* 60, no. 4 (December 2007): 376–7.

36   K.J. Wilson et al., "Shipping in the Canadian Arctic, *Canadian Ice Service and the Institute of Ocean Sciences* (2004). For more recent reactions, see Paul Waldie, "Baffinland CEO says No to Shipping Ore through Northwest Passage," *Globe and Mail*, October 17, 2013.

37   Transport Canada, "Zone Date System," http://www.tc.gc.ca/eng/marinesafety/debs-arctic-acts-regulations-zds-chart-2014.htm.

38   Arctic Council, *Arctic Marine Shipping Assessment 2009 Report (AMSA)*, 5.

39   AMSA, 31.

40   Laurence C. Smith and Scott R. Stephenson, "New Trans-Arctic Shipping Routes Navigable by Mid-Century," *Proceedings of the National Academy of Sciences of the United States of America* 110, no. 3 (March 2013).

41   Lasserre, *China and the Arctic: Threat or Cooperation*, 6–7.

42   "Little Interest in Ice-Free Northwest Passage," *BC Hydro*, June 29, 2010.

43   Frédéric Lasserre and Sébastien Pelletier, "Polar Super Seaways? Maritime Transport in the Arctic: An Analysis of Shipowners' Intentions," *Journal of Transport Geography* 19 (2011): 1465–73.

44   The survey was conducted in September 2013. Interviews were conducted with the following firms:

COSCO; CSCL; Chipolbrok; Winland Shipping, Tongli Shipping, Suns Shipping; West Line; Dandong Shipping Group; Lufeng Shipping; Shangdong Mou Ping Ocean Shipping; Shandong Ocean Shipping; Tianjin Harvest Shipping Co.; Zhongchang Marine Shipping Co.; Ningbo Silver Star; Maritime Shipping Co., Ningbo Jun Hao Ocean Shipping; Nanjing Henglong Shipping Co.; Uniwill Shipping Co.; King Far East

Shipping; Evertop Intel Shipping; Harmony Maritime Inc.; Pacific Glory Shipping; Liao Yuan Shipping Co.; and SITC Shipping.

45   A SWOT analysis is a planning method used to evaluate the strengths, weaknesses, opportunities, and threats involved in a project.

46   Leagh Beveridge et al., "Interest of Asian Shipping Companies in Navigating the Arctic," *Polar Science* 10, no. 3 (September 2016).

47   Ibid.

48   Ibid.

49   Linyan Huang, Frédéric Lasserre, and Olga Alexeeva, "Is China's Shipping Interest for the Arctic Driven by Arctic Shipping Potential?," *Asian Geographer*, online edition (December 2014): 9.

50   Fednav, "First Arctic Cargo Shipped through the Northwest Passage," September 19, 2014, http://www.fednav.com/.

51   NORDREG, Arctic Traffic Statistics (2013, 2014, 2015).

52   Government of Nunavut Bureau of Statistics, "Population Estimates 2014" (2014).

53   Frédéric Lasserre and Linyan Huang, "China's Strategy in the Arctic: Threatening or Opportunistic?," *Polar Record* (2015): 5.

54   Lajeunesse, "A New Mediterranean?"

55   Bob Weber, "Little Interest in Arctic Shipping," *Canadian Press*, June 30, 2010.

56   Claes Lykke Ragner, "The Northern Sea Route," *Nordin Association's Yearbook* (2008).

57   Katarzyna Zysk, "Russia's Arctic Strategy: Ambitions and Constraints," *Joint Force Quarterly* (April 2010): 105.

58   Andrey Vokuev, "Russia Opens First Arctic Search and Rescue Center," *Barents Observer*, August 27, 2013.

59   Trude Pettersen, "46 Vessels through Northern Sea Route," *Barents Observer*, November 23, 2012.

60   Northern Sea Route Information Office, Transit Statistics, www.arctic-lio.com/nsr_transits.

61   Quoted in Jakobson, *China Prepares for an Ice-Free Arctic*, 7.

62   Gazprom Marketing and Trading, "Gazprom Successfully Completes the World's first LNG Shipment through the Northern Sea Route," December 6, 2012.

63   Malte Humpert, "The Future of the Northern Sea Route – A "Golden Waterway" or a Niche Trade Route," The Arctic Institute, September 15, 2011.

64   Costas Paris, "Ship Travels Arctic from China to Europe," *Wall Street Journal Online*, August 19, 2013.

65   Sovcomflot, "Sovcomflot Group and China National Petroleum Corporation Become Strategic Partners," November 22, 2010; Nong Hong, "The Melting Arctic and its

Impact on China's Maritime Transport," *Research in Transportation Economics* 35, no. 1 (2012): 50–7.

66   Atle Staalesen, "To Yamal with World's Most Powerful LNG Carriers," *Barents Observer*, November 11, 2014.

67   RT.com, "China to Ship up to 15% of Trade through the Arctic," March 18, 2013.

68   Wu Weibing, "Some Shipping Experiences on the Northeast Passage" [北极东北航道航行体会], Marine Technology [航海技术] 4 (2016).

69   Ibid.

70   Mia Bennett, "China's Silk Road Plans Could Challenge Northern Sea Route," *CryoPolitics*, December 29, 2014.

71   Ibid.

72   "Northern Sea Route Traffic Plummets," *Radio Canada, Eye on the Arctic*, December 16, 2014.

73   Hutchison Port Holdings, "Ports," www.hph.com/.

74   CentralAmericaData, "China's Coscon Launches New Multimodal Service in Panama," July 8, 2008.

75   "Piraeus Port has Further Investment Planned," *Port Technology International*, June 28, 2013.

76   Latin Ports, "COSCO Pacific Wants to Continue Investing in Overseas Ports," March 26, 2014.

77   Canada, Department of Foreign Affairs and International Trade, *Statement on Canada's Arctic Foreign Policy*.

78   David Wright, *The Panda Readies to Meet the Polar Bear*, 1–2.

79   On China's straight baseline claim see Hyun-Soo Kim, "The 1992 Chinese Territorial Sea Law in Light of the UN Convention," *International and Comparative Law Quarterly* 43, no. 4 (1994): 899. This phenomenon is widespread – for a broader look at Asian claims see Sam Bateman and Clive Schofield, "State Practice Regarding Straight Baselines in East Asia: Legal, Technical and Political Issues in a Changing World," *Conference on Difficulties Implementing the Provisions of UNCLOS*, Monaco, October 16–17, 2008.

80   See, for example, Zou Keyuan, *Law of the Sea in East Asia: Issues and Prospects* (New York: Routledge, 2005); Shicun Wu and Mark Valencia, eds., *UN Convention on the Law of the Sea and the South China Sea* (New York: Routledge, 2016); Katherine Morton, "China's Ambition in the South China Sea: Is a Legitimate Maritime Order Possible?" *International Affairs* 92, no. 4 (2016): 909–40; Zhou Fangyin, "Between Assertiveness and Self-Restraint: Understanding China's South China Sea Policy," *International Affairs* 92, no. 4 (2016): 869–90.

81   Lincoln E. Flake, "Russia and China in the Arctic: A Team of Rivals," *Strategic Analysis* 37, no. 6 (2013): 685.

82 James Manicom interview with Guo Peiqing, Qingdao, November 20, 2012.

83 Yang Jian, "China and Arctic Affairs," *Arctic Yearbook* (2012).

84 Linda Jakobson and Jingchao Peng, *China's Arctic Aspirations*, SIPRI Policy Paper 34 (November 2012), v–vi, 15–16. By contrast, Japan and South Korea are more likely to be sympathetic to American and European legal perspectives on transit through the Northwest Passage, although neither country is particularly interested in the prospect of actually using the passage for shipping. James Manicom, Conversation with MOFA official, July 27, 2011.

85 Rob Huebert, "The Shipping News Part II," *International Journal* 58, no. 3 (Summer 2003): 302.

86 Rob Huebert, "The Coming Arctic Maritime Sovereignty Crisis," *Arctic Bulletin* (World Wildlife Fund) 2, no. 4 (July 2004): 24.

87 Franklyn Griffiths, "The Shipping News," *International Journal*, 58, no. 2 (Spring 2003). For a similar argument, see Andrea Charron, "The Northwest Passage: Is Canada's Sovereignty Floating Away?" *International Journal* 60, no. 3 (2005): 831–48.

88 Lajeunesse, "A New Mediterranean?" 536–7.

89 As far back as 1971 Pierre Trudeau rejected any implications that Canada might seek to close those waters to foreign ships, the prime minister stated: "to close off those waters and to deny passage to all foreign vessels in the name of Canadian sovereignty, as some commentators have suggested, would be as senseless as placing barriers across the entrances to Halifax and Vancouver harbours." Prime Minister's Statement in the Throne Speech, House of Commons Debates (October 24, 1969).

90 Lajeunesse, "A New Mediterranean?," 537.

91 Laurence C. Smith and Scott R. Stephenson, "New Trans-Arctic Shipping Routes Navigable by Mid-Century," Proceedings of the National Academy of Sciences of the United States of America 110, no. 3 (March 2013).

92 Peter Kikkert, "Promoting National Interests and Fostering Cooperation: Canada and the Development of a Polar Code," *Journal of Maritime Law and International Commerce* 43, no. 3 (July 2012): 319.

93 Ibid., 330.

94 Atle Staalensen, "For China, Barents Region Comes Closer," *Barents Observer*, February 8, 2013.

95 Staalensen, "For China, Barents Region Comes Closer."

96 Guo Peiqing, "The Arctic is Not Desolate" [北极并不冷清], *Huanqiu* 17 (September 2008) quoted in Jakobson, *China Prepares for an Ice-Free Arctic*, 11.

97 Presentation to the Second Sino-Canadian Exchange on Arctic Issues. Non-attributed according to Chatham House rules. See also Olya Gayazova, "China's Rights in the Marine Arctic," *International Journal of Marine and Coastal Law* 28, no. 1 (2013): 61–95; and Jiayu Bai, "The IMO Polar Code: The Emerging Rules of Arctic Shipping Governance," *International Journal of Marine and Coastal Law* 30, no. 4 (2015): 674–99.

98   This was highlighted by Vice Foreign Minister Zhang Ming at the China Country Session of the Third Arctic Circle Assembly; Ministry of Foreign Affairs of the PRC, "Keynote Speech by Vice Foreign Minister Zhang Ming at the China Country Session of the Third Arctic Circle Assembly," Speech to the Third Arctic Circle Assembly, Iceland, October 17, 2015.

Chapter 4 - Arctic Resources and China's Rising Demand

1   Konstantin Garibov and Igor Denisov, "Norway May Shut China out of the Arctic Council," *Voice of Russia*, January 30, 2012.

2   Wayne Arnold, "China's Global Mining Play is Failing to Pan Out," *Wall Street Journal*, September 15, 2014.

3   The most frequently cited estimate for oil and gas supplies is also among the most bullish: United States Geological Survey, "Circum-Arctic Resource Appraisal: Estimates of Undiscovered Oil and Gas North of the Arctic Circle" (2008).

4   See Vlado Vivoda and James Manicom, "Oil Import Diversification in Northeast Asia: A Comparison between China and Japan," *Journal of East Asian Studies* 11, no. 2 (Summer 2011): 223–54.

5   Olga V. Alexeeva and Frédéric Lasserre, "The Snow Dragon: China's Strategies in the Arctic," *China Perspectives* 3 (2012): 66–8.

6   Wang Kuan-Hsung quoted in Wendell Minnick, "Ice Station Dragon: China's Strategic Arctic Interest," *Defense News*, May 16, 2011.

7   See, for example, Roger W. Robinson, "China's Long-Term Arctic Strategy," *Inside Policy* (September 2013).

8   DFAIT, *Statement on Canada's Arctic Foreign Policy: Exercising Sovereignty and Promoting Canada's Northern Strategy Abroad* (August 2010): 11.

9   DFAIT, *Statement on Canada's Arctic Foreign Policy*, 4, 11, 14.

10   Government of Canada, "Fact Sheet: China," October, 2104, http://www. canadainternational.gc.ca/china-chine.

11   APFC, "National Opinion Poll: Canadian Views on Asia – Executive Summary," 2012, 14–28.

12   Lasserre, *China and the Arctic: Threat or Cooperation*, 7.

13   USGS, "90 Billion Barrels of Oil and 1,670 Trillion Cubic Feet of Natural Gas Assessed in the Arctic," *USGS Newsroom*, July 23, 2008, http://www.usgs.gov/newsroom/.

14   Jonathan Seymour, *Canadian Arctic Shipping Assessment*, 7; Robert M. Bone, *The Geography of the Canadian North: Issues and Challenges*, 2nd ed. (Don Mills: Oxford University Press, 2003), 105.

15   Floyd Roland, "Arctic Energy Resources Will Be Needed," *Embassy*, November 6, 2008.

16   All numbers in USD and calculated from 2005 to 2013, based on amounts produced by the Heritage Foundation's "China Global Investment Tracker," http://www.heritage. org/research/projects/china-global-investment-tracker-interactive-map.

17   Quoted in Jane George, "The Global Mining Industry Arrives in Nunavut," *Nunatsiaq News*, April 6, 2011.

18   Deloite, *Tracking the Trends 2013: The Top 10 Issues Mining Companies May Face in the Coming Year* (2013), 4.

19   Alana Wilson, Fred McMahon, and Miguel Cervantes, *Survey of Mining Companies 2012/2013* (Vancouver: Fraser Institute, 2013), 9.

20   Ibid., 65–7.

21   Deloite, 3–4; Liezel Hill and Doug Alexander, "Canadian Bankers Feeling the Pain of Decimated Mining Sector," *Financial Post*, July 7, 2013.

22   Wilson et al., 72.

23   "Go East. Far East," *Arctic Journal*, November 26, 2013.

24   Jane George, "Iron Ore Rush Set to Start in Nunavik," *Nunatsiaq News*, March 21, 2011; "Chinese Steel Giant Ready to Help Finance Nunavik Iron Mine," *Nunatsiaq News*, December 20, 2011. On Plan Nord, see Government of Québec, "Plan Nord," http://www.plannord.gouv.qc.ca/. On the scaling-back of the plan in 2015, see Peter Hadekel, "New Plan Nord Calls for Smaller Investment as Metal, Mineral Prices Tumble," *Montreal Gazette*, April 8, 2015.

25   Jane George, "Nunavik Mine Owes $72 Million to Creditors; Chinese Owners Turn Project over to Toronto Bank" *NunatsiaqOnline*, August 14, 2013.

26   "MV Nunavik: From Quebec to China via the Northwest Passage," *NunatsiaqOnline*, September 22, 2014.

27   James Munson, "China North: Canada's Resources and China's Arctic Long Game," *iPolitics*, December 31, 2012.

28   Government of Yukon, "Wolverine Property," *Yukon Mineral Update* (2008), 192.

29   Munson, "China North."

30   Jane George, "MMG Promises Jobs Galore for Western Nunavut," *Nunatsiaq Online*, October 1, 2012.

31   Jim Bell, "Nunavut Adds Huge Grays Bay Road-Port Scheme to its Shipping List," *Nunatsiaq News*, February 29, 2016.

32   Ibid.

33   Pav Jordan, "Nunavut Mining Rush Attracts China-Backed MMG" *Globe and Mail*, September 4, 2012.

34   Ironbark Zinc, "Ironbark Zinc in New Partnership with China's NFC to Progress Citronen," *Arctic Journal* Press Release, April 15, 2014 and Greenland Minerals and Energy, "Greenland Minerals Signs Memorandum of Understanding with China's NFC, to form Fully-Integrated Global Rare Earth Supply Chain," *Arctic Journal* Press Release, May 24, 2014.

35   Statsministeriet, "The Greenland Self-Government Arrangement," http://www.stm. dk/_p_13090.html. The website explains: "The Self-Government Act contains a provision regarding Greenland's access to independence. The provision stipulates that if the people of Greenland take a decision in favour of independence, negotiations are to commence between the Danish Government and Naalakkersuisut regarding the introduction of independence for Greenland. An agreement between the Danish Government and Naalakkersuisut regarding the introduction of independence for Greenland is to be concluded with the consent of Inatsisartut and is to be endorsed by a referendum in Greenland. Furthermore, the agreement is to be concluded with the consent of the Folketing, cf. Section 19 of the Danish Constitution. Independence for Greenland implies that Greenland assumes sovereignty over the Greenland territory."

36   Charles M. Perry and Bobby Andersen, *New Strategic Dynamics in the Arctic Region* (Washington: Institute for Foreign Policy Analysis, 2012), 78.

37   "China, Denmark Eye Closer Relationship," *Global Times*, April 25, 2014; Zhu Xiaolei, "The Danish Arctic Ambassador: China is Expected to Have More Participation in Arctic Development" [丹麦北极大使: 愿中国更多参与北极开发], *Global Time News* [环球网], February 18, 2014.

38   Andreas Jakobsen, "Copenhagen Zoo to Borrow Two Pandas from China," *Copenhagen Post*, April 24, 2014.

39   Pu Jun, "Greenland Lures China's Miners with Cold Gold," *CaixinOnline*, July 12, 2014. Pu notes that "the culture gap is wide but some of the 56,000 people who live in Greenland will get a chance to understand China's culture when Chinese labor crews arrive." He also notes that, as of 2011, "many of Greenland's imported mine workers are Canadians, working for Canadian mining companies."

40   London Mining, "FAQ – Isua Project," www.londonmining.com/operations/greenland/ faqs.

41   John Vidal, "Climate Change Brings New Risks to Greenland, says PM Aleqa Hammond," *Guardian*, January 23, 2014.

42   Terry Macalister, "Greenland Government Falls as Voters Send Warning to Mining Companies," *Guardian*, March 15, 2013.

43   Ibid.

44   Kevin McGwin, "To the Polls," *Arctic Journal*, October 1, 2014.

45   Kevin McGwin, "The Coalition of the Willing," *Arctic Journal*, December 4, 2014.

46   Svein Magnason, "Continued Disagreement over Uranium Mining," *Nora Region Trends*, October 8, 2014.

47   Matthew Willis and Duncan Depledge, "How We Learned to Stop Worrying about China's Arctic Ambitions: Understanding China's Admission to the Arctic Council, 2004," *Handbook of the Politics of the Arctic*, eds. Leif Christian Jensen and Geir Hønneland (Northampton: Edward Elgar Publishing Limited, 2015), 773.

48   Pu Jun, "Greenland Lures China's Miners with Cold Gold."

49 Holman et al. and Annie Gilroy, "Must-Know: Factors Driving down the Price Outlook for Iron Ore," *Yahoo Finance*, October 27, 2014.

50 "China Environmental Measures' Impact on Steel and Iron Ore," *Wood Mackenzie*, March 28, 2014.

51 Kevin McGwin, "Editor's Briefing | Another One Bites the Ore," *Arctic Journal*, December 9, 2014.

52 Nicholas Van Praet, "Cliffs Natural Resources Retreats from Canadian Disaster," *Globe and Mail*, November 20, 2014.

53 Bob Weber, "Tories Mull a Chinese Plan for Izok Corridor That Could Bring Billions of Dollars to Nunavut," *Financial Post*, December 8, 2012; London Mining, Press Release, November 3, 2014, www.londonmining.com.

54 Du Juan, "General Nice Group to Take Over Greenland Mine," *China Daily*, January 13, 2015.

55 London Mining, "ISUA Overview," www.londonmining.com.

56 Nicolas van Praet, "Cliffs Natural Resources Retreats from Canadian Disaster."

57 Cecilia Jamasmie, "Iron Ore War: Rio Tinto 'Not Standing Still' over BHP's Production Boost," *Mining.com*, October 9, 2014; Vale SA, "Vale's Performance in 3Q14," Corporate Presentation (2014).

58 Ben Blanchard and David Stanway, "China to 'Declare War' on Pollution, Premier Says," *Reuters*, March 4, 2014.

59 Ibid.

60 Holman Fenwick Willan et al.

61 "China Environmental Measures' Impact on Steel and Iron Ore," *Wood Mackenzie*, March 28, 2014.

62 Keith Tan, "Iron Ore Pellet Premiums to Remain Firm into 2014 on Demand Growth," *Platts*, December 11, 2013.

63 Vale SA, "Quarterly Earnings, 2Q2013," July 31, 2014.

64 Holman Fenwick Willan et al.

65 Frik Els, "Iron Ore Price Surges," *Mining.com*, December 4, 2014.

66 Keith Bradsher, "China Restarts Rare Earth Shipments to Japan," *Global Business*, November 19, 2010.

67 Keith Bradsher, "Chasing Rare Earths, Foreign Companies Expand in China," *New York Times*, August 24, 2011.

68 Carol Matlack, "Chinese Workers in Greenland?" *Bloomberg Businessweek*, February 10, 2013.

69 Paula Briscoe, "Greenland – China's Foothold in Europe?" Council on Foreign Relations, February 1, 2013.

70 Greenland Minerals and Energy, Press Release, March 24, 2014.

71 Molycorp, "Molycorp Reports Fourth Quarter and Full Year 2013 Financial Results," March 3, 2104; Lynas Corporation, "Capital Raising and Business Update," May 5, 2014; Tim Worstall, "Why Lynas Corp Is Struggling; The Great Rare Earth Shortage Is Truly Over," *Forbes*, March 8, 2014.

72 For instance, a return to the REE prices of 2011 would make Great Western Minerals' Steenkampskraal mine (South Africa) profitable and bring 1,512 tons/a online; Avalon Resource's Nechalacho mine in the NWT with a capacity of 10,000 tons/a and Quest Rare Minerals' project at Strange Lake (Northern Quebec) with a capacity of 10,4000 tons/a: Great Western Minerals, "Steenkampskraal Feasibility Study," May 12, 2014; Avalon, "Project Fact sheet: Nechalacho, Thor Lake," April 16, 2013; and Quest Rare Minerals, "Developing a World-Class Rare Earth Project in Canada," October, 2014.

73 Briscoe, "Greenland-China's Foothold in Europe?"

74 Ólafur Ragnar Grímsson, "Why the Arctic Matters," Keynote Address to the Arctic Imperative Summit, June 20, 2011.

75 See, for example, Kevin McGwin, "Game of Alliances," *Arctic Journal*, March 7, 2014.

76 Marc Lanteigne and Su Ping, "China's Developing Arctic Policies: Myths and Misconceptions," *Journal of China and International Relations* 3, no. 1 (2015): 3–4.

77 Ministry of Foreign Affairs of the People's Republic of China, "Premier Wen Jiabao Holds Talks with His Icelandic Counterpart Sigurdardottir," April 21, 2012.

78 Anne-Marie Brady, "Polar Stakes: China's Polar Activities as a Benchmark for Intentions," *China Brief* 12, no. 14 (July 19, 2012). In reference to China's fifth CHINARE expedition in 2012, a spokesperson in the Icelandic office of President Grimsson stated "The (Chinese) journey indicates a growing interest in the melting of the ice in the northern regions and how climate change is affecting the globe and the future of all nations." Jon Viglundson and Alister Doyle, "First Chinese Ship Crosses Arctic Ocean Amid Record Melt," *Reuters*, August 17, 2012.

79 Du Juan, "CNOOC Licensed to Seek Arctic Oil," *China Daily*, March 4, 2014.

80 Jesse Guite Hastings, "The Rise of Asia in a Changing Arctic: A View from Iceland," *Polar Geography* 37, no. 3 (October 2014): 222.

81 Andrew Higgins, "Teeing Off at Edge of the Arctic? A Chinese Plan Baffles Iceland," *New York Times*, March 23, 2013.

82 On this, see Huang Ding and Zhao Ningning, "Arctic Governance and China's Participation – An Analysis Based on the Theory of International Public Goods [北极治理与中国参与——基于国际公共品理论的分析], *Wuhan University Journal (Philosophy & Social Sciences)* 3 [武汉大学学报(哲学社会科学版] (2014).

83 Transparency International, "Corruption Perceptions Index 2014: Results" (2014), http://www.transparency.org/cpi2014/results.

84 See, for example, Roger W. Robinson, "China's Long Con in the Arctic," *Macdonald Laurier Institute Commentary* (September 2013). On this theme more generally, see Matthew Willis and Duncan Depledge, "How We Learned to Stop Worrying about China's Arctic Ambitions: Understanding China's Admission to the Arctic Council,

2004–2013," in *Handbook of the Politics of the Arctic*, eds. Leif Christian Jensen and Geir Hønneland (Cheltenham, UK: Edward Elgar, 2015), 768.

85   Higgins, "Teeing Off at Edge of the Arctic?"

86   Nong Honga, "Emerging Interests of Non-Arctic Countries in the Arctic: a Chinese Perspective," *Polar Journal* 4, no. 2 (November 2014).

87   Jesse Guite Hastings, "The Rise of Asia in a Changing Arctic: A View from Iceland," *Polar Geography* 37, no. 3 (2014): 215.

88   USGS, "Circumpolar Resource Appraisal: Estimates of Undiscovered Oil and Gas North of the Arctic Circle," *USGS Fact Sheet* (Washington: US Geological Survey, 2008).

89   Katarzyna Zysk, "Russia's Arctic Strategy: Ambitions and Constraints," *Joint Force Quarterly* 57, no. 2 (April 2010): 105.

90   Thomas Nilsem, "Discovers Kara Sea Oil a Week before Sanctions Hit," *Barents Observer*, September 29, 2014.

91   Peter Hobson and Sam Skove, "Rosneft Asks for $49 Billion From State Welfare Fund to Survive Sanctions," *Moscow Times*, October 22, 2014.

92   Alexander Panin, "Russia Plans Giant State Oil Services Company to Replace Western Firms," *Moscow Times*, October 12, 2014.

93   "China Won't Support Sanctions against Moscow," *RT.com*, September 23, 2014.

94   Dina Gusovsky, "Should America Worry about a China-Russia Axis?" *CNBC*, October 22, 2014.

95   Rakteem Katakey and Will Kennedy, "Russia Lets China into Arctic Rush as Energy Giants Embrace," *Bloomberg*, May 25, 2013.

96   Jane Perlez, "As Russia Remembers War in Europe, Guest of Honor is From China," *New York Times*, May 8, 2015.

97   Mia Bennett, "China-Russia Gas Deal Creates Arctic Winners and Losers," *CryoPolitics*, June 25, 2014.

98   "Russia's Rosneft offers ONGC Videsh Ltd Stake in Vankor Oilfield," *Economic Times*, October 5, 2014.

99   This is a rough comparison for illustrative purposes only – it should be kept in mind that a big part of the Nexen acquisition was its potential for future production.

100 James Paton and Aibing Guo, "Russia, China Add to US$400B Gas Deal with Second Pact," *Financial Post*, November 10, 2014.

101 Denmark, Ministry of Foreign Affairs, "Oil and Gas Newsletter," February 2014, 22.

102 Selina Williams and Daniel Gilbert, "Total Looks to China to Finance Russian Gas Project Amid Sanctions," *Wall Street Journal*, September 22, 2014.

103 James Marson and Andrey Ostroukh, "Gazprom Secures $2.17 Billion Loan from Bank of China," *Wall Street Journal*, March 3, 2016.

104   Lincoln E. Flake, "Russia and China in the Arctic: A Team of Rivals," *Strategic Analysis* 37, no. 6 (2013): 682. See also Katarzyna Zysk, "Asian Interests in the Arctic: Risks and Gains for Russia," *Asia Policy* 18, no. 1 (2014): 30–8.

105   Liu Fangqi, "Arctic Oil and Gas Development and the Status of the Latest Trends in Equipment and Technology" [北极油气开发现状及装备技术最新动向], *China Ship Survey* [中国船检] 10 (2016).

106   Morena Skalamra, "China Can't Solve Russia's Energy Technology Trap," *Diplomat*, February 11, 2015; Xue Liu et al., "Recent Progress in Arctic Oil and Gas Exploitation Research" [北极油气勘探开发技术最新进展研究], *Ocean Development and Management* [海洋开发与管理] 1 (2014).

107   Tom Røseth, "Russia's China Policy in the Arctic," *Strategic Analysis* 38, no. 6 (2014): 855; Lincoln E. Flake, "Russia and China in the Arctic: A Team of Rivals," 686.

108   Mia Bennett, "China-Russia Gas Deal Creates Arctic Winners and Losers."

109   Geoffrey Morgan, "IEA says Canadian LNG Costs among Highest in the World – Neck and Neck with Australia," *Financial Post*, November 13, 2014.

110   Centre for Energy, *Canada: NWT Statistics*, www.centreforenergy.ca/FactsStats/ statistics.asp?template=5,13.

111   Graham Chandler, "Stranded Gas," *Up Here Business* (June 2008). For more on this period see Tom Kennedy, *Quest: Canada's Search for Arctic Oil* (Reidmore, 1988).

112   "Yukon: CNOOC funds Northern Cross at Eagle Plain," *Oil & Gas Journal*, July 1, 2011; Northern Cross, "Developing Energy for Yukoners" (2015), http://www. northerncrossyukon.ca/.

113   Chris Windeyer, "There and Back Again," *Up Here Business*, February 2013, 27.

114   Lasserre, *China and the Arctic*, 7.

115   Q. Li, "The Situation and Challenges for Deep Water Oil and Gas Exploration and Exploitation in China [我国海洋深水油气开发面临的挑战], *Zhongguo Haishang Youqi* 18, no. 2 (April 2006), quoted in Jakobson, *China Prepares for an Ice-Free Arctic*, 8.

116   See, for example, Keltie Voutier et al., "Sustainable Energy Development in Canada's Mackenzie Delta-Beaufort Sea Coastal Region," *Arctic* 61, no. 1 (2008): 105.

117   See, for example, Chinese National Petroleum Company's emerging relationship with Sovcomflot discussed in chapter 4.

118   Ron Bousso, "Oil Projects Worth More than $150-Billion Face the Axe in 2015 Because of Plunging Prices," *Financial Post*, December 4, 2014.

119   Guy Quenneville, "Chevron puts Arctic Drilling Plans on Hold Indefinitely," *CBC News*, December 18, 2014; Quenneville, "Tough Oil, Easy Decision," *Arctic Journal*, January 18, 2015.

120   Quenneville, "Tough Oil, Easy Decision."

121   See, for example, Li Hui, "The Dream of the Arctic Gas and Oil Might Break [北极油气 开发或将梦碎], *Sinopecnews* [中国石化报], March 6, 2015.

122 See, for example, Li Jie, "The Study on the International Development Mechanism of the Arctic Gas and Oil Exploitation" [北极地区油气资源开发国际合作机制研究], *Wuhan University International Law Review* [武大国际法评论] 2 (2014); Zhu Mingya et al. "The Impact of Arctic Gas and Oil Exploitation on China and the World Energy Network [北极油气资源开发对世界能源格局和中国的潜在影响], *Ocean Development and Management* [海洋开发与管理] 4 (2015).

123 Kevin McGwin, "Oil: Bucking the Trend," *Arctic Journal*, January 15, 2015.

124 Njord Wegge, "The Emerging Politics of the Arctic Ocean. Future Management of the Living Marine Resources, *Marine Policy* 55 (2015): 337.

125 MELAW, Second Sino-Canadian Exchange on the Arctic, Halifax, June 25–26, 2012, Final Workshop Report, December 2012 and Oceans North International, "More than 2,000 Scientists Worldwide Urge Protection of Central Arctic Ocean Fisheries," http://www.oceansnorth.org/arctic-fisheries-letter.

126 Boris Worm and David Vanderzwaag, "High Seas Fisheries: Troubled Waters, Tangled Governance, and Recovery Prospects," *Behind the Headlines* 64, no. 5 (2007).

127 Some commentators encourage Canada to engage the international community to enact a regulatory framework that ensures "fair and transparent management of fisheries in accordance with the Code of Conduct for Responsible Fishing." See, for example, Rob Huebert and Brooks Yeager, *A New Sea* (WWF, 2008), 10–12. Experts propose various governance models, including an Arctic regional seas framework agreement, a regional ocean management organization, or a protected area designation. See, for example, Oran Young, "Whither the Arctic? Conflict or Cooperation in the Circumpolar North," *Polar Record* 45, no. 1 (January 2009): 180.

128 Gloria Galloway, "Canada Siding with US, Denmark on High Arctic Fishing Moratorium," *Globe and Mail*, February 23, 2014; Daniel Ahrens, "Breaking the Ice: The Politics of the Arctic Council," *Berkeley Political Review*, November 22, 2014.

129 Jim Bell, "Nunavut Fishing Reps Rap Feds over Docks, Quota," *Nunatsiaq News*, March 21, 2008.

130 Thandlwe Vela, "'Exceptional' Winter Ice Fishery," *Nunatsiaq News*, February 18, 2013; Justin Nobel, "Cold Winter Equals Big Dollars for Pangnirtung Fishermen," *Nunatsiaq News*, April 24, 2012.

131 Zhou YingQi, "The Chinese Perspective," *The Arctic in World Affairs: A North Pacific Dialogue on Arctic Marine Issues*, eds. Oran R. Young, Jong Deog Kim, and Yoon Hyung Kim (Seoul: Korea Maritime Institute, 2012), 213–20.

132 "China, Russia Blocked Plan for Giant Antarctic Sea Reserve, Activists Say," *CTV News*, October 31, 2014.

133 DFAIT, *Statement on Canada's Arctic Foreign Policy*, 7.

134 A peaceful framework was agreed to at the Ilulissat declaration in 2008.

135 Walter Gibbs, "Russia and Norway Reach Accord on Barents Sea," *New York Times*, April 10, 2010, A10.

136 Sergei Lavrov and Jonas Gahr Støre, "Canada, Take Note: Here's How to Resolve Maritime Disputes," *Globe and Mail*, September 21, 2010.

137 Xiao, Yang, "The Arctic Council Open its Gate without Letting Anyone In – The Logic of the Monroe Doctrine [排他性开放:北极理事会的"门罗主义"逻辑], *Pacific Journal* [太平洋学报] 9 (2014).

138 Luo Jianwen, "Navy Major General: China Cannot Afford to Lose Out on Developing the Arctic Ocean," *Zhongguo Xinwen*, August 28, 2010.

139 Gordon Chang, "China's Arctic Play," *Foreign Policy*, March 9, 2010.

140 Linda Jakobson, "China Prepares for an Ice-Free Arctic," *SIPRI Insights on Peace and Security* 2 (March 2010).

141 Luo, "Navy Major General." For a similar case see Shengjun Zhang and Li Xing, "Chinese Energy Security and the Positioning of China's Arctic Strategy" [中国能源安全与中国北极战略定位], *International Observations* [国际观察] (2010).

142 Workshop Report, "Sino-Canadian Workshop on the Arctic," February 25–27, 2010, Beijing/Shanghai.

143 See, for example, Linda Jakobsen, *China Prepares for an Ice-Free Arctic*; Wright, *The Dragon Eyes the Top of the World*.

144 Aldo Chircop, "The Emergence of China as a Polar-Capable State," *Canadian Naval Review* 7, no. 1 (Spring 2011), 14.

145 Ted McDorman, Presentation to the First Sino-Canadian Workshop, February 2010, Beijing.

146 Permanent Mission of the Republic of Indonesia, United Nations, No. 480/POL-703/VII/10 (July 8, 2010).

147 On Li Zhenfu's statement to this effect see David Wright, *The Panda Readies to Meet the Polar Bear: China and Canada's Arctic Sovereignty Challenge* (Calgary: Canadian Defence and Foreign Affairs Institute, March 2011), 8–9.

148 Investment Canada Act, Part IV, 25.2 (1).

149 Claudia Cattaneo, "Why China's Mood is Souring on Canada's Oil Patch," *Financial Post*, July 10, 2014.

150 Nathan Vanderklippe, "Nexen Deal Comes Back to Haunt CNOOC," *Globe and Mail*, December 3, 2013.

151 Willis and Depledge, "How We Learned to Stop Worrying," 767–8.

152 "Stephen Harper Raises Human Rights Concerns with Chinese President Xi Jinping," *CBC News*, November 9, 2014; and Steven Chase, "Challenges with China Can't 'Just be Pretended Away,' Harper says in one-on-one Interview," *Globe and Mail*, December 17, 2004.

153 On the conditions of the resource curse, see Philippe Le Billon, ed., *Geopolitics of Resource Wars: Resource Dependence, Governance and Violence* (London: Frank Cass, 2005).

154 Perry and Andersen, *New Strategic Dynamics in the Arctic Region*, 80.

155 Quoted in Andrew Ward and Sylvia Pfeifer, "Greenland Sees Oil as Key to Independence," *Financial Times*, August 26, 2010.

156 Mary Simon, "Inuit and the Canadian Arctic: Sovereignty Begins at Home," *Journal of Canadian Studies* 43, no. 2 (2009): 250–60; Inuit Circumpolar Council, "Circumpolar Declaration on Sovereignty in the Arctic" (2009); Jessica Shadian, *The Politics of Arctic Sovereignty: Oil, Ice, and Inuit Governance* (London: Routledge, 2014).

157 "Circumpolar Agreement Affirms Inuit Development Rights," *Indian Country Today Media Network*, May 26, 2011.

158 "Circumpolar Inuit Declaration on Resource Development Principles in Inuit Nunaat," May 11, 2011. The declaration states that "Inuit welcome the opportunity to work in full partnership with resource developers, governments and local communities in the sustainable development of resources of Inuit Nunaat, including related policy-making, to the long-lasting benefit of Inuit and with respect for baseline environmental and social responsibilities."

159 Ministry of Foreign Affairs of the PRC, "Keynote Speech by Vice Foreign Minister Zhang Ming at the China Country Session of the Third Arctic Circle Assembly," Speech to the Third Arctic Circle Assembly, Iceland, October 17, 2015.

Chapter 5 - China and Arctic Governance: Uncertainty and Potential Friction

1 Ministry of Foreign Affairs of the PRC, "Keynote Speech by Vice Foreign Minister Zhang Ming at the China Country Session of the Third Arctic Circle Assembly," Speech to the Third Arctic Circle Assembly, Iceland, October 17, 2015.

2 DFAIT, *Statement on Canada's Arctic Foreign Policy: Exercising Sovereignty and Promoting Canada's Northern Strategy Abroad* (August 2010).

3 Ibid.

4 "Charting New Arctic Waters," *Toronto Star*, August 21, 2010.

5 Steven Chase, "Only Arctic Nations Should Shape the North, Harper Tells The Globe," *Globe and Mail*, January 17, 2014.

6 See, for example, Workshop Report, "Sino-Canadian Workshop on the Arctic," held in Beijing/Shanghai, February, 25–27, 2010, and Final Workshop Report, "Second Sino-Canadian Exchange on the Arctic," held in Halifax, June 25–26, 2012.

7 See, for example, Li Zhenfu "A Northeast Asian Perspective on the Greater Arctic" [大北极视角下的泛东北亚], China Ship Survey [中国船检] 8 (2016); Meng Zhenrong, "The Competition in the Arctic and China's Response" [北极之争与中国应对], *Intelligence* [才智] 2 (2016).

8 Hi Zhenyue cited in Caitlin Campbell, "China and the Arctic: Objectives and Obstacles," *US-China Economic and Security Review Commission Staff Research Report*, April 13, 2012, 3.

9   Yang Jian, "China and Arctic Affairs," *Arctic Yearbook* (2012), emphasis added.

10   Chinese presentation to the Second Sino-Canadian Exchange on the Arctic, held in Halifax, June 25–26, 2012, identity withheld according to Chatham House rules.

11   Jian Yang, "The Integration of Non-Arctic Factors and the Mechanism of Arctic Governance" [域外因素的嵌入与北极治理机制], *Journal of Social Sciences* [社会科学] 1 (2014).

12   Linda Jakobson and Jingchao Peng, *China's Arctic Aspirations*, SIPRI Policy Paper 34 (Stockholm: Stockholm International Peace Research Institute, November 2012), 11.

13   Jakobson and Peng, *China's Arctic Aspirations*, 12.

14   David Curtis Wright, *The Dragon Eyes the Top of the World: Arctic Policy Debate and Discussion in China* (Newport: Naval War College Press, China Maritime Studies Institute, 2011), 2.

15   See for instance: Guo Zhen, "China's Ocean Rights in the Arctic – Based on an Analysis of UNCLOS [中国在北极的海洋权益及其维护——基于《联合国海洋法公约》的分析], *Theoretical Studies on PLA Political Work* [军队政工理论研究] 1 (2014).

16   In his review of China's Arctic interests for Defence Research and Development Canada, Kyle Christensen seems to have examined these authors and not the other side of the debate. See "China in the Arctic: Potential Developments Impacting China's Activities in an Ice-Free Arctic," *On Track* (Conference of Defence Associations Institute) (Winter 2010–11): 19–20. His report "China in the Arctic: China's Interests and Activities in an Ice-Free Arctic" (DRDC CORA LR 2010-210) is now available online at http://publications.gc.ca/collections/collection_2016/rddc-drdc/D68-6-196-2011-eng.pdf.

17   Sanjay Chaturvedi, "Geopolitical Transformations," 232.

18   Ed Struzik, "As the Far North Melts, Calls Grow for Arctic Treaty," *Yale Environment 360*, June 14, 2010; Rob Huebert, "The Need for an Arctic Treaty: Growing from the United Nations Convention on the Law of the Sea," *Ocean Yearbook* 23 (2009); Hans H. Hertell, "Arctic Melt: The Tipping Point for an Arctic Treaty," *Georgetown International Environmental Law Review* 21 (2009): 565–91; Timo Koivurova and Erik J. Molenaar, *International Governance and Regulation of the Marine Arctic: Overview and Gap Analysis* (Oslo: World Wildlife Foundation, 2009).

19   The Arctic Governance Project, "Arctic Governance in an Era of Transformative Change: Critical Questions, Governance Principles, Ways Forward," April 14, 2010. Bridget Larocque of the Gwitch'in Council International criticized the Arctic Governance project proposals as flawed. She was reported stating that "the report was directed by people who don't live in the Arctic and that their steering committee sidelined the Arctic Council's indigenous permanent participants." She also noted that the Arctic Council was completing its own review. Jane George, "Group Touts Big Makeover for Arctic Council," *Nunatsiaq News*, May 20, 2010.

20   This section draws from James Manicom and P. Whitney Lackenbauer, "Demystifying China's Arctic Ambitions: What Can We Expect from China in the Arctic?," a paper presented to the international symposium *China and the World after the 18th NCCPC*,

held in Montreal, February 21–22, 2013; "The Chinese Pole," *Policy Options* (May 2013); and "East Asian States, the Arctic Council and International Relations in the Arctic," *CIGI Policy Brief* 26 (April 2013).

21 DFAIT, Statement on Canada's Arctic Foreign Policy, 9.

22 Timo Koivurova and David Vanderzwaag, "The Arctic Council at 10 Years: Retrospect and Prospects," *UBC Law Review* 40, no. 1 (2008): 122; Arctic Council, "About the Arctic Council," http://www.arctic-council.org/index.php/en/about-us.

23 Arctic Athabaskan Council (AAC), "Europe and the Arctic: A View From the Arctic Athabaskan Council," Presentation to Nordic Council of Ministers, Arctic Conference: Common Concern for the Arctic, Ilulissat, Greenland (September 9–11, 2008), 3.

24 Oran R. Young, "Governing the Arctic: From Cold War Theatre to Mosaic of Cooperation," *Global Governance* 11 (2005): 11.

25 David Vanderzwaag in Workshop Report, "Sino-Canadian Workshop on the Arctic," Beijing/Shanghai, February 25–27, 2010.

26 Arctic Council, "Working Groups," http://www.arctic-council.org/index.php/en/about-us/working-groups. Working Groups also regularly invite guests or experts to attend their meetings. Several Task Forces, appointed at the Ministerial meetings to work on specific issues for a limited amount of time, also operate within the framework of the Arctic Council. The Task Forces are active until they have produced the desired results, at which point they become inactive. In May 2011, the Nuuk Declaration also established an Ecosystem-based Management Experts Group *to recommend further activities in this field for consideration by the Senior Arctic Officials before the end of the Swedish chairmanship.*

27 For Inuit perspectives on the EU seal ban, see the Inuit Circumpolar Council website at: www.inuitcircumpolar.com. Another controversial aspect of the EU's application related to the European Commission's first Communication specifically on the Arctic on November 20, 2008 (IP/08/1750), which proposed the need for an Antarctic-like treaty. This directly contradicted the Illulissat Declaration by the Arctic coastal states announced on May 28, 2008.

28 Steven Chase, "Q&A with Harper: No Previous Government Has 'Delivered More in the North,'" *Globe and Mail*, January 17, 2014.

29 Chircop, "The Emergence of China as a Polar-Capable State," 13.

30 Jakobson and Peng, *China's Arctic Aspirations*, 13.

31 Lincoln E. Flake, "Russia and China in the Arctic: A Team of Rivals," *Strategic Analysis* 37, no. 6 (2013): 681.

32 Denmark, "Programme for the Danish Chairmanship of the Arctic Council 2009–2011," April 29, 2009.

33 Norway, Minister of Foreign Affairs Jonas Gahr Støre, "The Arctic: Norwegian Policy and International Cooperation," speech made August 30, 2010.

34 Steven Lee Myers, "Arctic Council Adds 6 Nations as Observer States, Including China," *New York Times*, May 15, 2013.

35   Matthew Willis and Duncan Depledge, "How We Learned to Stop Worrying about China's Arctic Ambitions: Understanding China's Admission to the Arctic Council, 2004" *Handbook of the Politics of the Arctic*, eds. Leif Christian Jensen and Geir Hønneland (Northampton: Edward Elgar, 2015), 765, 786.

36   The Nuuk Ministerial Meeting also decided to adopt the recommendations of the Senior Arctic Officials on the role and criteria for observers to the Arctic Council (SAO Report, May 2011). The SAO Report acknowledges at the outset that "Since the establishment of the Arctic Council participation by observers has been a valuable feature through their provision of scientific and other expertise, information and financial resources. The involvement of observers should enhance and complement the unique and critical role of permanent participants in the Arctic Council." As for the role of observers, it resolved that "decisions at all levels in the Arctic Council are the exclusive right and responsibility of the eight Arctic states with the involvement of the permanent participants." Once observer status has been granted to them, the primary role of observers is "to observe the work of the Arctic Council" and "continue to make relevant contributions through their engagement in the Arctic Council primarily at the level of working groups." Observers are allowed to propose projects through an Arctic state or a permanent participant "but financial contributions from observers to any given project may not exceed the financing from Arctic states, unless otherwise decided by the SAOs."

37   Lincoln E. Flake, "Russia and China in the Arctic: A Team of Rivals," 681.

38   Statement by H.E. Ambassador Lan Lijun at the Meeting between the Swedish Chairmanship of the Arctic Council and observers, November 6, 2012.

39   Willis and Depledge, "How We Learned to Stop Worrying," 766.

40   Ibid.

41   Ibid.

42   Cheng, "Arctic Aspirations." In addition, Cheng Baozhi of the Shanghai Institute for International Studies cast the new criteria as an attempt by the Member States to raise "The Political Threshold in Order to Stop Non-Arctic States Interfering in Arctic [Affairs]." Quoted in Jakobson and Peng, *China's Arctic Aspirations*, 14.

43   Arctic Council, "Observers."

44   Guo Peiqing, "An Analysis of New Criteria for Permanent Observer Status on the Arctic Council and the Road of Non-Arctic States to Arctic," draft article, *KMI International Journal of Maritime Affairs and Fisheries* 4, no. 2 (2012): 4, 6. Peiqing also raises specific concerns related to subjects such as excessive straight baselines, outer continental shelf claims, and LOSC Article 234.

45   Peiqing, "An Analysis of New Criteria," 11–14.

46   James Manicom and P. Whitney Lackenbauer, "The Chinese Pole," *Policy Options* 34, no. 4 (April–May 2013): 12–15. See also Kristofer Bergh, "Arctic Cooperation Must Become More Inclusive," SIPRI Essay (July/August 2011).

47   Lasserre, *China and the Arctic: Threat or Cooperation*, 11.

48 The literature is Elizabeth Economy and Michel Oksenberg, eds. *China Joins the World: Progress and Prospects* (New York: Council on Foreign Relations, 1999); Alastair Iain Johnston and Robert S. Ross, eds., *Engaging China: The Management of an Emerging Power* (London: Routledge, 1999); Harold K. Jacobson and Michel Oksenberg, *China's Participation in the IMF, the World Bank and GATT: Toward a Global Economic Order* (Ann Arbor: University of Michigan Press, 1990); Alastair Iain Johnston, *Social States: China in International Institutions, 1980–2000* (Princeton: Princeton University Press, 2009); Ann Kent, *Beyond Compliance: China, International Organizations and Global Security* (Stanford: Stanford University Press, 2007).

49 Nina Hachigan, *China's Engagement in the International System: In the Ring, But Punching Below Its Weight* (Washington, DC: Center for American Progress, 2009).

50 Quoted in Jakobson and Peng, *China's Arctic Aspirations*, 14.

51 Yoshinobu Takei, "Who Governs the Arctic Ocean? A Reply from an International Law Perspective," *Ocean Policy Studies* 9 (July 2011): 62–8.

52 Cheng Baozhi, "Arctic Aspirations," *Beijing Review* 4, August 24, 2011.

53 Frédéric Lasserre and Linyan Huang, "China's Strategy in the Arctic: Threatening or Opportunistic?" *Polar Record* 53, no. 1 (2017): 31-42.

54 Jin Kai, "Can China Build a Community of Common Destiny?" *Diplomat*, November 28, 2013.

55 See, for example, Huang Dung and Baolin Zhu, "Arctic Governance Mechanisms and Innovation, A "Community of Destiny" Concept [基于"命运共同体"理念的北极治理机制创新], *Exploration and Free Views* [探索与争鸣] 3 (2016); Huang Ding and Chong Zhang, "China's Participation in Arctic Governance – A Perspective Based on Institutional Neoliberalism" [中国参与北极治理的价值分析基于新自由制度主义的视角], *Wuhan University Journal* [武汉大学学报(哲学社会科学版] 3 (2016).

56 Chaturvedi, "Geopolitical Transformations," 251.

57 Patricia A.L. Cochran, ICC Chair on behalf of Inuit in Greenland, Canada, Alaska, and Chukotka, "Circumpolar Inuit Declaration on Arctic Sovereignty," adopted by the Inuit Circumpolar Council (April 2009).

58 Despite the official assurances that the core of Canada's Northern Strategy is first and foremost about people, Northern indigenous groups have expressed concerns about their involvement in national and international decision-making. Inuit representatives, for example, have suggested that the government agenda prioritizes investments in defence and resource development at the expense of environmental protection and improved social and economic conditions. They insist that "sovereignty begins at home" and that the primary challenges are domestic human security issues, requiring investments in infrastructure, education, and health care. As such, indigenous voices add to the complexity of the Canadian message projected to the rest of the world. See, for example, Inuit Qaujisarvingat/Inuit Knowledge Centre, *Nilliajut: Inuit Perspectives on Sovereignty, Patriotism, and Security* (Ottawa: Inuit Tapiriit Kanatami and the Walter and Duncan Gordon Foundation, 2013). The Inuit Circumpolar Council's transnational *Circumpolar Inuit Declaration on Sovereignty in the Arctic* (2009) emphasized that "the inextricable linkages between issues of sovereignty and

sovereign rights in the Arctic and Inuit self-determination and other rights require states to accept the presence and role of Inuit as partners in the conduct of international relations in the Arctic." The declaration envisions the Inuit playing an active role in all deliberations on environmental security, sustainable development, militarization, shipping, and socio-economic development.

59   Peter Kikkert, "Rising above the Rhetoric: Northern Voices and the Strengthening of Canada's Capacity to Maintain a Stable Circumpolar World," *Northern Review* 33 (2009): 8.

60   DFAIT, *Statement on Canada's Arctic Foreign Policy* (August 2010).

61   Jim Bell, "Aglukkaq Stresses 'People-First' Approach to Arctic Council," *Nunatsiaq News*, October 29, 2012.

62   Quoted in "China, Korea, EU Woo Arctic Council at Norway Conference," *Nunatsiaq News*, January 22, 2013.

63   Lisa Gregoire, "Arctic Council Should Be Cautious about New Observer Hopefuls," *Nunatsiaq News*, February 1, 2013.

64   Timo Koivurova, "Sovereign States and Self-Determining Peoples: Carving Out a Place for Transnational Indigenous Peoples in a World of Sovereign States," *International Community Law Review* 12 (2010).

65   Inuit Tapiriit Kanatami (ITK), *An Integrated Arctic Strategy* (2008), 12.

66   Cochran. While regional institutions involving non-Arctic states "can provide useful mechanisms for international exchange and cooperation," the Inuit declaration on sovereignty also insists that "the conduct of international relations in the Arctic and the resolution of international disputes in the Arctic are not the sole preserve of Arctic states or other states, they are also within the purview of the Arctic indigenous peoples. The development of international institutions in the Arctic, such as multi-level governance systems and indigenous people's organizations must transcend Arctic states' agenda on sovereignty and sovereignty rights and the traditional monopoly claimed by states in the area of foreign affairs."

67   In August 2010, for example, the Qikiqtani Inuit Association secured an injunction to halt seismic testing in Lancaster Sound on the grounds that this activity could affect whales, polar bears and other marine life and change migration patterns. "Inuit Win Injunction on Seismic Testing," *CBC News*, August 8, 2010. In December 2006, Nunavut Tunngavik Inc. filed a $1 billion lawsuit against the government of Canada for breach of contract, arguing that Canada "is not living up to its implementation responsibilities and is therefore violating the Nunavut Land Claims Agreement (NLCA)" and "keeps Inuit dependent and in a state of financial and emotional despair despite promises made when the NLCA was signed in 1993." NTI, "NTI Launches Lawsuit against Government of Canada for Breach of Contract," December 6, 2006.

68   Jakobson and Peng, *China's Arctic Aspirations*, 14–15.

69   Donat Pharand, "Arctic Waters and the Northwest Passage: A Final Revisit," *Ocean Development and International Law* 38, nos. 1–2 (2007): 59.

70   See, for example, Huang Ding and Chong Zhang, "China's Participation in Arctic Governance - A Perspective Based on Institutional Neoliberalism" [中国参与北极治理的价值分析基于新自由制度主义的视角], *Wuhan University Journal* [武汉大学学报 (哲学社会科学版) 3 (2016); Lu Jing, "An Analysis of the Arctic Governance Dilemma and Coordination [北极治理困境与协同治理路径探析],International Studies [国际问题研究] 5 (2016).

71   Oran R. Young, "Governing the Arctic: From Cold War Theatre to Mosaic of Cooperation," *Global Governance* 11 (2005): 10, 14.

72   Lawson Brigham, "The Fast-Changing Maritime Arctic," US Naval Institute *Proceedings* (May 2010): 57; Shih-Ming Kao, Nathaniel S. Pearre, and Jeremy Firestone, "Adoption of the Arctic Search and Rescue Agreement: A Shift of the Arctic Regime toward a Hard Law Basis?" *Marine Policy* 36, no. 3 (2012): 832–8; Heather Exner-Pirot, "Defence Diplomacy in the Arctic: The Search and Rescue Agreement as a Confidence Builder," *Canadian Foreign Policy Journal* 18, no. 2 (2012): 195–207; Arctic Council, "Agreement on Cooperation on Marine Oil Pollution Preparedness and Response in the Arctic" (2013).

73   See, for example, Thomas Axworthy, Timo Koivurova, and Waliul Hasanat, eds., *The Arctic Council: Its Place in the Future of Arctic Governance* (Toronto: Walter & Duncan Gordon Foundation, 2012); Lassi Heininen, Heather Exner-Pirot, and Joel Plouffe, eds., *2016 Arctic Yearbook – The Arctic Council: 20 Years of Regional Cooperation and Policy Shaping* (Northern Research Forum, 2016); Douglas Nord, *The Changing Arctic: Creating a Framework for Consensus Building and Governance within the Arctic Council* (Houndmills: Palgrave Macmillan, 2016); Oran R. Young, "The Arctic Council at Twenty: How to Remain Effective in a Rapidly Changing Environment," *University of California Irvine Law Review* 6 (2016): 99–120.

74   An example is the Arctic Circle, a new international assembly launched by Iceland in April 2013. See Duncan Depledge and Klaus Dodds, "Bazaar Governance: Situating the Arctic Council," in *Governing Arctic Change: Global Perspectives*, eds. Kathrin Keil and Sebastian Knecht (London: Palgrave Macmillan, 2017), 141–60. On the Arctic Circle as a challenge for Canada, see Paul Koring, "New Arctic Group Gives Canada Political Competition," *Globe and Mail*, April 15, 2013.

75   Valur Ingimundarsona, "Managing a Contested Region: The Arctic Council and the Politics of Arctic Governance," *Polar Journal* 3, no. 1 (2014): 194.

76   Frédéric Lasserre has also argued that "engaging China and supporting the admission of other countries as observers at the Arctic Council could prove useful for Canada in keeping its own agenda prominent in cooperation discussions ... working on building common grounds with China and taking its concerns and interests into account could prove profitable inasmuch as China, in turn, consider Canada's specific interests in the Arctic." Lasserre, *China and the Arctic: Threat or Cooperation*, 11. See also Piotr Graczyk, Małgorzata Śmieszek, Timo Koivurova, and Adam Stępień, "Preparing for the Global Rush: The Arctic Council, Institutional Norms, and Socialisation of Observer

Behaviour," in *Governing Arctic Change: Global Perspectives*, eds. Kathrin Keil and Sebastian Knecht (London: Palgrave Macmillan, 2017), 121–40.

77 Statement by H.E. Ambassador Lan Lijun at the Meeting between the Swedish Chairmanship of the Arctic Council and observers.

Chapter 6 - The Way Ahead

1 DFAIT, Statement on Canada's Arctic Foreign Policy, 23.

2 Chaturvedi, "Geopolitical Transformations," 240.

3 The first part of this overview of the Trudeau government's agenda is derived from P. Whitney Lackenbauer and Suzanne Lalonde, "Searching for Common Ground in Evolving Canadian and EU Arctic Strategies," in *The European Union and the Arctic*, ed. Nengye Liu (Leiden: Brill, 2017), 119-171.

4 See, for example, Matthew Bondy: "Justin Trudeau is Putting the 'Liberal' Back in 'Canadian Foreign Policy,'" *Foreign Policy*, October 21, 2015; Lee Berthiaume, "A Return to Multilateralism," *National Post*, December 29, 2015; Stéphane Dion, "On 'Responsible Conviction' and Liberal Foreign Policy," *Maclean's*, March 29, 2016. On the new government's main priorities and their relationship to the North, see Thomas Axworthy, "In the North, Justin Trudeau Can Accomplish Great Things," *Toronto Star*, March 6, 2016.

5 Prime Minister of Canada, "Ministerial Mandate Letters," http://pm.gc.ca/eng/ministerial-mandate-letters.

6 Gloria Galloway, "Canada Drops Opposition to UN Indigenous Rights Declaration," *Globe and Mail*, May 9, 2016.

7 Ken Coates and Bill Favel, "Embrace of UNDRIP Can Bring Aboriginal Canada and Ottawa Closer Together," *iPolitics*, May 19, 2016.

8 Jason Fekete, "Justin Trudeau Says Canada 'Is Back at Climate-Change Meeting,'" *National Post*, November 30, 2015.

9 Liberal Party of Canada, "A New Plan for Canada's Environment and Economy" (August 2015), https://www.liberal.ca/files/2015/08/A-new-plan-for-Canadas-environment-and-economy.pdf. On the muzzling of government scientists, see for example Verlyn Klinkenborg, "Silencing Scientists," *New York Times*, September 21, 2013; Jonathon Gatehouse, "When Science Goes Silent," *Maclean's*, May 3, 2013; Margaret Munro, "Unmuzzling Government Scientists Is Just the First Step," *Globe and Mail*, October 26, 2015; Mark Hume, "Federal Scientists Eager to Share Their Research Now That Muzzles Are Off," *Globe and Mail*, November 8, 2015.

10 Canadian Press, "Trudeau on Climate Targets: 'Canada's Efforts Will Not Cease,'" *Maclean's*, April 22, 2016.

11 "US-Canada Joint Statement on Climate, Energy, and Arctic Leadership," March 10, 2016.

12 After PM Harper "ordered a rewrite of Canada's international claim for Arctic seabed rights to include the North Pole" in December 2013, Trudeau (as Liberal leader) noted:

"I am going to defer to scientists. There has been an awful lot of work done over the past years, and even decades, on mapping out the undersea floor of the North Pole to align with the United Nations regulations ... And I don't know that it is a place where we need necessarily to have political interference. I trust our scientists and oceanographers in terms of how we're mapping it." Steven Chase, "Turf War with Russia Looms over Ottawa's Claim to Arctic Seabed," *Globe and Mail*, December 5, 2013.

13   See, for example, Borgerson and Byers, "Arctic Front in the Battle to Contain Russia"; Levon Sevunts, "Canada's Defence Review and the Arctic," *Radio Canada International*, April 8, 2016.

14   See, for example, Ernie Regehr, "A Nuclear-Weapon-Free Zone and Cooperative Security in the Arctic," Simons Foundation Disarming Arctic Security Project, October 14, 2014; Thomas Axworthy, "A Proposal for an Arctic Nuclear Weapon-Free Zone," *Yearbook of Polar Law* 4, no. 1 (2012): 87–139; Michael D. Wallace and Steven Staples, *Ridding the Arctic of Nuclear Weapons: A Task Long Overdue* (Ottawa: Rideau Institute, February 2010).

15   In highlighting the need for "an agile, responsive, and well-equipped military force that can effectively defend Canada and North America," and by mentioning the Arctic in particular, there is no indication that Arctic defence, security, and safety will be downgraded in importance. Instead, the Liberal party promised to make investments in the Royal Canadian Navy to be a "top priority," including completing the six Arctic and offshore patrol ships (AOPS) announced by the Conservatives and the construction of more icebreakers (presumably for the Canadian Coast Guard). Liberal Party of Canada, "Defence Platform [2015]," https://www.liberal.ca/realchange/royal-canadian-navy/.

16   See P. Whitney Lackenbauer, "Towards a Comprehensive Approach: Defence, Security, and Safety," in *North of 60: Toward a Renewed Canadian Arctic Agenda*, eds. John Higginbotham and Jennifer Spence (Waterloo: Centre for International Governance Innovation, 2016), 50–4.

17   While the Harper Conservatives had suspended almost all bilateral contact with Russia after the latter invaded Crimea in March 2014, Dion stressed that this extreme stand deviated from the actions of the US and other G7 partners. "We also need to think about our national interests because Russia is our neighbour in the Arctic," the minister explained. Lee Berthiaume, "Canada Ready to Re-engage with Russia, Iran, Despite Differences, Dion Says," *Ottawa Citizen*, November 11, 2015. During the election campaign in October 2015, Trudeau had told reporters that, if he became prime minister, he would "tell off" Putin "directly to his face" after accusing the Russian leader of "being dangerous" in eastern Europe, "irresponsible and harmful" in the Middle East, and "unduly provocative" in the Arctic. Canadian Press, "Justin Trudeau Would Tell Off 'Bully' Vladimir Putin 'Directly to His Face' If He Becomes Prime Minister," *National Post*, October 13, 2015.

18   In January 2016, Dion reiterated that Canada hoped to resume dialogue with Russia, despite that country's military aggression in Ukraine, and cited the Arctic as a region where Canada would benefit from reengagement with its circumpolar neighbour. Scott Borgerson and Michael Byers, "The Arctic Front in the Battle to Contain Russia," *Wall Street Journal*, 8 March 2016. See also Matthew Fisher, "Allies Wait for Great Defence Commitment from Canada While Russia Militarizes the Arctic," *National Post*,

February 4, 2016; Eva Salinas and Hannah Hoag [in conversation with Rob Huebert and Heather Exner-Pirot], "Canada Wants to Reopen Dialogue with Russia," *Arctic Deeply*, February 17, 2016.

19　See, for example, Kari Roberts, "Why Russia Will Play by the Rules in the Arctic," *Canadian Foreign Policy Journal* 21, no. 2 (2015): 112–28; Adam Lajeunesse and Whitney Lackenbauer, "Canadian Arctic Security: Russia's Not Coming," *OpenCanada/ Arctic Deeply*, April 19, 2016, https://www.opencanada.org/features/canadian-arctic-security-russias-not-coming/; Lackenbauer, "Canada & Russia: Toward an Arctic Agenda," *Global Brief* (Summer/Fall 2016): 21–5.

20　Thomas Axworthy, "In the North, Justin Trudeau Can Accomplish Great Things," *Toronto Star*, March 6, 2016.

21　"US-Canada Joint Statement on Climate, Energy, and Arctic Leadership," 10 March 2016, http://www.pm.gc.ca/eng/news/2016/03/10/us-canada-joint-statement-climate-energy-and-arctic-leadership#sthash.XjRoT2R7.dpuf.

22　"US-Canada Joint Statement on Climate, Energy, and Arctic Leadership," December 20, 2016, http://pm.gc.ca/eng/news/2016/12/20/united-states-canada-joint-arctic-leaders-statement.

23　"US-Canada Joint Statement on Climate, Energy, and Arctic Leadership," 10 March 2016.

24　Conservation of Arctic Flora and Fauna (CAFF) Working Group, *Arctic Biodiversity Assessment 2013: Report for Policy Makers* (Akureyri: CAFF, 2013), 8, 10.

25　"US-Canada Joint Statement on Climate, Energy, and Arctic Leadership," 10 March 2016.

26　Indigenous and Northern Affairs Canada (INAC), "Shared Arctic Leadership Model Engagement 2016: Discussion Guide," October 7, 2016, https://www.aadnc-aandc.gc.ca/eng/1475862863810/1475862891382. See also Sima Sahar Zerehi, "Mary Simon Named Minister of Indigenous Affairs' Special Representative on Arctic," *CBC News*, August 5, 2016,

27　See Inuit Circumpolar Council Canada, "Application of Indigenous Knowledge in the Arctic Council," http://www.inuitcircumpolar.com/application-of-indigenous-knowledge-in-the-arctic-council.html; Arctic Council Participants, "Ottawa Traditional Knowledge Principles" (2014), http://www.saamicouncil.net/fileadmin/user_upload/Documents/Eara_dokumeanttat/Ottawa_TK_Principles.pdf.

28　"US-Canada Joint Statement on Climate, Energy, and Arctic Leadership," March 10, 2016.

29　"US-Canada Joint Statement on Climate, Energy, and Arctic Leadership," December 20, 2016.

30　"Select Actions Being Taken under the United States-Canada Joint Arctic Leaders' Statement," December 20, 2016, http://pm.gc.ca/eng/news/2016/12/20/select-actions-being-taken-under-united-states-canada-joint-arctic-leaders-statement.

31　According to the Nunavut Impact Review Board (NIRB), the Nunavut Marine Council (NMC) was established in 2012 by Section 15.4.1 of the *Nunavut Land Claims Agreement* (NLCA), "which allows the Nunavut Impact Review Board, the Nunavut Water Board, the Nunavut Planning Commission and the Nunavut Wildlife Management Board to, together as the NMC, or individually advise and make recommendations to other government agencies regarding the marine areas of the Nunavut Settlement Area." Pursuant to the NLCA, the Canadian government "must consider such advice and recommendations in making decisions which affect marine areas," with the objective of ensuring "the ongoing protection and wise use of the marine areas for the long-term benefit of Inuit and the rest of the public of Nunavut and Canada, in a manner consistent with the principles of *Inuit Qaujimajatuqangit* and of the Nunavut Land Claims Agreement." NIRB, "Nunavut Marine Council," http://www. nirb.ca/marine-council. See also NMC, "What is the Nunavut Marine Council?," http:// www.nunavutmarinecouncil.com/node/30.

32 "US-Canada Joint Statement on Climate, Energy, and Arctic Leadership," March 10, 2016.

33 "Declaration Concerning the Prevention of Unregulated High Seas Fishing in the Central Arctic Ocean," Oslo, July 16, 2015, https://www.regjeringen.no/globalassets/ departementene/ud/vedlegg/folkerett/declaration-on-arctic-fisheries-16-july-2015.pdf.

34 "US-Canada Joint Statement on Climate, Energy, and Arctic Leadership," March 10, 2016.

35 On this context, see Sarah Gulas, Mitchell Downton, Kareina D'Souza, Kelsey Hayden, and Tony R. Walker, "Declining Arctic Ocean Oil and Gas Developments: Opportunities to Improve Governance and Environmental Pollution Control," *Marine Policy* 75 (2017): 53–61.

36 "US-Canada Joint Statement on Climate, Energy, and Arctic Leadership," December 20, 2016.

37 Heather Exner-Pirot also suggests that the December joint statement also shows a realignment of Canadian Arctic foreign policy with US priorities, as well as the influence of environmental groups such as WWF and Oceans North Canada which, she observes, "Boast Alumni Currently in Senior Canadian Government Roles." Exner-Pirot, "Six Takeaways from this Week's US-Canada joint Arctic Statement," *OpenCanada*, December 22, 2016.

38 This objective stresses that "all Indigenous Peoples in the Arctic are vital to strengthening and supporting US and Canadian sovereignty claims," and both countries "commit to working in partnership to implement land claims agreements to realize the social, cultural and economic potential of all Indigenous and Northern communities." Priority areas include renewable energy and efficiency alternatives to diesel; community climate change adaptation; "innovative options for housing and infrastructure"; and action to improve mental wellness, education, Indigenous languages, and skill development, particularly among Indigenous youth. "US-Canada Joint Statement on Climate, Energy, and Arctic Leadership," March 10, 2016.

39 Sima Sahar Zerehi, "Trudeau-Obama Shared Arctic Leadership Model a Hit with Inuit and Environmental Groups," *CBC News*, March 11, 2016, http://www.cbc.ca/news/ canada/north/trudeau-obama-washington-visit-arctic-promises-1.3486076.

40 "US-Canada Joint Statement on Climate, Energy, and Arctic Leadership," March 10, 2016.

41 Exner-Pirot, "Six Takeaways from this Week's US-Canada Joint Arctic Statement."

42 On this characterization of the Conservative government's agenda see, for example, Lisa Williams, "Canada, the Arctic, and Post-national Identity in the Circumpolar

World," *Northern Review* 33 (2011): 113–31; Whitney Lackenbauer, "Harper's Arctic Evolution," *Globe and Mail*, August 20, 2013; Petra Dolata, "A New Canada in the Arctic? Arctic Policies under Harper," *Études canadiennes/Canadian Studies – Revue interdisciplinaire des études canadiennes en France* 78 (2015): 131–54; Jerald Sabin, "North's Liberal Vote a Rebuke of Harper's Arctic Policy," *CBC News*, October 21, 2015, http://www.cbc.ca/news/canada/north/opinion-sabin-arctic-policy-election-1.3280899; Wilfrid Greaves, "Thinking Critically about Security and the Arctic in the Anthropocene," The Arctic Institute, March 22, 2016, http://www.thearcticinstitute. org/thinking-critically-about-security-and-the-arctic-in-the-anthropocene/; Heather Nicol, "Ripple Effects: Devolution, Development and State Sovereignty in the Canadian North," in *Future Security of the Global Arctic: State Policy, Economic Security and Climate*, ed. Lassi Heininen (Basingstoke: Palgrave Macmillan, 2016), 99–120.

43   See P. Whitney Lackenbauer and Ryan Dean, eds., *Canada's Northern Strategy under the Harper Conservatives: Key Speeches and Documents on Sovereignty, Security, and Governance, 2006–15*, Documents on Canadian Arctic Sovereignty and Security (DCASS) No. 6 (Calgary and Waterloo: Centre for Military, Strategic and Security Studies/Centre on Foreign Policy and Federalism/Arctic Institute of North America, 2016).

44   Address by Parliamentary Secretary Goldsmith-Jones, on behalf of Minister Dion, marking the twentieth anniversary of the Arctic Council, Ottawa, September 29, 2016, http://news.gc.ca/web/article-en.do?nid=1131189.

45   "The Arctic Council at 20 Years: More Necessary than Ever," address by Parliamentary Secretary Pamela Goldsmith-Jones at Arctic Circle Assembly, October 8, 2016, Reykjavik, Iceland, http://news.gc.ca/web/article-en.do?nid=1139819.

46   Evans, *Engaging China*, 75.

47   Ibid, 98–9.

48   Mulroney, *Middle Power, Middle Kingdom*, 291.

49   Peter Edwards, "Chinese Media Swoons over Justin Trudeau, the 'Future of Canada,'" *Toronto Star*, September 2, 2016.

50   Ibid.

51   Doug Saunders, "What Are Justin Trudeau's End-Game Ambitions with China?," *Globe and Mail*, September 23, 2016.

52   Deborah Wilson, "Goodwill Visit by Chinese Navy Draws Crowds, Questions," *CBC News*, December 17, 2016.

53   Andy Blanchford, "Canada to Apply to Join China-Backed Asian Infrastructure Investment Bank," *Global News*, August 31, 2016.

54   Catherine Tunney, "Chrystia Freeland Set for Trade Talks with China in 2017," *CBC News*, December 30, 2016.

55   Nathan Vanderklippe, "With Trump Presidency, Some See Chance for Canada to Embrace China," *Globe and Mail*, December 12, 2016.

56 Robert D'A. Henderson, "Liberals' China Dilemma," *Diplomat & International Canada*, October 4, 2016.

57 Doug Saunders, "What Are Justin Trudeau's End-Game Ambitions with China?," *Globe and Mail*, September 23, 2016; Henderson, "Liberals' China Dilemma."

58 Saunders, "What Are Justin Trudeau's End-Game Ambitions?"

59 For a poignant discussion of Chinese state and corporate espionage and the risks to Canadian security, see Mulroney, *Middle Power, Middle Kingdom*, 160–70.

60 Jakobson, *China Prepares For an Ice-Free Arctic*, 7.

61 China maintains a fleet of ten nuclear submarines, none of which have been designed for under-ice operations. It should be remembered that developing this capability took the Soviet and American navies decades of practice.

62 Chinese official's presentation, "Second Sino-Canadian Exchange on Arctic Issues," June 25–26, 2012, speaker's identity withheld pursuant to Chatham House rules.

63 Chen translation of Baranikova, "China's Arctic Policy."

64 See, for example, Wang Ru, "China and Canada Expect More Collaboration on the Arctic," *China Daily*, March 26, 2015.

65 Cheng Baozhi, "Arctic Aspirations," *Beijing Review* 4, August 24, 2011.

66 Luo Jianwen, "Navy Major General: China Cannot Afford to Lose Out on Developing the Arctic Ocean," *Zhongguo Xinwen*, August 28, 2010.

67 Thomas J. Christensen, "Fostering Stability or Creating a Monster? The Rise of China and US Policy toward East Asia," *International Security* 31, no. 1 (Summer 2006): 81–126.

68 Timothy Wright, "China's New Arctic Stratagem: A Strategic Buyer's Approach to the Arctic," *Journal of Military and Strategic Studies* 15, no. 1 (2013): 8.

69 David Curtis Wright, *The Dragon Eyes the Top of the World: Arctic Policy Debate and Discussion in China* (Newport: Naval War College Press, China Maritime Studies Institute, 2011), 38.

70 Evelyn Goh, "Great Powers and Hierarchical Order in Southeast Asia: Analyzing Regional Security Strategies," *International Security* 32, no. 3 (2007–08): 113–57.

71 Alistair Iain Johnston, *Cultural Realism: Strategic Culture and Grand Strategy in Chinese History* (Princeton: Princeton University Press, 1996).

72 See P. Whitney Lackenbauer and Rob Huebert, "Premier Partners: Canada, the United States and Arctic Security," *Canadian Foreign Policy Journal* 20, no. 3 (Fall 2014): 320–33.

73 See, for example, Hannah Hoag, "Expert View: How the Outcome of the US Election Affects the Arctic," *Arctic Deeply*, November 9, 2016; Jane George, "Donald Trump's Arctic: More Heat, Development and Militarization," *Nunatsiaq News*, November 9, 2016; Rob Huebert, "What Donald Trump's Presidency Might Mean for the Arctic," *Arctic Deeply*, December 14, 2016; John Higginbotham, "What Does 'America First' Mean for the Canada-US Bond over the Arctic," *OpenCanada*, January 6, 2017.

74 P. Whitney Lackenbauer and Adam Lajeunesse, "Canadian Security and Safety in the Arctic: Probable Challenges, Practical Responsibilities," *Canadian Naval Review* 10, no. 2 (Fall 2014): 10–15; Lackenbauer, "Towards a Comprehensive Approach: Defence, Security, and Safety," in *North of 60: Toward a Renewed Canadian Arctic Agenda*, ed. John Higginbotham and Jennifer Spence (Waterloo: Centre for International Governance Innovation, 2016), 50–4.

75 See the articles and chapters by P. Whitney Lackenbauer and Adam Lajeunesse: "The Canadian Armed Forces in the Arctic: Building Appropriate Capabilities," *Journal of Military and Strategic Studies* 16, no. 4 (March 2016): 7–66; "The Emerging Arctic Security Environment: Putting the Military in Its (Whole of Government) Place," in *Whole of Government through an Arctic Lens*, ed. P. Whitney Lackenbauer and Heather Nicol (Kingston: CDA Press, forthcoming 2017); "Sovereignty, Security and Canada's Northern Strategy under Prime Minister Harper," in *Canada's Northern Strategy under Stephen Harper*, eds. Klaus Dodds and Mark Nuttall (Edmonton: University of Alberta Press, forthcoming).

76 Marc Lantrigne, *China's Emerging Arctic Strategies: Economics and Institutions* (Reykjavik: Institute of International Affairs, 2014), ii.

Bibliography

Government Publications

Canada, Denmark, Norway, The Russian Federation, and the United States. *Ilulissat Declaration*. Adopted at the Arctic Ocean Conference, Ilulissat, Greenland (May 27–29, 2008).

Canada. "Fact Sheet: China" (October, 2104), http://www.canadainternational.gc.ca/china-chine.

Canada. Department of Finance. *Budget 2008: Responsible Leadership* (2008).

Canada. Department of Foreign Affairs and International Trade. *Statement on Canada's Arctic Foreign Policy: Exercising Sovereignty and Promoting Canada's Northern Strategy Abroad* (August, 2010).

Canada. House of Commons. *Debates.*

Canada. *Investment Canada Act.*

Canada. Minister of Indian Affairs and Northern Development. *Canada's Northern Strategy: Our North, Our Heritage, Our Future* (July, 2009).

Canada. Prime Minister's Office. "Prime Minister Harper Announces the John G. Diefenbaker Icebreaker Project" (August 28, 2008), http://pm.gc.ca/eng/media.asp?id=2258.

Canada. Transport Canada. "Zone Date System," http://www.tc.gc.ca/eng/marinesafety/debs-arctic-acts-regulations-zds-chart-2014.htm.

Denmark. "Programme for the Danish Chairmanship of the Arctic Council 2009–2011" (April 29, 2009).

Denmark. Ministry of Foreign Affairs. "Oil and Gas Newsletter" (February, 2014).

Greenland. Statsministeriet. "The Greenland Self-Government Arrangement" (2009).

Indonesia. Permanent Mission of the Republic of Indonesia. United Nations. No. 480/POL-703/VII/10 (July 8, 2010).

Northwest Territories. Centre for Energy. *Canada: NWT Statistics*, http://www.centreforenergy.ca/FactsStats/statistics.asp?template=5.13.

Nunavut. Bureau of Statistics. "Population Estimates 2014" (2014).

Nunavut Impact Review Board (NIRB), "Nunavut Marine Council," http://www.nirb.ca/marine-council.

Nunavut Marine Council (NMC), "What is the Nunavut Marine Council?," http://www.nunavutmarinecouncil.com/node/30.

People's Republic of China and the governments of the ASEAN States. *"Declaration on the Conduct of Parties in the South China Sea"* (2002).

People's Republic of China. Chinese Arctic & Antarctic Administration, http://www.chinare.gov.cn/en.

People's Republic of China. Ministry of Commerce. "Commercial Operation Outlook of North Pole Navigation Routes" [北极航道商业化运营的前景] (September 11, 2013).

People's Republic of China. Ministry of Foreign Affairs. "China's View on Arctic Cooperation" (July 30, 2010), http://www.fmprc.gov.cn/eng/wjb/zzjg/tyfls/tfsxw/t812046.ahtm.

People's Republic of China. Ministry of Foreign Affairs. "Premier Wen Jiabao Holds Talks with His Icelandic Counterpart Sigurdardottir" (April 21, 2012).

People's Republic of China. PRIC. "Polar Information Centre," http://www.pric.gov.cn/enindex.asp?sortid=14.

People's Republic of China. State Oceanic Administration People's Republic of China. "The Main Duties of the State Oceanic Administration" [国家海洋局主要职责] (April 9, 2010).

People's Republic of China. State Oceanic Administration. *China National Offshore Development Report 2011* (2011).

Québec. "Plan Nord," http://www.plannord.gouv.qc.ca/.

United States. Office of the Press Secretary. "Remarks by President Obama to the Australian Parliament" (November 17, 2011).

United States. The White House. *Sustaining US Global Leadership: Priorities for 21st Century Defence* (Washington DC, 2012).

United States. United States Geological Survey. "90 Billion Barrels of Oil and 1.670 Trillion Cubic Feet of Natural Gas Assessed in the Arctic." *USGS Newsroom* (July 23, 2008).

United States. United States Geological Survey. "Circum-Arctic Resource Appraisal: Estimates of Undiscovered Oil and Gas North of the Arctic Circle" (2008).

United States. United States Geological Survey. "Circumpolar Resource Appraisal: Estimates of Undiscovered Oil and Gas North of the Arctic Circle." *USGS Fact Sheet* (Washington: US Geological Survey, 2008).

Yukon. "Wolverine Property." *Yukon Mineral Update* (2008).

Monographs, Edited Volumes, and Research Reports

Arctic Climate Impact Assessment. *Impacts of a Warming Arctic: ACIA Overview Report.* Cambridge: Cambridge University Press, 2004.

Bone, Robert M. *The Geography of the Canadian North: Issues and Challenges*, 2nd edition. Don Mills: Oxford University Press, 2003.

Brady, Anne-Marie. "China's Antarctic Interests." In *The Emerging Politics of Antarctica*, edited by Anne-Marie Brady, 31–49. Abingdon: Routledge, 2012.

Burles, Mark, and Abram Shulsky. *Patterns in China's Use of Force: Evidence from History and Doctrinal Writings.* Santa Monica: RAND, 2000.

Byers, Michael. *Who Owns the Arctic?* Vancouver: Douglas & McIntyre, 2009.

Callahan, William A. *Contingent States: Greater China and Transnational Relations.* Minneapolis: University of Minnesota Press, 2004.

Campbell, Caitlin. "China and the Arctic: Objectives and Obstacles." *US-China Economic and Security Review Commission Staff Research Report* (April 13, 2012).

Canadian Polar Commission. *International Polar Year Canadian Science Report: Highlights* Ottawa: Canadian Polar Commission, 2012.

———. *The State of Northern Knowledge in Canada.* Ottawa: Canadian Polar Commission, 2014.

Chan, Wai-Shin, and Zoe Knight. "China's Rising Climate Risk: The 20 Questions Investors Need to Ask." *HSBC Global Research* (2011).

Chaturvedi, Sanjay. "Geopolitical Transformations: 'Rising' Asia and the Future of the Arctic Council." In *The Arctic Council: Its Place in the Future of Arctic Governance*, edited by Thomas S. Axworthy, Timo Koivurova, and Waliul Hasanat. Toronto: Munk-Gordon Arctic Security Program and the University of Lapland, 2012.

Clark, Ian. *The Post-Cold War: Order: The Spoils of Peace.* Oxford: Oxford University Press, 2001.

Coates, Ken, P. Whitney Lackenbauer, Bill Morrison, and Greg Poelzer. *Arctic Front: Defending Canada in the Far North.* Toronto: Thomas Allen & Son Ltd., 2008.

Coen, Ross. *Breaking Ice for Arctic Oil: The Epic Voyage of the SS Manhattan through the Northwest Passage* Anchorage: University of Alaska Press, 2012.

Council of Canadian Academies. *Vision for the Canadian Arctic Research Initiative: Assessing the Opportunities* (2008).

Economy, Elizabeth, and Michel Oksenberg, eds. *China Joins the World: Progress and Prospects*. New York: Council on Foreign Relations, 1999.

Emmerson, Charles. *The Future History of the Arctic*. New York: Public Affairs, 2010.

Friedberg, Aaron. *A Contest for Supremacy: China, America, and the Struggle for Mastery in Asia*. New York: W.W. Norton, 2011.

Gill, Bates. "Two Steps Forward, One Step Back: The Dynamics of Chinese Non-proliferation and Arms Control Policy Making in the Era of Reform." In *The Making of Chinese Foreign and Security Policy in the Era of Reform*, edited by David M. Lampton. Stanford: Stanford University Press, 2001.

Griffiths, Franklyn, Rob Huebert, and P. Whitney Lackenbauer. *Canada and the Changing Arctic: Sovereignty. Security and Stewardship*. Waterloo: Wilfrid Laurier University Press, 2011.

Hachigan, Nina. *China's Engagement in the International System: In the Ring, But Punching Below its Weight*. Washington, DC: Center for American Progress, 2009.

Higginbotham, John, Andrea Charron, and James Manicom. "Canada-US Arctic Marine Corridors and Resource Development." *CIGI Policy Brief* 24 (November, 2012).

Huebert, Rob, and Brooks Yeager. *A New Sea*. WWF, 2008.

Jacobson, Harold K., and Michel Oksenberg. *China's Participation in the IMF, the World Bank and GATT: Toward a Global Economic Order*. Ann Arbor: University of Michigan Press, 1990.

Jakobson, Linda. *China Prepares for an Ice-Free Arctic*. Stockholm: Stockholm International Peace Research Institute, 2010.

Jakobson, Linda, and Jingchao Peng. *China's Arctic Aspirations*. SIPRI Policy Paper No. 34. Stockholm: Stockholm International Peace Research Institute, November, 2012.

Jisi, Wang. "China's Search for a Grand Strategy." In *China 3.0*, edited by Mark Leonard. European Council on Foreign Relations, November 2012.

Johnston, Alastair Iain. *Social States: China in International Institutions, 1980–2000*. Princeton: Princeton University Press, 2009.

———. *Cultural Realism: Strategic Culture and Grand Strategy in Chinese History*. Princeton: Princeton University Press, 1996.

———. *Social States: China in International Institutions 1980–2000*. Princeton: Princeton University Press, 2008.

Johnston, Alastair Iain, and Paul Evans. "China's Engagement with Multilateral Security Institutions." In *Engaging China: The Management of an Emerging Power*, edited by Alastair Iain Johnston and Robert S. Ross. London: Routledge, 1999.

Kennedy, Tom. *Quest: Canada's Search for Arctic Oil*. Reidmore, 1988.

Kent, Ann. *Beyond Compliance: China. International Organizations and Global Security*. Stanford: Stanford University Press, 2007.

———. *China, the United Nations and Human Rights: The Limits of Compliance*. Philadelphia: University of Philadelphia Press, 1999.

Keyuan, Zou. *Law of the Sea in East Asia: Issues and Prospects*. New York: Routledge, 2005.

Klare, Michael T. *Resource Wars*. New York: Henry Holt & Co., 2002.

Koivurova, Timo, and Erik J. Molenaar. *International Governance and Regulation of the Marine Arctic: Overview and Gap Analysis*. Oslo: World Wildlife Foundation, 2009.

Lantrigne, Marc. *China's Emerging Arctic Strategies: Economics and Institutions*. Reykjavik: Institute of International Affairs, 2014.

Lasserre, Frédéric. *China and the Arctic: Threat or Cooperation Potential for Canada?* Toronto: Canadian International Council, 2010.

Lawrence, Susan V. "China's Political Institutions and Leaders in Charts." *CRS Report to Congress*. R43303 (November 12, 2013).

Le Billon, Philippe, ed. *Geopolitics of Resource Wars: Resource Dependence, Governance and Violence*. London: Frank Cass, 2005.

Manicom, James, and P. Whitney Lackenbauer. "Canada's Northern Strategy and East Asian Interests in the Arctic." *Centre for International Governance Innovation (CIGI) East Asia-Arctic Paper Series*. December 2013.

———. "East Asian States, the Arctic Council and International Relations in the Arctic." *CIGI Policy Brief* 26 (April, 2013).

Mearsheimer, John J. *The Tragedy of Great Power Politics*. New York: W.W. Norton & Co., 2001.

Mulvenon, James. "Chinese Nuclear and Conventional Weapons." In *China Joins the World: Progress and Prospects*, edited by Elizabeth Economy and Michel Oksenberg. New York: Council on Foreign Relations, 1999.

National Research Council. *Abrupt Impacts of Climate Change: Anticipating Surprises*. Washington, DC: The National Academies Press, 2013.

NSERC/SSHRC. "From Crisis to Opportunity: Rebuilding Canada's Role in Northern Research." Ottawa: 2000.

Owen, Nick. "Disputed South China Sea Oil in Context." In *Maritime Energy Resources in Asia: Energy and Geopolitics*, edited by Clive Schofield. Washington, DC: The National Bureau of Asia Research, 2011.

Perry, Charles M., and Bobby Andersen. *New Strategic Dynamics in the Arctic Region*. Washington, DC: Institute for Foreign Policy Analysis, 2012.

Review Commission Staff Research Report. "China and the Arctic: Objectives and Obstacles." *US-China Economic and Security* 13 (April 2012).

Shadian, Jessica. *The Politics of Arctic Sovereignty: Oil, Ice, and Inuit Governance*. London: Routledge, 2014.

Swaine, Michael D., and Ashley J. Tellis. *Interpreting China's Grand Strategy: Past, Present and Future*. Santa Monica: RAND, 2000.

T., Qu, Jun Wu, Haiwen Zhang, and Shunlin Liu, eds. "Research on Arctic Issues" [北极问题研究] Beijing: Ocean Press, June 2011.

The Organisation for Economic Co-operation and Development. *OECD Economic Surveys: China 2013*. OECD Publishing, 2013.

Wahl, M.E.B., and Erik Kristoffersen. "Speed Optimization for Very Large Crude Carriers: Potential Savings and Effects of Slow Steaming." Master's Thesis: *Norwegian School of Economics*, 2012.

Wilson, Alana, Fred McMahon, and Miguel Cervantes. *Survey of Mining Companies 2012/2013* Vancouver: Fraser Institute: 2013.

Wilson, K.J., J. Falkingham, H. Melling, and R. De Abreu. "Shipping in the Canadian Arctic." *Canadian Ice Service and the Institute of Ocean Sciences*, 2004.

Wright, David Curtis. *The Dragon Eyes the Top of the World: Arctic Policy Debate and Discussion in China*. Newport: Naval War College Press, China Maritime Studies Institute, 2011.

——. *The Panda Readies to Meet the Polar Bear: China and Canada's Arctic Sovereignty Challenge*. Calgary: Canadian Defence & Foreign Affairs Institute, 2011.

Ying Qi, Zhou. "The Chinese Perspective." In *The Arctic in World Affairs: A North Pacific Dialogue on Arctic Marine Issues*, edited by Oran R. Young, Jong Deog Kim, and Yoon Hyung Kim, 84–9. Seoul: Korea Maritime Institute, 2012.

Zellen, Barry Scott. *Arctic Doom, Arctic Boom: The Geopolitics of Climate Change in the Arctic*. Santa Barbara: Praeger, 2009.

Articles

Aibo, Dong, Chen Chang, and Yao Shi. "China and Russia to Build a Large-Scale Upgrade of the Arctic Ocean 'Golden Waterway' Freight Hub." [中俄共建港口提升北极"黄金水道"成色]. *Pearl River Water Transport* [珠江水运] 20 (2014).

Alexeeva, Olga, and Frédéric Lasserre. "China and the Arctic." *Arctic Yearbook* (2012): 80–90.

———. "The Snow Dragon: China's Strategies in the Arctic." *China Perspectives* 3 (2012): 66–8.

Bennetta, Mia M. "North by Northeast: Toward an Asian-Arctic Region," *Eurasian Geography and Economics* 55, no. 1 (August 2014): 71–93.

Bergh, Kristofer. "Arctic Cooperation Must Become More Inclusive." SIPRI Essay (July/August 2011).

Borgerson, Scott. "Arctic Meltdown: The Economic and Security Implications of Global Warming." *Foreign Affairs* 87, no. 2 (March–April 2008): 63–77.

Brigham, Lawson. "The Fast-Changing Maritime Arctic." US Naval Institute *Proceedings* (May 2010): 54–9.

Buszynski, Leszek. "ASEAN, the Declaration on Conduct and the South China Sea." *Contemporary Southeast Asia* 25, no. 3 (2003): 343–62.

Buszynski, Leszek. "The South China Sea: Oil, Maritime Claims, and US-China Strategic Rivalry." *Washington Quarterly* 35, no. 2 (2012): 139–56.

Buzan, Barry. "China in International Society: Is Peaceful Rise Possible?" *Chinese Journal of International Politics* 3 (2010): 5–36.

Chang, Felix K. "Beyond the Unipolar Moment: Beijing's Reach in the South China Sea." *Orbis* 40, no. 3 (1996): 353–74.

Chen, Gang. "China's Emerging Arctic Strategy." *Polar Journal* 2, no. 2 (2012): 358–71.

Chin, Gregory, and Ramesh Thakur. "Will China Change the Rules of Global Order?" *The Washington Quarterly* 33, no. 4 (2010): 119–38.

Chircop, Aldo. "The Emergence of China as a Polar-Capable State." *Canadian Naval Review* 7, no. 1 (Spring 2011): 9–14.

Christensen, Thomas J. "Fostering Stability or Creating a Monster? The Rise of China and US Policy toward East Asia." *International Security* 31, no. 1 (Summer 2006): 81–126.

Comiso, Josefino C. "Accelerated Decline in the Arctic Sea Ice Cover." *Geophysical Research Letters* 35 (2008): 1–6.

Dannreuther, Roland. "Asian Security and China's Energy Needs." *International Relations of the Asia-Pacific* 3, no. 2 (2003): 197–219.

Dawson, J., M.E. Johnston, E.J. Stewart. "Governance of Arctic Expedition Cruise Ships in a Time of Rapid Environmental and Economic Change" *Ocean & Coastal Management* 89 (2014): 88–99.

Deming, Huang, and Zhang Cheng. "The Legal Issues of the Arctic Outer Continental Shelf Boundary from the Perspective of China's Overseas Security" [中国海

外安全利益视角下的北极外大陆架划界法律问题], *Nanjing Journal of Social Sciences* [南京社会科学] 7 (2014): 84–102.

Ding, Huang, and Baolin Zhu. "Arctic Governance Mechanisms and Innovation, A 'Community of Destiny' Concept" [基于"命运共同体"理念的北极治理机制创新]. *Exploration and Free Views* [探索与争鸣] 3 (2016).

Ding, Huang, and Ningning Zhao. "Arctic Governance and China's Participation – An Analysis Based on the Theory of International Public Goods [北极治理与中国参与——基于国际公共品理论的分析]. *Wuhan University Journal (Philosophy & Social Sciences)* 3 [武汉大学学报(哲学社会科学版] (2014).

Ding, Huang, and Zhang Chong. "China's Participation in Arctic Governance – A Perspective Based on Institutional Neoliberalism" [中国参与北极治理的价值分析基于新自由制度主义的视角], *Wuhan University Journal* [武汉大学学报(哲学社会科学版] 3 (2016).

Fangqi, Liu. "Arctic Oil and Gas Development and the Status of the Latest Trends in Equipment and Technology [北极油气开发现状及装备技术最新动向], *China Ship Survey* [中国船检] 10 (2016).

Flake, Lincoln E. "Russia and China in the Arctic: A Team of Rivals." *Strategic Analysis* 37, no. 6 (2013): 261–7.

Foot, Rosemary. "Chinese Strategies in a US-Hegemonic Global Order: Accommodating and Hedging." *International Affairs* 82, no. 1 (2006): 77–97.

Frolov, Viacheslav A. "China's Armed Forces Prepare for High-Tech Warfare." *Defense & Foreign Affairs Strategic Policy* 26, no. 1 (1998): 7–8.

Furuichi, Masahiko, and Natuhiko Otsuka. "Proposing a Common Platform of Shipping Cost Analysis of the Northern Sea Route and the Suez Canal Route." *Maritime Economics & Logistics* 17, no. 1 (2014): 1–23.

Gadihoke, Neil. "Arctic Melt: The Outlook for India." *Maritime Affairs* 8, no. 1 (Summer 2012): 4–5.

Gang Chen, "China's Emerging Arctic Strategy," *Polar Journal* 2, no. 2 (2012): 358–71.

Goh, Evelyn. "Great Powers and Hierarchical Order in Southeast Asia: Analyzing Regional Security Strategies." *International Security* 32, no. 3 (2007–08): 113–57.

Goldstein, Avery. "Power Transitions, Institutions, and China's Rise in East Asia: Theoretical Expectations and Evidence," *The Journal of Strategic Studies* 30, nos. 4–5 (August–October 2007): 639–82.

Griffiths, Franklyn. "The Shipping News." *International Journal* 58, no. 2 (Spring 2003): 257–82.

Guo, Hongyan. "Inquiries on the Northwest Passage" [论西北航道的通行制度]. *Journal of CUPL* [中国政法大学学报] 6 (2015): 83–92.

Guo, Peiqing. "The Arctic is Not Desolate" [北极并不冷清]. *Huanqiu* 17 (September 2008).

———. "An Analysis of New Criteria for Permanent Observer Status on the Arctic Council and the Road of Non-Arctic States to Arctic." Draft Article. *KMI International Journal of Maritime Affairs and Fisheries* 4, no. 2 (2012): 21–38.

Hastings, Jesse Guite. "The Rise of Asia in a Changing Arctic: A View from Iceland." *Polar Geography* 37, no. 3 (October, 2014): 215–33.

Hertell, Hans H. "Arctic Melt: The Tipping Point for an Arctic Treaty." *Georgetown International Environmental Law Review* 21 (2009): 565–91.

Ho, Joshua. "The Implications of Arctic Sea Ice Decline on Shipping." *Marine Policy* 34, no. 3 (2010): 713–15.

———. "The Opening of the Northern Sea Route." *Maritime Affairs* 7, no. 1 (2010): 106–20.

Holland, Marika, Cecilia M. Bitz, and Bruno Tremblay. "Future Abrupt Reductions in the Summer Arctic Sea Ice." *Geophysical Research Letters* 33 (2006): 1–5.

Hong, Nong. "Emerging Interests of Non-Arctic Countries in the Arctic: A Chinese Perspective." *Polar Journal* 4, no. 2 (Nov. 2014): 271–86.

———. "The Melting Arctic and Its Impact on China's Maritime Transport." *Research in Transportation Economics* 35, no. 1 (2012): 50–7.

Huang, Linyan, Frédéric Lasserre, and Olga Alexeeva. "Is China's Interest for the Arctic Driven by Arctic Shipping Potential?" *Asian Geographer* 32, no. 1 (2015): 1–13.

Huebert, Rob. "The Need for an Arctic Treaty: Growing from the United Nations Convention on the Law of the Sea." *Ocean Yearbook* 23 (2009): 27–39.

———. "The Shipping News Part II: How Canada's Arctic Sovereignty Is on Thinning Ice." *International Journal* 58, no. 3 (Summer 2003): 295–308.

Huebert, Rob, and P. Whitney Lackenbauer. "Premier Partners: Canada, the United States and Arctic Security." *Canadian Foreign Policy Journal* 20, no. 3 (Winter 2015): 1–14.

Hua, Xu. "Comments on Chapter 2: Chinese Perspective." In *The Arctic in World Affairs: A North Pacific Dialogue on the Future of the Arctic – 2012 North Pacific Arctic Conference Proceedings*, edited by Oran Young, Jong Deog Kim, and Yoon Hyung Kim, 84–9. Seoul: Korea Maritime Institute and East-West Center, 2012.

Humpert, Malte. "The Future of the Northern Sea Route – A 'Golden Waterway' or a Niche Trade Route." The Arctic Institute (September 15, 2011).

Ikenberry, John. "Power and Liberal Order: America's Postwar World Order in Transition." *International Relations of the Asia-Pacific* 5, no. 2 (2005): 133–95.

———. "The Rise of China and the Future of the West." *Foreign Affairs* (January–February 2008).

Ingimundarsona, Valur. "Managing a Contested Region: The Arctic Council and the Politics of Arctic Governance." *Polar Journal* 3, no. 1 (2014): 183–98.

Jakobson, Linda. "China Prepares for an Ice-Free Arctic." *SIPRI Insights on Peace and Security* 2010, no. 2 (March 2010).

Ji, You. "The Revolution in Military Affairs and China's Strategic Thinking." *Contemporary Southeast Asia* 21, no. 3 (1999): 352–5.

Jian, Yang. "China and Arctic Affairs." *Arctic Yearbook* (2012).

Jianmin, Shou, and Feng Yuan. "A Study on Container Transport Potential of Northeast Arctic Channel Based on Shipping Cost" [基于航运成本的北极东北航道集装箱运输潜力研究]. *Journal of Polar Research* [极地研究] 27, no. 1 (2015): 65–73.

Jie, Li. "The Study on the International Development Mechanism of Arctic Gas and Oil Exploitation" [北极地区油气资源开发国际合作机制研究]. *Wuhan University International Law Review* [武大国际法评论] 1 (2015).

Jing, Lu. "An Analysis of the Arctic Governance Dilemma and Coordination [北极治理困境与协同治理路径探]. *International Studies* [国际问题研究] 5 (2016).

Jisi, Wang. "China's Search for a Grand Strategy." *Foreign Affairs* (March/April 2011).

Johnston, Alastair Iain. "Treating International Institutions as Social Environments." *International Studies Quarterly* 45, no. 4 (2001): 487–515.

Jun, Wu, and Wu Leizhao. "An Analysis of China's Ocean Rights in the Arctic – Based on the Perspective of International Maritime Law [中国北极海域权益分析——以国际海洋法为基点的考量] *Wuhan University Journal* (Philosophy & Social Sciences) [武汉大学学报(哲学社会科学版] 67, no. 3 (2014).

Khoo, Nicholas, Michael L.R. Smith, and David Shambaugh. "Correspondence: China Engages Asia? Caveat Lector." *International Security* 30, no. 1 (2005): 196–213.

Kikkert, Peter. "Promoting National Interests and Fostering Cooperation: Canada and the Development of a Polar Code." *Journal of Maritime Law and International Commerce* 43, no. 3 (July 2012): 319–34.

———. "Rising above the Rhetoric: Northern Voices and the Strengthening of Canada's Capacity to Maintain a Stable Circumpolar World." *Northern Review* 33 (2009): 29–45.

Kim, Hyun-Soo. "The 1992 Chinese Territorial Sea Law in Light of the UN Convention." *International and Comparative Law Quarterly* 43, no. 4 (1994): 894–904.

Kirton, John, and Don Munton. "The *Manhattan* Voyages and Their Aftermath." In *Politics of the Northwest Passage*, edited by Franklyn Griffiths, 67–97. Kingston: McGill-Queen's University Press, 1987.

Koivurova, Timo. "Sovereign States and Self-Determining Peoples: Carving Out a Place for Transnational Indigenous Peoples in a World of Sovereign States." *International Community Law Review* 12 (2010): 191–212.

Koivurova, Timo, and David Vanderzwaag. "The Arctic Council at 10 Years: Retrospect and Prospects." *UBC Law Review* 40, no. 1 (2008): 121–94.

Kraska, James. "International Security and International Law in the Northwest Passage," *Vanderbilt Journal of Transnational Law* 42 (2009): 1109–32.

Kugler, Jacek. "The Asian Ascent: Opportunity for Peace or Precondition for War?" *International Studies Perspectives* 7 (2006): 36–42.

Lackenbauer, P. Whitney. "Mirror Images? Canada, Russia, and the Circumpolar World." *International Journal* 65, no. 4 (Autumn, 2010): 879–97.

———. "India's Emerging Arctic Interests." In *Arctic Yearbook 2013*, edited by Lassi Heininen, 1–24. Akureyri, Iceland: University of the Arctic/Northern Research Forum, 2013.

———. "Canadian Responses to Asian Interests in the Arctic." *Asia Policy* 18 (July 2014): 22–9.

———. "Canada's Northern Strategy and East Asian Interests in the Arctic." In *East-Asia-Arctic Relations: Boundary, Security and International Politics*, edited by Ken Coates and Kimie Hara, 78–117. Waterloo: Centre for International Governance Innovation, 2014.

Lackenbauer, P. Whitney, and Andrew F. Cooper. "The Achilles Heel of Canadian Good International Citizenship: Indigenous Diplomacies and State Responses in the Twentieth Century." *Canadian Foreign Policy Journal* 13, no. 3 (2007): 99–119.

Lackenbauer, P. Whitney, and James Manicom. "Asian States and the Arctic: National Perspectives on Regional Governance." In *The Handbook of the Politics of the Arctic*, edited by Geir Hønnelan. Cheltenham, UK: Edward Elgar, 2015.

Lackenbauer, P. Whitney, and Rob Huebert. "Premier Partners: Canada, the United States and Arctic Security." *Canadian Foreign Policy Journal* 20, no. 3 (Fall 2014): 320–33.

Lajeunesse, Adam. "A New Mediterranean? Arctic Shipping Prospects for the 21st Century." *Journal of Maritime Law and Commerce* 43, no. 44 (October 2012): 521–39.

Lajeunesse, Adam, and P. Whitney Lackenbauer. "China's Mining Interests in the North American Arctic." In *Governing the North American Arctic: Lessons from the Past, Prospects for the Future*, edited by Dawn Berry and Halbert Jones. London: Palgrave MacMillan, 2015.

———. "Sovereignty, Security, and Arctic Development." *Journal of Ocean Technology* 9, no. 2 (summer 2014): 114–15.

Lalonde, Suzanne, and Frédéric Lasserre. "The Position of the United States on the Northwest Passage: Is the Fear of a Precedent Warranted?" *Ocean Development and International Law* 44, no. 1 (2013): 28–72.

Lalonde, Suzanne, and Michael Byers. "Who Controls the Northwest Passage?" *Vanderbilt Journal of Transnational Law* 42 (2009): 1133–1210.

Lanjun, Gao. "Arctic Security Governance: Nature, Challenge and Solution" [北极地区的安全治理问题:内涵、困境与应对]. *Seeker* [求索] 11 (2015).

Lanteigne, Marc. "China's Maritime Security and the 'Malacca Dilemma.'" *Asian Security* 4, no. 2 (2008): 143–61.

Lasserre, Frédéric. "Case Studies of Shipping along Arctic Routes: Analysis and Profitability Perspectives for the Container Sector," *Transportation Research Part A* 66 (2014): 144–61.

Lasserre, Frédéric, and Linyan Huang. "China's Strategy in the Arctic: Threatening or Opportunistic?" *Polar Record* 53, no. 1 (2017): 31-42.

Lasserre, Frédéric, and Olga Alexeeva. "The Snow Dragon: China's Strategies in the Arctic." *China Perspectives* 3 (2012): 61–8.

Lasserre, Frédéric, and Sébastien Pelletier. "Polar Super Seaways? Maritime Transport in the Arctic: An Analysis of Shipowners' Intentions." *Journal of Transport Geography* 19 (2011): 1465–73.

Legro, Jeffrey W. "What Will China Want: The Future Intentions of a Rising Power." *Perspectives on Politics* 5, no. 3 (2007): 515–34.

Leilei, Zhou, and Shuolin Huang. "A Comparative Study of the Northwest Passage and the Northeast Passage [加拿大西北航道与俄罗斯北方海航道管理的对比研究]. *Chinese Journal of Polar Research* [极地研究] 26, no. 4 (2014): 515–21.

Lenton, Timothy M. "Arctic Climate Tipping Points." *AMBIO* 41, no. 1 (2012): 10–22.

Li, Mingjiang. "Rising from Within: China's Search for a Multilateral World." *Global Governance* 17 (2011): 331–51.

Li, W., C. Yang, D. Nebert, R. Raskin, P. Houser, H. Wu, Z. Li. "Semantic-Based Web Service Discovery and Chaining for Building an Arctic Spatial Data Infrastructure." *Computers & Geosciences* 37, no. 1 (2011): 1752–62.

Li, Z. "Obstacles to China's Participation in the International Arctic Route Mechanism and Countermeasures" [中国参与北极航线国际机制的障碍及对策]. Zhongguo Hanghai. 32, no. 2 (June 2009): 98–102.

Liu, Miaojia, and Jacob Kronbak. "The Potential Economic Viability of using the Northern Sea Route (NSR) as an Alternative Route between Asia and Europe." *Journal of Transport Geography* 18, no. 3 (2010): 434–44.

Liu, Xue, Wang Xuemei, Ling Xiaoliang, Zheng Wei, Wang Liwei. "Recent Progress in Arctic Oil and Gas Exploitation Research" [北极油气勘探开发技术最新进

展研究]. *Ocean Development and Management* [海洋开发与管理] 1 (2014): 37–41.

Lykke Ragner, Claes. "The Northern Sea Route." *Nordin Association's Yearbook* (2008): 114–27.

Ma, Jianmin, Hayley Hung, Chongguo Tian, and Roland Kallenborn. "Revolatilization of Persistent Organic Pollutants in the Arctic Induced by Climate Change." *Nature Climate Change* 1, no. 5 (2011): 255–60.

Malik, J. Mohan. "China and the Nuclear Non-Proliferation Regime." *Contemporary Southeast Asia* 22, no. 3 (2000): 445–78.

Manicom, James. "Beyond Boundary Disputes: Understanding the Nature of China's Challenge to Maritime East Asia." *Harvard Asia Quarterly* 12, nos. 3–4 (2010): 46–53.

Manicom, James, and P. Whitney Lackenbauer. "The Chinese Pole." *Policy Options* (April–May 2013): 16-18.

———. "East Asian States and the Pursuit of Arctic Council Membership." In *East Asia-Arctic Relations: Boundary, Security and International Politics*, edited by Ken Coates and Kimie Hara, 199–216. Waterloo: Centre for International Governance Innovation, 2014.

Mingya, Zhu, Ping Ying, and Shufeng He. "The Impact of Arctic Gas and Oil Exploitation on China and the World Energy Network [北极油气资源开发对世界能源格局和中国的潜在影响], *Ocean Development and Management* [海洋开发与管理] 4 (2015): 1–7.

Pelletier, Sébastien, and Frédéric Lasserre. "Les Chinois dans l'Arctique: une présence qui ne date pas d'hier – Analyse de l'incident de Tuktoyaktuk, TNO." *Monde Chinois* 41 (2015): 109–29.

Pen, Jinchao, and Njord Wegge. "China's Bilateral Diplomacy in the Arctic." *Polar Geography* 38, no. 3 (2015).

Perovich, D.K.B., Bonnie Light, Hajo Eicken, Kathleen F. Jones, Kay Runciman, Son V. Nghiem. "Increasing Solar Heating of the Arctic Ocean and Adjacent Seas, 1979–2005: Attribution and Role in the Ice-Albedo Feedback." *Geophysical Research Letters* 34, no. 19 (2007): 1–5.

Pharand, Donat. "Arctic Waters and the Northwest Passage: A Final Revisit." *Ocean Development and International Law* 38, nos. 1–2 (2007): 3–69.

———. "The Arctic Waters and the Northwest Passage: A Final Revisit." *Ocean Development & International Law* 38, nos. 1–2 (2007): 3–69.

Pu, Xiaoyu. "Socialization as a Two-Way Process: Emerging Powers and the Diffusion of International Norms." *Chinese Journal of International Politics* (2012): 1–27.

Q., Li. "The Situation and Challenges for Deep Water Oil and Gas Exploration and Exploitation in China" [我国海洋深水油气开发面临的挑战]. *Zhongguo Haishang Youqi* 18, no. 2 (April 2006).

Robinson, Roger W. "China's Long Con in the Arctic." *Macdonald Laurier Institute Commentary* (September 2013).

———. "China's Long-Term Arctic Strategy." *Inside Policy* (September 2013).

Røseth, Tom. "Russia's China Policy in the Arctic." *Strategic Analysis* 38, no. 6 (2014): 841–59.

Salameh, Mamdouh G. "China. Oil and the Risk of Regional Conflict." *Survival* 37, no. 4 (1995–96): 133–46.

Shambaugh, David. "China Engages Asia: Reshaping the Regional Order." *International Security* 29, no. 3 (2004–05): 64–99.

Sharp, Todd. "The Implications of Ice Melt on Arctic Security." *Defence Studies* 11, no. 2 (June, 2011): 297–322.

Simon, Mary. "Inuit and the Canadian Arctic: Sovereignty Begins at Home," *Journal of Canadian Studies* 43, no. 2 (2009): 250–60.

Stewart, E.J., S.E.L. Howel, D. Draper, J. Yackel, and A. Tivy. "Sea Ice in Canada's Arctic: Implications for Cruise Tourism." *Arctic* 60, no. 4 (December 2007): 376–7.

Stohl. A., Z. Klimont, S. Eckhardt, K. Kupiainen, V.P. Shevchenko, V.M. Kopeikin, and A.N. Novigatsky. "Black Carbon in the Arctic: The Underestimated Role of Gas Flaring and Residential Combustion Emissions." *Atmospheric Chemistry and Physics* 13, no. 8 (2013): 8833–55.

Sun, Kai. "Beyond the Dragon and the Panda: Understanding China's Engagement in the Arctic." *Asia Policy* 18 (2014): 46–51.

———. "China's Contribution to Arctic Governance [为北极治理作出中国贡献], *Journal of China Social Sciences* [中国社会科学报] (December 30, 2015).

———. "Comments on Chapter 4: Chinese Perspective." In *The Arctic in World Affairs: A North Pacific Dialogue on the Future of the Arctic – 2013 North Pacific Arctic Conference Proceedings*, edited by Oran Young, Jong Deog Kim, and Yoon Hyung Kim. Seoul: Korea Maritime Institute and East-West Center, 2013.

Takei, Yoshinobu. "Who Governs the Arctic Ocean? A Reply from an International Law Perspective." *Ocean Policy Studies* 9 (July, 2011): 62–8.

Teeple, Nancy. "A Brief History of Intrusions into the Canadian Arctic." *Canadian Army Journal* 12, no. 3 (Winter 2010): 45–68.

Thayer, Carlyle A. "Chinese Assertiveness in the South China Sea and Southeast Asian Responses." *Journal of Current Southeast Asian Affairs* 30, no. 2 (2011): 77–104.

Vivoda, Vlado, and James Manicom. "Oil Import Diversification in Northeast Asia: A Comparison between China and Japan." *Journal of East Asian Studies* 11, no. 2 (Summer 2011): 223–54.

Wang, Muyin, and James Overland. "A Sea Ice Free Summer Arctic within 30 Years?" *Geophysical Research Letters* 36, no. 7 (April 2009): 1–5.

Wang, Ru. "China and Canada Expect More Collaboration on the Arctic," *China Daily* (March 26, 2015).

Weibing, Wu. "Some Shipping Experiences on the Northeast Passage" [北极东北航道航行体会]. *Marine Technology* [航海技术] 4 (2016).

Wegge, Njord. "China in the Arctic: Interests, Actions and Challenges." *Nordlit* 32 (2014).

———. "The Emerging Politics of the Arctic Ocean. Future Management of the Living Marine Resources. *Marine Policy* 55 (2015): 331–8.

Willis, Matthew. "The Manhattan Incident Forty Years On: Re-assessing the Canadian Response." In *Canada and Arctic Sovereignty and Security: Historical Perspectives*, edited by P. Whitney Lackenbauer, 259–82. Calgary: Centre for Military and Strategic Studies, 2011.

Willis, Matthew, and Duncan Depledge. "How We Learned to Stop Worrying about China's Arctic Ambitions: Understanding China's Admission to the Arctic Council, 2004." In *Handbook of the Politics of the Arctic*, edited by Leif Christian Jensen and Geir Hønneland, 759–98. Northampton: Edward Elgar Publishing Limited, 2015.

Winton, M. "Does the Arctic Sea Ice have a Tipping Point." *Geophysical Research Letters* 33 (2006): 1–5.

Worm, Boris, and David Vanderzwaag. "High Seas Fisheries: Troubled Waters, Tangled Governance, and Recovery Prospects." *Behind the Headlines* 64, no. 5 (2007).

Wright, David Curtis. *The Dragon Eyes the Top of the World: Arctic Policy Debate and Discussion in China*. Newport: Naval War College Press, China Maritime Studies Institute, 2011.

Xu, Hua, Zhifang Yin, Dashan Jia, Fengjun Jin, and Hua Ouyang. "The Potential Seasonal Alternative of Asia-Europe Container Service via Northern Sea Route under the Arctic Sea Ice Retreat." *Maritime Policy and Management* 28, no. 5 (September 2011): 541–60.

Yang, Chaowei, Doug Nebert, and D.R. Fraser Taylor. "Establishing a Sustainable and Cross-Boundary Geospatial Cyber Infrastructure to Enable Polar Research." *Computers & Geosciences* 37 (2011): 1721–6.

Yang, Huigen. "Development of China's Polar Linkages." *Canadian Naval Review* 8, no. 3 (Fall 2012): 30–2.

Yang, Jian. "The Integration of Non-Arctic Factors and the Mechanism of Arctic Governance" [域外因素的嵌入与北极治理机制]. *Journal of Social Sciences* [社会科学] 1 (2014).

Young, Oran R. "Governing the Arctic: From Cold War Theatre to Mosaic of Cooperation." *Global Governance* 11 (2005).

———. "Review Article, The Future of the Arctic: Cauldron of Conflict or Zone of Peace?" *International Affairs* 87, no. 1 (2011): 185–93.

———. "Whither the Arctic? Conflict or Cooperation in the Circumpolar North." *Polar Record* 45, no. 1 (January 2009).

Yun, Luoqiao. "An Analysis of Arctic LNG Shipping Profitability and its Future [北极东北航道运输经济性与前景分析]. *Journal of Dalian Maritime University* [大连海事大学学报] 3 (2016).

Zhang, Shengjun, and Li Xing. "Chinese Energy Security and the Positioning of China's Arctic Strategy" [中国能源安全与中国北极战略定位]. *International Observations* [国际观察] (2010): 64–71.

Zhenfu, Li. "A Northeast Asian Perspective on the Greater Arctic" [大北极视角下的泛东北亚]. *China Ship Survey* [中国船检] 8 (2016).

———. "Obstacles and Countermeasures: China's Participation in International Mechanisms of the Arctic Route" [中参与北极航线际机制的障碍及对策]. China Navigation [中国航海] 32, no. 2 (2009).

Zhen, Guo. "China's Ocean Rights in the Arctic – Based on an Analysis of UNCLOS" [中国在北极的海洋权益及其维护——基于《联合国海洋法公约》的分析]. *Theoretical Studies on PLA Political Work* [军队政工理论研究] 15, no. 1 (2014): 136–40.

Zhenrong, Meng. "The Competition in the Arctic and China's Response [北极之争与中国应对]. *Intelligence* [才智] 2 (2016).

Zysk, Katarzyna. "Russia's Arctic Strategy: Ambitions and Constraints." *Joint Force Quarterly* 57, no. 2 (April 2010): 103–10.

Newspapers, Magazines, and Media

"Arctic Terror Threats Real: Security Agencies." *CBC News North*, November 10, 2010.

"Charting New Arctic Waters." *Toronto Star*, August 21, 2010.

"China, Denmark Eye Closer Relationship." *Global Times*, April 25, 2014.

"China Eclipses US and Biggest Trading Nation" *Bloomberg News*, February 10, 2013.

"China Environmental Measures' Impact on Steel & Iron Ore." *Wood Mackenzie*, March 28, 2014.

"China, Korea, EU Woo Arctic Council at Norway Conference." *Nunatsiaq News*, January 22, 2013.

"China, Russia Blocked Plan for Giant Antarctic Sea Reserve, Activists Say." *CTV NEWS*, October 31, 2014.

"China to Ship up to 15% of Trade through the Arctic." *RT*, March 18, 2013.

"China Won't Support Sanctions against Moscow." *RT*, September 23, 2014.

"China: Measures Aim to Bolster Control of Maritime Interests." *OSC Analysis*, May 31, 2007.

"China's Arctic Ambition." *Winnipeg Free Press*, October 25, 2014.

"China's 'Arctic Dream' Misread as 'The Dragon's Arctic Aspirations'" [中国"北极"梦想被误读为巨龙对北极的野心"]. *Global Times*, December 12, 2012.

"China's Navy Making Waves." *Calgary Herald*, October 1, 2007.

"Chinese Steel Giant Ready to Help Finance Nunavik Iron Mine." *Nunatsiaq New*, December 20, 2011.

"Circumpolar Agreement Affirms Inuit Development Rights." *Indian Country Today Media Network*, May 26, 2011.

"CPC Central Committee's Proposal on Formulating the 12th Five-Year Program on National Economic and Social Development." *Xinhua*, October 30, 2010.

"Go East. Far East." *Arctic Journal*, November 26, 2013.

"Harper Promises to Defend Arctic Sovereignty." *CBC News*, August 12, 2006.

"Harper Speaks up for Canada's Arctic." *Globe and Mail*, January 28, 2006.

"Icebreaker *Xuelong* Concludes Arctic Expedition." *China Daily*, September 27, 2012.

"Inuit Win Injunction on Seismic Testing." *CBC News*, August 8, 2010.

"Little Interest in Ice-Free Northwest Passage." *BC Hydro*, June 29, 2010.

"MV Nunavik: From Quebec to China via the Northwest Passage." *NunatsiaqOnline*, September 22, 2014.

"Northern Sea Route Traffic Plummets." *Radio Canada: Eye on the Arctic*, December 16, 2014.

"Piraeus Port Has Further Investment Planned." *Port Technology International*, June 28, 2013.

"Russia's Rosneft Offers ONGC Videsh Ltd Stake in Vankor Oilfield." *Economic Times*, October 5, 2014.

"Short and Sharp." *Economist*, June 16, 2012.

"Stephen Harper Raises Human Rights Concerns with Chinese President Xi Jinping." *CBC News*, November 9, 2014.

"Tough Oil, Easy Decision." *Arctic Journal*, January 18, 2015.

"Yukon: CNOOC Funds Northern Cross at Eagle Plain." *Oil & Gas Journal*, July 1, 2011.

Ahrens, Daniel. "Breaking the Ice: The Politics of the Arctic Council." *Berkeley Political Review*, November 22, 2014.

Arnold, Wayne. "China's Global Mining Play is Failing to Pan Out." *Wall Street Journal*, September 15, 2014.

Astill, James. "The Melting North." *Economist*, June 16, 2012.

Baozhi, Cheng. "Arctic Aspirations." *Beijing Review* 4, August 24, 2011.

Bell, Jim. "Aglukkaq Stresses 'People-First' Approach to Arctic Council." *Nunatsiaq News*, October 29, 2012.

———. "Nunavut Adds Huge Grays Bay Road-Port Scheme to Its Shipping List," *Nunatsiaq News*, February 29, 2016.

———. "Nunavut Fishing Reps Rap Feds over Docks, Quota." *Nunatsiaq News*, March 21, 2008.

Bennett, Mia. "China's Silk Road Plans Could Challenge Northern Sea Route." *CryoPolitics*, December 29, 2014.

———. "China-Russia Gas Deal Creates Arctic Winners and Losers." *CryoPolitics*, June 25, 2014.

Blanchard, Ben. "China Wants Ships to Use Faster Arctic Route Opened by Global Warming." *Reuters*, April 20, 2016.

Blanchard, Ben, and David Stanway. "China to 'Declare War' on Pollution, Premier Says." *Reuters*, March 4, 2014.

Blank, Stephen. "The Arctic: A Future Source of Russo-Chinese Discord?" *China Brief* 10, no. 24, December 3, 2010.

Boswell, Randy. "China Moves to Become Major Arctic Player." *Nunatsiaq News*, March 3, 2010.

Bradsher, Keith. "Chasing Rare Earths, Foreign Companies Expand in China." *New York Times,* August 24, 2011.

———. "China Restarts Rare Earth Shipments to Japan." *Global Business*, November 19, 2010.

Brady, Anne-Marie. "Polar Stakes: China's Polar Activities as a Benchmark for Intentions." *China Brief* 12, no. 14 (2012).

Briscoe, Paula. "Greenland – China's Foothold in Europe?" *Council on Foreign Relations*, February 1, 2013.

Buckley, Chris. "China Report Spells out 'Grim' Climate Change Risks." *Reuters*, January 17, 2012.

Byers, Michael. "Asian Juggernaut Eyes Our "Golden" Waterways." *Globe and Mail*, August 29, 2011.

Byers, Michael, and Scott Borgerson. "The Arctic Front in the Battle to Contain Russia." *Wall Street Journal*, March 8, 2016.

Cattaneo, Claudia. "Why China's Mood is Souring on Canada's Oil Patch." *Financial Post*, July 10, 2014.

CentralAmericaData. "China's COSCO Launches New Multimodal Service in Panama," July 8, 2008.

Chandler, Graham. "Stranded Gas." *Up Here Business* (June 2008).

Chang, Gordon. "China's Arctic Play." *Foreign Policy*, March 9, 2010.

Chase, Steven. "Challenges with China Can't 'Just Be Pretended Away.' Harper Says in One-on-One Interview." *Globe and Mail*, December 17, 2004.

———. "Only Arctic Nations Should Shape the North, Harper Tells The Globe." *Globe and Mail*, January 17, 2014.

———. "Q&A with Harper: No Previous Government Has 'Delivered More in the North.'" *Globe and Mail*, January 17, 2014.

Chen, Gang. "China's Emerging Arctic Strategy." *Polar Journal*, iFirst Article, 2012.

Darby, Andrew. "China, Japan Block Antarctic Fisheries Regulation as Rorts Continue." *Sydney Morning Herald*, December 3, 2014.

———. "China Moves in for the Krill." *Sydney Morning Herald*, April 12, 2015.

Dolata, Petra. "A New Canada in the Arctic? Arctic Policies under Harper," *Études canadiennes/Canadian Studies – Revue interdisciplinaire des études canadiennes en France* 78 (2015): 131–54.

Els, Frik. "Iron Ore Price Surges." *Mining.com*, December 4, 2014.

Erickson, Andrew S., and Adam P. Liff. "A Player But No Superpower." *Foreign Policy*, March 7, 2013.

Fangyuan, Guo, and Zhao Zhuqing. "Exploitation in the Arctic, China Cannot Be Left Behind" [开发北极, 中国不能落下]. *China Scientific Newspaper* [中国科学报], September 23, 2014.

Fenwick Willan, Holman. "Iron Ore: Soaring Supply and Dropping Demand Causing Concerns for Miners, Investors and Importers." *Lexology*, August 12, 2014.

———. "Must-Know: Factors Driving down the Price Outlook for Iron Ore." *Yahoo Finance*, October 27, 2014.

Francis, Diane. "Is the Arctic Poised to Become the Next Suez?" *National Post*, December 14, 2013.

Fravel, Taylor. "Hainan's New Fishing Rules: A Preliminary Analysis." *Diplomat*, January 10, 2014.

Galloway, Gloria. "Canada Siding with US, Denmark on High Arctic Fishing Moratorium." *Globe and Mail*, February 23, 2014.

Garibov, Konstantin, and Igor Denisov. "Norway May Shut China out of the Arctic Council." *Voice of Russia*, January 30, 2013.

George, Jane. "Arctic Borders Need Tighter Control, Former Commander Says." *Nunatsiaq News*, February 2, 2001.

———. "Group Touts Big Makeover for Arctic Council." *Nunatsiaq News*, May 20, 2010.

———. "Iron Ore Rush Set to Start in Nunavik." *Nunatsiaq News*, March 21, 2011.

———. "MMG Promises Jobs Galore for Western Nunavut." *Nunatsiaq Online*, October 1, 2012.

———. "Nunavik Mine Owes $72 Million to Creditors; Chinese Owners Turn Project over to Toronto Bank" *Nunatsiaq Online*, August 14, 2013.

———. "The Global Mining Industry Arrives in Nunavut." *Nunatsiaq News*, April 6, 2011.

Gibbs, Walter. "Russia and Norway Reach Accord on Barents Sea." *New York Times*, April 10, 2010.

Grant, Shelagh. "Troubled Arctic Waters." *Globe and Mail*, June 30, 2010.

Greaves, Wilfrid. "Thinking Critically about Security and the Arctic in the Anthropocene," The Arctic Institute, March 22, 2016, http://www.thearcticinstitute.org/thinking-critically-about-security-and-the-arctic-in-the-anthropocene/.

Gregoire, Lisa. "Arctic Council Should Be Cautious about New Observer Hopefuls." *Nunatsiaq News*, February 1, 2013.

Gusovsky, Dina. "Should America Worry about a China-Russia Axis?" *CNBC*, October 22, 2014.

Hadekel, Peter. "New Plan Nord Calls for Smaller Investment as Metal, Mineral Prices Tumble." *Montreal Gazette*, April 8, 2015.

Higgins, Andrew. "Teeing Off at Edge of the Arctic? A Chinese Plan Baffles Iceland." *New York Times*, March 23, 2013.

Hill, Liezel, and Doug Alexander. "Canadian Bankers Feeling the Pain of Decimated Mining Sector." *Financial Post*, July 7, 2013.

Hille, Katrin. "Hu Calls for China to Be 'Maritime Power.'" *Financial Times*, November 8, 2012.

Hobson, Peter, and Sam Skove. "Rosneft Asks for $49 Billion from State Welfare Fund to Survive Sanctions." *Moscow Times*, October 22, 2014.

Huebert, Rob. "Canada and China in the Arctic: A Work in Progress." *Meridian Newsletter*, 2012.

———. "Canada Must Prepare for the New Arctic Age." *Edmonton Journal*, August 4, 2008.

———. "Return of the Vikings." *Globe and Mail*, December 28, 2002.

———. "The Coming Arctic Maritime Sovereignty Crisis." *Arctic Bulletin* 2, no. 4 (July 2004).

Hui, Li. "The Dream of the Arctic Gas and Oil Might Break [极油气开发或将梦碎]. *Sinopecnews* [中国石化报], March 6, 2015.

Humpet, Malte, and Andreas Raspotnik. "From 'Great Wall to 'Great White North': Explaining China's Politics in the Arctic." *Longpost*, August 17, 2012.

Hunter, Iain. "The North No Longer Cold War Bulwark." *Times Colonist*, August 25, 2013.

International Crisis Group. "Stirring Up the South China Sea." *Asia Report* 223, 2012.

Jakobsen, Andreas. "Copenhagen Zoo to Borrow Two Pandas from China." *Copenhagen Post*, April 24, 2014.

Jakobson, Linda. "China: Potential Benefits of Arctic Melting." *University World News*, May 28, 2010.

Jamasmie, Cecilia. "Iron Ore War: Rio Tinto 'Not Standing Still' over BHP's Production Boost." *Mining.com*, October 9, 2014.

Jenkins, Nash. "China Could Be Preparing to Challenge Canada's Sovereignty over the Northwest Passage." *Time*, April 21, 2016.

Jiansong, Zhang. "China's Scientists Will Play a More Active Role in the Arctic Scientific Research" [中国科学家将在北极科学研究舞台办案更积极角色]. *Xinhua News* [新华网], January 24, 2015. Jianwen, Luo. "Navy Major General: China Cannot Afford to Lose Out on Developing the Arctic Ocean." *Zhongguo Xinwen*, August 28, 2010.

Jordan, Pav. "Nunavut Mining Rush Attracts China-Backed MMG.e " *Globe and Mail*, September 4, 2012.

Juan, Du. "CNOOC Licensed to Seek Arctic Oil." *China Daily*, March 4, 2014.

———. "General Nice Group to Take over Greenland Mine." *China Daily*, January 13, 2015.

Jun, Pu. "Greenland Lures China's Miners with Cold Gold." *CaixinOnline*, July 12, 2014.

Kai, Jin. "Can China Build a Community of Common Destiny?" *Diplomat*, November 28, 2013.

Katakey, Rakteem, and Will Kennedy. "Russia Lets China into Arctic Rush as Energy Giants Embrace." *Bloomberg*, May 25, 2013.

Keck, Zachary. "China's Building Second Aircraft Carrier." *Diplomat*, January 20, 2014.

———. "US Warns China against a South China Sea ADIZ." *Diplomat*, December 18, 2013.

Lackenbauer, P. Whitney. "Finding a Seat at the Top of the Globe." *Globe and Mail*, January 16, 2012.

———. "Harper's Arctic Evolution; By Shifting Focus from Sovereignty to Responsible Development, the Prime Minister Could Cement a Legacy." *Globe and Mail*, August 20, 2013.

———. "Push to Reform Arctic Council Raises as Many Questions as It Solves." iPolitics, February 17, 2012.

———. "The World Wants an Arctic In." *National Post*, May 7, 2013.

Lackenbauer, P. Whitney, and Adam Lajeunesse. "More Ships in the Northwest Passage Will Boost Our Arctic Claim." *Globe and Mail*, January 5, 2015.

Lavrov, Sergei, and Jonas Gahr Støre. "Canada, Take Note: Here's How to Resolve Maritime Disputes." *Globe and Mail*, September 21, 2010.

Li, Yizhi, and Xuan Zhang. "International Observation: China's Cooperation with Northern Europe in the Arctic Has Had Steady Progress" [国际观察: 中国与北欧国家北极合作稳步推进]. *Xinhua Web* [新华网], June 4, 2016.

Macalister, Terry. "Greenland Government Falls as Voters Send Warning to Mining Companies." *Guardian*, March 15, 2013.

Magnason, Svein. "Continued Disagreement over Uranium Mining." *Nora Region Trends*, October 8, 2014.

Marson, James, and Andrey Ostroukh. "Gazprom Secures $2.17 Billion Loan From Bank of China." *Wall Street Journal*, March 3, 2016.

Matlack, Carol. "Chinese Workers in Greenland?" *Bloomberg Businessweek*, February 10, 2013.

McGwin, Kevin. "Game of Alliances." *Arctic Journal*, March 7, 2014.

———. "Editor's Briefing: Another One Bites the Ore." *Arctic Journal*, December 9, 2014.

———. "Oil: Bucking the Trend." *Arctic Journal*, January 15, 2015.

———. "The Coalition of the Willing." *Arctic Journal*, December 4, 2014.

———. "To the Polls." *Arctic Journal*, October 1, 2014.

Minnick, Wendell. "Ice Station Dragon: China's Strategic Arctic Interest." *Defense News*, May 16, 2011.

Morgan, Geoffrey. "IEA says Canadian LNG Costs among Highest in the World – Neck and Neck with Australia." *Financial Post*, November 13, 2014.

Munson, James. "China North: Canada's Resources and China's Arctic Long Game." *iPolitics*, December 31, 2012.

Myers, Steven Lee. "Arctic Council Adds 6 Nations as Observer States, Including China." *New York Times*, May 15, 2013.

Ng, Teddy. "Xi Sets Out Priorities for Foreign Policy." *South China Morning Post*, October 26, 2013.

Nicol, Heather. "Ripple Effects: Devolution, Development and State Sovereignty in the Canadian North." In *Future Security of the Global Arctic: State Policy, Economic Security and Climate*, edited by Lassi Heininen, 99–120. Basingstoke: Palgrave Macmillan, 2016.

Nilsem, Thomas. "Discovers Kara Sea Oil a Week before Sanctions Hit." *Barents Observer*, September 29, 2014.

Nobel, Justin. "Cold Winter Equals Big Dollars for Pangnirtung Fishermen." *Nunatsiaq News*, April 24, 2012.

NTI, "NTI Launches Lawsuit against Government of Canada for Breach of Contract," December 6, 2006.

Panin, Alexander. "Russia Plans Giant State Oil Services Company to Replace Western Firms." *Moscow Times*, October 12, 2014.

Paris, Costas. "Ship Travels Arctic from China to Europe." *Wall Street Journal Online*, August 19, 2013.

Paton, James, and Aibing Guo. "Russia, China Add to US$400B Gas Deal with Second Pact." *Financial Post*, November 10, 2014.

Perlez, Jane. "As Russia Remembers War in Europe, Guest of Honor is From China." *New York Times*, May 8, 2015.

Pettersen, Trude. "46 Vessels through Northern Sea Route." *Barents Observer*, November 23, 2012.

———. "China to Release Guidebook on Arctic Shipping." *Barents Observer*, June 20, 2014.

Plumer, Brad. "These 20 Cities Have the Most to Lose from Rising Sea Levels." *Washington Post Wonkblog*, August 20, 2013.

Pomereu, Jean de. "China Spreads Its Polar Wings: Investing in Infrastructure." *Science Poles*, December 5, 2012.

Qian, Wang. "New Icebreaker Planned by 2016: Officials." *China Daily*, January 6, 2014.

Quenneville, Guy. "Chevron Puts Arctic Drilling Plans on Hold Indefinitely." *CBC News*, December 18, 2014.

Ragsdale, Rose. "Mining News: Big Projects Advance in Kitikmeot Region." *North of 60 Mining News* 19, no. 21, May 25, 2014.

Robinson, Roger W. "China's 'Long Con' in the Arctic Must Be Countered." *Ottawa Citizen*, September 14, 2013.

Roland, Floyd. "Arctic Energy Resources Will Be Needed." *Embassy*, November 6, 2008.

Sabin, Jerald. "North's Liberal Vote a Rebuke of Harper's Arctic policy," *CBC News*, October 21, 2015, http://www.cbc.ca/news/canada/north/opinion-sabin-arctic-policy-election-1.3280899

Singh, Bhavna. "China and the Arctic: The Next 'Strategic' Frontline." *Institute of Peace & Conflict Studies*, November 9, 2012.

Shan, Lei, and Yin Jinyin. "An Analysis of Arctic Oil and Gas Exploitation and Strategic Thinking [北极油气开发现状分析与战略思考. 中国矿业]. *China Mining Magazine* 23, no. 2 (2014).

Sibley, Robert. "Canada Ignores Arctic Sovereignty at its Peril." *Ottawa Citizen*, October 2, 2015.

Skalamra, Morena. "China Can't Solve Russia's Energy Technology Trap." *Diplomat*, February 11, 2015.

Sloan, Elinor. "Responding to China's Military Build-Up." *OpenCanada.org*. Canadian International Council, March 20, 2013.

Spears, Joseph. "A Snow Dragon in the Arctic." *Asia Times Online*, February 8, 2011.

———. "The Snow Dragon Moves into the Arctic Ocean Basin." *China Brief* 11, no. 2, January 28, 2011.

Spegele, Brian, and Jeremy Page. "Beijing to Shake Up Foreign-Policy Team." *Wall Street Journal*, March 10, 2013.

Staalensen, Atle. "For China, Barents Region Comes Closer." *Barents Observer*, February 8, 2013.

———. "To Yamal with World's Most Powerful LNG Carriers." *Barents Observer*, November 11, 2014.

Storey, Ian. "China's Malacca Dilemma." *China Brief* 6, no. 8 (2006).

Struzik, Ed. "As the Far North Melts, Calls Grow for Arctic Treaty." *Yale Environment 360*, June 14, 2010.

———. "Canada Urged to take Lead in Polar Research." *Edmonton Journal*, February 25, 2009.

———. "The True North Strong and Free but Not Cheap." *Toronto Star*, December 1, 2007.

Stuster, J. Dana. "The Case for Canamerica: The Far-Out, Incredibly Earnest Argument for Why the US Should Merge with its Northern Neighbor." *Foreign Policy*, October 3, 2013.

Suthren, Victor. "Sinking the Navy in Afghanistan." *Ottawa Citizen*, November 2, 2006.

Tan, Keith. "Iron Ore Pellet Premiums to Remain Firm into 2014 on Demand Growth." *Platts*, December 11, 2013.

Thayer, Carl. "China's New Fishing Regulations: An Act of State Piracy?" *Diplomat*, January 13, 2014.

Van Praet, Nicholas. "Cliffs Natural Resources Retreats from Canadian Disaster." *Globe and Mail*, November 20, 2014.

Vanderklippe, Nathan. "Nexen Deal Comes Back to Haunt CNOOC." *Globe and Mail*, December 3, 2013.

Vela, Thandlwe. "'Exceptional' Winter Ice Fishery." *Nunatsiaq News*, February 18, 2013.

Vidal, John. "Climate Change Brings New Risks to Greenland, says PM Aleqa Hammond." *Guardian*, January 23, 2014.

Viglundson, Jon, and Alister Doyle. "First Chinese Ship Crosses Arctic Ocean amid Record Melt." *Reuters*, August 17, 2012.

Vokuev, Andrey. "Russia Opens First Arctic Search and Rescue Center." *Barents Observer*, August 27, 2013.

Waldie, Paul. "A Reality Check on the Northwest Passage 'Boom.'" *Globe and Mail*, January 7, 2014.

———. "Baffinland CEO Says No to Shipping Ore through Northwest Passage." *Globe and Mail*, October 17, 2013.

Wang, Xiaoyi. "American Media: Russia Has Changed Its Mind and Has Started to Attract China to Arctic Exploitation" [美媒: 俄转变立场, 吸引中国开发北极]. *Wangyi Finance* [网易财经], October 3, 2016.

Ward, Andrew, and Sylvia Pfeifer. "Greenland Sees Oil as Key to Independence." *Financial Times*, August 26, 2010.

Weber, Bob. "Little Interest in Arctic Shipping." *Canadian Press*, June 30, 2010.

———. "Tories Mull a Chinese Plan for Izok Corridor That Could Bring Billions of Dollars to Nunavut." *Financial Post*, December 8, 2012.

Welch, David A. "What's an ADIZ: Why the United States, Japan, and China Get it Wrong." *Foreign Affairs*, December 9, 2013.

Williams, Lisa. "Canada, the Arctic, and Post-national Identity in the Circumpolar World." *Northern Review* 33 (2011): 113–31.

Williams, Selina, and Daniel Gilbert. "Total Looks to China to Finance Russian Gas Project amid Sanctions." *Wall Street Journal*, September 22, 2014.

Windeyer, Chris. "There and Back Again." *Up Here Business*, February, 2013.

Worstall, Tim. "Why Lynas Corp Is Struggling; The Great Rare Earth Shortage Is Truly Over." *Forbes*, March 8, 2014.

Wright, David. "Canada Must Stand Up against China's Increasing Claim to Arctic." *Calgary Herald*, March 7, 2011.

Xiaolei, Zhu. "The Danish Arctic Ambassador: China is Expected to Have More Participation in Arctic Development" [丹麦北极大使: 愿中国更多参与北极开发]. *Global Time News* [环球网], February 18, 2014.

Xinhuanet. "China to Further Explore Antarctic, Deep This Year," February 9, 2016.

Yundt, Heather. "Canada's North Becomes a Battlefield in Arctic Video Game." *Nunatsiaq News*, February 9, 2012.

Conference Proceedings and Speeches

Arctic Athabaskan Council. "Europe and the Arctic: A View from the Arctic Athabaskan Council." Presentation to Nordic Council of Ministers. *Arctic Conference: Common Concern for the Arctic*, Ilulissat, Greenland, September 9–11, 2008.

Bateman, Sam, and Clive Schofield. "State Practice Regarding Straight Baselines in East Asia: Legal, Technical and Political Issues in a Changing World." *Conference on Difficulties Implementing the Provisions of UNCLOS*, Monaco, October 16–17, 2008.

Brady, Anne-Marie. "The Emerging Economies of Asia and Antarctica: Challenges and Opportunities." In *Australia's Antarctica: Proceedings of the Symposium to Mark 75 Years of the Australian Antarctic Territory*, edited by Julia Jabour, Marcus Haward, and Tony Press. Institute for Marine and Antarctic Studies, Occasional Paper no. 2, 2012.

Christensen, Kyle D. "China in the Arctic: Potential Developments Impacting China's Activities in an Ice-Free Arctic." *On Track Conference of Defence Associations Institute* (November 2010).

Grímsson, Ólafur Ragnar. "Why the Arctic Matters." Keynote Address. *Arctic Imperative Summit*, June 20, 2011.

Homer-Dixon, Thomas. "Climate Change, the Arctic, and Canada: Avoiding Yesterday's Analysis of Tomorrow's Crisis." *Securing Canada's Future in a Climate-Changing World*. National Round Table on the Environment and the Economy, October 30, 2008.

Lackenbauer, P. Whitney. "Demystifying China's Arctic Ambitions: What Can We Expect from China in the Arctic?" *China and the World after the 18th NCCPC*, Montreal, February 21–22, 2013.

Ministry of Foreign Affairs of the PRC. "Keynote Speech by Vice Foreign Minister Zhang Ming at the China Country Session of the Third Arctic Circle Assembly." Speech to the Third Arctic Circle Assembly, Iceland, October 17, 2015.

Norwegian Minister of Foreign Affairs Jonas Gahr Støre. "The Arctic: Norwegian Policy and International Cooperation," Speech, August 30, 2010.

Simon, Mary. "The Arctic and Northern Dimensions of World Issues." *Canada-UK Colloquium*, Iqaluit, November 4, 2010.

Smith, Laurence C., and Scott R. Stephenson. "New Trans-Arctic Shipping Routes Navigable by Mid-Century." *Proceedings of the National Academy of Sciences of the United States of America* 110, no. 3 (March 2013).

Statement by H.E. Ambassador Lan Lijun at the Meeting between the Swedish Chairmanship of the Arctic Council and Observers, November 6, 2012.

Sun, Kai. "China & the Arctic: China's Interests and Participation in the Arctic." *Workshop on East Asian-Arctic Relations*, Whitehorse, March 2–3, 2013.

Watt-Cloutier, Sheila. "Connectivity: The Arctic – The Planet." *Oslo Sophie Prize Ceremony*, June 15, 2005.

"Workshop Report." *Second Sino-Canadian Exchange on the Arctic*, Halifax, June 25–26, 2012.

"Workshop Report." *Sino-Canadian Workshop on the Arctic*, Beijing and Shanghai, February 25–27, 2010.

Industry Publications and News Releases

Avalon. "Project Fact Sheet: Nechalacho, Thor Lake," April 16, 2013.

Deloite. *Tracking the Trends 2013 The Top 10 Issues Mining Companies May Face in the Coming Year* (2013).

Gazprom Marketing and Trading. "Gazprom Successfully Completes the World's First LNG Shipment through the Northern Sea Route." December 6, 2012, http://www.gazprom-mt.com/.

Greenland Minerals and Energy. "Greenland Minerals Signs Memorandum of Understanding with China's NFC to form Fully-Integrated Global Rare Earth Supply Chain." *Arctic Journal* Press Release, May 24, 2014.

Greenland Minerals and Energy. Press Release, March 24, 2014.

Hutchison Port Holdings. "Ports," www.hph.com/

Ironbark Zinc. "Ironbark Zinc in New Partnership with China's NFC to Progress Citronen." *Arctic Journal* Press Release, April 15, 2014.

LatinPorts. "COSCO Pacific Wants to Continue Investing in Overseas Ports." March 26, 2014.

London Mining. "FAQ – Isua Project." http://www.londonmining.com.

———. "ISUA Overview." www.londonmining.com.

———. Press Release, November 3, 2014, www.londonmining.com

Lynas Corporation. "Capital Raising and Business Update." May 5, 2014.

Molycorp. "Molycorp Reports Fourth Quarter & Full Year 2013 Financial Results," March 3, 2104.

Northern Cross. "Developing Energy for Yukoners" (2015), http://www. northerncrossyukon.ca/.

Northern Sea Route Information Office, www.arctic-lio.com/nsr_transits.

Quest Rare Minerals. "Developing a World-Class Rare Earth Project in Canada." October 2014.

Sovcomflot. "Sovcomflot Group and China National Petroleum Corporation become Strategic Partners," November 22, 2010.

Vale SA. "Vale's Performance in 3Q14." Corporate Presentation (2014).

———. "Quarterly Earnings, 2Q2013." July 31, 2014.

Other

Arctic Council, http://www.arctic-council.org/

Arctic Governance Project. "Arctic Governance in an Era of Transformative Change: Critical Questions, Governance Principles, Ways Forward," April 14, 2010.

Asia Pacific Foundation of Canada. *2012 National Opinion Poll: Canadian Views on Asia* (2012).

———. *2016 National Opinion Poll: Canadian Views on Asia* (2016).

Central Intelligence Agency. "World Factbook: China," https://www.cia.gov/library/publications/the-world-factbook/.

Ekos Research Associates. *Rethinking the Top of the World: Arctic Security Public Opinion Survey.* January 2011.

Fednav. "First Arctic Cargo Shipped through the Northwest Passage," September 19, 2014, http://www.fednav.com/.

Heritage Foundation. "China Global Investment Tracker," http://www.heritage.org/research/projects/china-global-investment-tracker-interactive-map.

Intergovernmental Panel on Climate Change. *Climate Change 2014: Impacts, Adaptation, and Vulnerability*, http://www.ipcc.ch/.

International Chamber of Commerce. "IMB Piracy & Armed Robbery Map 2012." http://www.icc-ccs.org.

International Energy Agency. *China's Worldwide Quest for Energy Security* (2000).

Interview with Guo Peiqing in Qingdao, November 20, 2012.

Inuit Circumpolar Council, www.inuitcircumpolar.com.

Inuit Circumpolar Council. "Circumpolar Inuit Declaration on Resource Development Principles in Inuit Nunaat," May 11, 2011.

Inuit Circumpolar Council Chair on Behalf of Inuit in Greenland, Canada, Alaska, and Chukotka. "Circumpolar Inuit Declaration on Arctic Sovereignty." Adopted by the Inuit Circumpolar Council (April 2009).

Inuit Qaujisarvingat/Inuit Knowledge Centre. *Nilliajut: Inuit Perspectives on Sovereignty, Patriotism, and Security.* Ottawa: Inuit Tapiriit Kanatami and the Walter & Duncan Gordon Foundation, 2013.

Inuit Tapiriit Kanatami. *An Integrated Arctic Strategy* (2008).

Inuit Tapiriit Kanatami and Inuit Circumpolar Council (Canada). "Europe and the Arctic." *Building Inuit Nunaat.* Ottawa: 2007.

Manicom, James. Conversation with MOFA official, July 27, 2011.

National Intelligence Council. *Global Trends 2030: Alternative Worlds* (December 2012), http://www.dni.gov/files/documents/GlobalTrends_2030.pd.

NORDREG, Arctic Traffic Statistics 2013, 2014, 2015.

Oceans North International. "More than 2,000 Scientists Worldwide Urge Protection of Central Arctic Ocean Fisheries," http://www.oceansnorth.org/arctic-fisheries-letter.

Transparency International. "Corruption Perceptions Index 2014: Results" (2014), http://www.transparency.org/cpi2014/results.

United Nations. *Convention on the Law of the Sea.* Signed December 10, 1982 at Montego Bay, Jamaica. Came into effect November 16, 1994.

United Nations Environment Programme. "Revised Draft Decision on Sustainable Development of the Arctic Region." February 1, 2008.

Wahl, M.E.B., and Erik Kristoffersen. "Speed Optimization for Very Large Crude Carriers: Potential Savings and Effects of Slow Steaming." Master's thesis, Norwegian School of Economics (2012).

World Bank. "Multipolarity: The New Global Economy" (2011).

Wright, Timothy Curtis. "China's Race towards the Arctic: Interests, Legitimacy, and Canadian Security Implications." Master's Thesis, University of Calgary (2014).

———. "Rhetoric in Chinese Media, Overseas Diplomats, and PLA Officials." Unpublished research report, March 25, 2013.

Index

climate change (*continued*)
  motivating Chinese Arctic interest, 12, 14–15, 25, 38, 47–48, 51, 54
  resource development, 142
  sea-ice loss, 52
  shipping, 65
  threat multiplier, 52
  tipping point, 53
  trans-regional issue, 22, 25, 54, 133, 140
continental shelf, 65, 67, 134
  Canada's extended continental shelf claim, 4, 7, 48, 123–25, 156
  Chinese activities on, 68
  Chinese respect for claims, 13
  excessive claims, 25
  See also sovereignty; United Nations Convention on the Law of the Sea (UNCLOS)
cooperation, 2, 22, 65, 154
  Arctic Council as vehicle, 140–43
  Arctic opportunities, 14–15, 22, 51, 77, 168, 170
  Canadian policy, 4–6, 90–91, 153, 156
  China and Indigenous Northerners, 149–50
  China-Iceland, 113
  Chinese policy, 44, 47, 50, 65, 67, 96, 131
  climate change, 74
  Law of the Sea Convention (LOSC), 68
  Russia-China, 87–88
  science, 13, 23, 59, 64–66
  search and rescue, 152
  shipping, 94

D

Dai Bingguo, 29, 41
Denmark, 3
  See also Greenland; Hans Island
Depledge, Duncan, 139–40
Dion, Stéphane, 156–157, 161

E

East China Sea, 33, 41
environment, 6, 133, 119
  and China, 22, 38–39, 44, 56, 65–68, 79, 96, 110, 138, 142
  Indigenous perspectives, 150, 160, 164, 173;
  protecting, 5, 7, 25, 33, 81, 96, 111, 136–37, 155, 158–59, 162, 167–68, 172
  See also climate change; science; sustainable development
Erickson, Andrew, 28
Evans, Paul, 21–22, 162, 164
exclusive economic zones (EEZs), 14, 69, 114, 123
Exner-Pirot, Heather, 160

F

Feng Yuan, 75
fisheries, 4, 121–22, 171
Flake, Lincoln, 92
Fournier, Mélanie, 83
Francis, Diane, 13, 35
Friedberg, Aaron, 45

G

Gang Chen, 8, 27, 35–36, 39–41, 45
Gao Zhiguo, 49, 66, 124
Goldsmith-Jones, Pamela, 1, 161–62
Greenland, 6, 81, 100,103, 109, 111–13, 126–28, 145, 147, 173
  mining, 105–12
  See also Denmark
Griffiths, Franklyn, 93
Grímsson, Ólafur Ragnar, 113
Guo Peiqing, 66, 76, 92, 96, 135, 143–44

H

Hammond, Aleqa, 107–8
Han Jun, 164
Han Xudong, Colonel, 165
Hans Island, 3

Harper, Stephen, 2, 4–5, 21, 90, 127, 132, 138,153–55, 161–64
Ho, Joshua, 54
Homer-Dixon, Thomas, 52
Hu Jintao, 38, 76, 148
Huebert, Robert, 3, 9, 10, 11, 13, 50, 62, 93, 132, 136
Huigen Yang, 48, 56, 63–64, 66–67, 88

I

icebreakers, 12–13, 58–59, 70–71, 87–89, 117, 159, 169
See also Xue Long
Iceland, 17, 67, 74, 100, 113–14, 126, 136, 139, 145, 173
Ikenberry, John, 30
India, 18, 37, 44, 58, 102, 145
Indigenous peoples
  Arctic Council, 136, 141, 145, 149
  Canadian policy, 1, 5, 7, 48–49, 155–58, 160–61
  Chinese interests, 69, 170
  Chinese support for, 129, 149–50
  Circumpolar Inuit Declaration on Sovereignty, 128, 151
  Climate change, 52–53, 148, 157
  development, 167
  free, prior and informed consent, 155
  governance, 148, 159
  knowledge, 172
  land use and occupancy, 150
  Permanent participants, 136
  seal products, 138
  shipping, 158–59
  UN Declaration on the Rights of Indigenous Peoples, 128
  welfare, 12
  See also Inuit; Inuit Circumpolar Council; Inuit Tapiriit Kanatami (ITK)
International Maritime Organization (IMO), 95–96, 134, 147
international polar year, 7, 23, 47–48, 57, 63–64, 71
Inuit, 53, 105–8, 112, 127–28, 145, 149–50, 160–61

indigenous knowledge, 157–58, 168, 172
  See also Inuit Circumpolar Council, Inuit Tapiriit Kanatami (ITK)
Inuit Circumpolar Council (ICC), 145, 150, 158
Inuit Tapiriit Kanatami (ITK), 128, 149

J

Jakobson, Linda, 14, 25, 44, 66, 69, 75, 92, 134, 138–39, 143, 151, 171
Jingchao Peng, 25, 70, 92, 134

K

Kai Sun, 66
Kerry, John, 139
Kielsen, Kim, 108
Kikkert, Peter, 149
Kirkegaard, Jens-Erik, 103
Kitikmeot Inuit Association, 105
Kleist, Kuupik, 107, 111–12

L

Lackenbauer, P. Whitney, 14, 144, 152
Lan Lijun, 140, 142–43
Lasserre, Frédéric, 13–14, 62, 81, 83, 85, 147
Lavorv, Sergei, 123
Le Li, Colonel, 99
Li Keqiang, 110, 163–64
Li Yuanchao, 41
Lidegaard, Martin, 106
Liff, Adam, 28
Linyan Huang, 83, 147
Liqi Chen, 60
Liu Huirong, 69
Liu Pengfei, 78
Liu Zhenmin, 15, 48

M

Manhattan SS, 77–78
Manicom, James, 14, 144, 152
migrant workers, 107–8
Ming, Zhang, 47, 128; 131

Chinese investments, 11
Chinese policy, 15, 22, 25, 47, 55, 99
connection to growing Chinese strength,
    50
continental shelf, 123
cooperation, 13–14, 22, 56, 122, 142–43,
    168–69
fishing, 159
funding, 58–56, 71
Indigenous knowledge, 172
International Polar Year, 63
marine research, 49, 56, 68–69, 122
natural sciences emphasis, 61
    sea-ice work, 48
social science research, 65–68, 150
specialization, 70
See also Antarctica; climate change;
    environment; Polar Research In-
    stitute of China (PRIC); Xue Long
security, 15, 31, 77
    Arctic Council, 152
    Canadian policy, 45, 90, 161
    Chinese policy, 29
    Chinese threat to Arctic security, 11, 22,
        31, 62, 91
    energy security, 36, 38, 76, 102, 156
    maritime security, 37
    non-conventional security, 38, 52, 156,
        173
    Greenland, 106, 112
    implications of ice-free Arctic, 52
    regional security, 91, 135, 165
    resource development, 164–65
    US-China, 162–63, 173
Setchin, Igor, 88
Shanghai Institutes of International Studies
    (SIIS), 56–57, 92
Shell, 116, 120–21
shipping, 22, 24, 26, 66, 73, 94, 132, 136,
    140, 142, 166, 173–74
    AMSA, 81, 87
    Arctic Council, 145, 147
    Canada corridors, 158–59
        Canadian sovereignty, 13, 73, 91,
            93–94
    China as a trading nation, 74
    China preparing to use Arctic routes, 13

China-Russia cooperation, 87–89
Chinese policy, 14–16, 25, 67, 69, 76, 88
distance and savings, 74, 75, 77
hydrocarbons, 77
Indigenous peoples, 150
just in time delivery, 80
new shipping routes, 9, 45, 49, 64–65,
    77, 143
piracy, 76
Polar Code, 95–96
regulations, 14, 86, 94, 166
shipping company survey, 81–85
strategic value, 76
transpolar, 113, 132
See also Indigenous peoples; Northern
    Sea Route (NSR); Northwest
    Passage; South Korea
Shou Jianmin, 75
Sibley, Robert, 1
Simon, Mary, 6, 128, 158
South China Sea, 13, 32–34, 37, 39, 41–42,
    92, 97
South Korea
    Arctic Council, 139, 145
    cooperation in science, 59, 64
    ship construction, 10
    spending, 58
sovereignty, 127–27, 141, 143–44, 150–51,
    170
    Canadian position, 2–7, 13–16, 52, 85,
        131–32, 138, 156, 161
    Chinese position, 22, 26, 27–29, 33, 44,
        59–60, 76–79, 85–86, 90–94, 97,
        133–35, 140, 165, 170–74
    Law of the Sea (UNCLOS)
    perceived threats to Canadian position,
        2–4, 8–13
    and shipping, 23–24, 73–79
    US position on Canadian sovereignty,
        77–78, 91, 94
    See also continental shelf; Northwest
        Passage; shipping; United Na-
        tions Convention on the
state-owned enterprises (SOEs), 6, 20, 21,
    41, 99, 101–3, 105, 115, 118–21, 126,
    128, 164, 167, 170, 173

Biographies

P. Whitney Lackenbauer, PhD, is a Professor in the Department of History and co-director of the Centre on Foreign Policy and Federalism at St. Jerome's University in the University of Waterloo, Ontario. He is the 2017-18 Killam Visiting Scholar at the University of Calgary; an adjunct professor at the Frost Centre for Canadian Studies & Indigenous Studies at Trent University; and Honorary Lieutenant-Colonel of 1st Canadian Ranger Patrol Group with sixty patrols spanning Yukon, Northwest Territories, and Nunavut. A prolific author, Dr Lackenbauer specializes in Arctic policy, history, sovereignty, and governance issues; modern Canadian political, military, and diplomatic history; and Indigenous-state relations in Canada.

Adam Lajeunesse, PhD, is the Irving Shipbuilding Chair in Canadian Arctic Marine Security at the Mulroney Institute of Government, St. Francis Xavier University, Nova Scotia. He is also a fellow of the Canadian Global Affairs Institute and the Centre for the Study of Security and Development. He is a regular lecturer at the NATO Defence College (Rome) and the Canadian Forces College (Toronto) as well as a frequent speaker on northern security issues for academic, government, and military audiences. Dr. Lajeunesse is the author of the award-winning political history *Lock, Stock and Icebergs: A History of Arctic Maritime Sovereignty* (UBC Press, 2016) as well as publications on a range of subjects including northern security, development, shipping, governance, and maritime policy.

James Manicom, PhD, completed his doctoral degree at Flinders University in Adelaide, Australia. His research interests lie in the areas of maritime security, Asia-Pacific international relations, and geopolitics in the Arctic. He is the author of *Bridging Troubled Waters: China, Japan and Maritime Order in the East China Sea* (Georgetown University Press, 2014). The views expressed in this work are his own.

Frédéric Lasserre, PhD, is Professor at the Department of Geography at Laval University, Quebec, and director of the Quebec Council for Geopolitical Studies. He has conducted extensive research in the field of maritime border disputes, water management and on Arctic geopolitics. Since 2008, he has coordinated a multidisciplinary research team on the impacts of climate change on Arctic governance, with a particular focus on navigation, resources and sovereignty disputes. He is the editor of *Passages et mers arctiques : Géopolitique d'une région en mutation* (Presses de l'Université du Québec, 2010).